Process and Analysis

Whitehead, Hartshorne, and the Analytic Tradition

EDITED BY
George W. Shields

STATE UNIVERSITY OF NEW YORK PRESS

Published by
State University of New York Press, Albany

Printed in the United States of America

For information, address State University of New York Press,
90 State Street, Suite 700, Albany, NY 12207

Production by Cathleen Collins
Marketing by Michael Campochiaro

Library of Congress Cataloging in Publication Data

Process and analysis : Whitehead, Hartshorne, and the analytic tradition / edited by George W. Shields.
p. cm.—(SUNY series in philosophy)
Includes bibliographical references and index.
ISBN 0-7914-5573-4 (alk. paper)—ISBN 0-7914-5574-2 (pbk. : alk. paper)
1. Whitehead, Alfred North, 1861–1947. 2. Hartshorne, Charles, 1897–
3. Process philosophy. 4. Analysis (Philosophy) I. Shields, George W. II. Series

B1674.W354 P76 2002
146'.4—dc21

2002021054

10 9 8 7 6 5 4 3 2 1

PROCESS AND ANALYSIS

SUNY series in Philosophy
George R. Lucas Jr., editor

Dedicated
to
the Memory of
Bowman Lafayette Clarke
(1927–1997)
and
Charles Hartshorne
(1897–2000)

Contents

Preface

The concept for this volume had its very first beginnings in conversations I had with contributor George "Larry" Goodwin many years ago when I was putting the last touches on my Ph.D. dissertation at The University of Chicago. In fact I have retained the title that we originally envisioned. Unfortunately, for both of us, the rigors of college teaching and somewhat later administration quelled any serious efforts at following through on that initial project. The idea surfaced again while I was driving David Ray Griffin, who had just delivered a lecture at Kentucky State University, back to the Louisville airport in April 1994. I then confessed to David that one of my main intellectual ambitions was to foster greater conversation between analytic and process philosophers. He seemed to think that this was a worthy goal (I was at the time unaware of how deeply involved David was in thinking about current analytic philosophy of mind), and he suggested that I contact Lewis S. Ford about putting together a Special Focus issue of *Process Studies* devoted to the interface of analytic and process philosophy. Lewis was very supportive of the idea as were all of the original invitees (Richard M. Gale, George Lucas, Leemon McHenry—who engaged me in a lively correspondence—and Nicholas Rescher). Three years later, after much work, such a Special Focus was published in Volume 25, the commemorative issue in honor of Professor Charles Hartshorne's 100th birthday. That issue was the "seed" of the much expanded, much revised, and distinctive presentation published here.

I have many, many persons to thank, including some who were not directly involved in this project but whose support and influences are inseparable from the philosopher I have become, and about whom I feel a special obligation:

As always, my first debt is to my wife Marsha (a gifted teacher who is the "real brain" of the family) and to our precious daughter Kirstin Lorraine, both of whom have provided "a place where love abounds."

Some of the deepest motivations for this project were shaped long ago in varying degrees by former professor/mentors whom I have never thanked in writing. Given a spate of recent retirements, I am especially moved to do so now:

I should at once thank my former professors at The University of Chicago, especially Manley Thompson (who shared my interest in the Peirce-Hartshorne relationship), the late great Alan Donagan (who taught a superb course on Wittgenstein and served as coadviser of my dissertation), and David Tracy (also a dissertation adviser who for me will always truly embody the appellation "*learned* theologian"). The Chicago of my doctoral student days (1977–1981) was indeed a spirited place, where student colleagues in the Department of Philosophy pushed me in the direction of analytic thought and student colleagues in Divinity debated the merits of process philosophy and theology in a lively way; it was an exciting period when (in addition to the luminaries mentioned above) courses were available from none other than Donald Davidson, Stephen Toulmin, and Paul Ricoeur. Given such variegated influences, the motivations for organizing a volume in comparative philosophy like this one are not as difficult to understand as it may first appear.

I must also warmly thank my outstanding undergraduate professors at the University of Louisville (an *alma mater* I proudly share with *Journal of Speculative Philosophy* editor Carl Hausman): the recently retired John Flodstrom (in whose Kant seminar I came to study Hartshorne's work carefully for the first time while researching a term thesis on "Kant's Critique of the Ontological Argument"), Jim Massey (for whom I read Hartshorne in an honors course on recent philosophical theology), Melvin Greer (a fine teacher and efficient philosophy department head), but especially the just retired Charles F. Breslin and the late great Richard L. Barber. Professor Breslin is simply the most erudite person I have ever met *anywhere*. This includes philosophers, cultural historians, and scientists I have encountered from Oxford to Chicago to Berkeley to Toronto to Claremont. Perhaps more than anything else, he taught me the importance and value of being interdisciplinary and "pluralistic" in attitude—an attitude I hope this volume embodies—and long before anyone was using the expression "postmodernist." He was as at home in discussing Frege's philosophy of language or set theory or the nuances of Carl Prantl's historiography of logic as he was in discussing Ricoeur's hermeneutics or the latest translations from the Husserl archives or Karl Barth's *Church Dogmatics* or Dutch treatises on medieval history or the novels of Thomas Mann. (As his former students will all attest, I am not exaggerating; he exhibited that kind of reach.) But Richard Barber, the justly named University Distinguished Teaching Professor of Philosophy and Humanities-in-Medicine, became my true mentor. How deeply grateful I am that he was able to attend my 1987 Presidential Address on the topic of logicofatalism before the Kentucky Philosophical Association (later published in the *Southern Journal of Philosophy*) where I had the opportunity to thank him quite publicly for the extraordinary graduate level tutorial we undertook together in symbolic logic. A specialist in logic at Yale, who studied with none other than that Whiteheadian master of the subject—Frederic Fitch—his dissertation was regarded by Rulon Wells decades later (in personal correspondence) as the best work ever written at that institution on the topic of logical possibility and related issues in modal logic. The logic tutorial—which Professor Barber extended for up to six months so that we could range from classical syllogistic to quantificational calculi to metatheorems to Goedel—was nothing less than the "doorway" to my studies in the analytic tradition. Furthermore, our course together on F. H. Bradley helped me enormously in understanding the historical context that shaped Whitehead's *Process and Reality* (on this see contributor Leemon McHenry's fine study entitled *Whitehead and Bradley: A Comparative Analysis* [Albany: State University of New York press, 1992]), and, of course, in better understanding one foil surrounding Hartshorne's work on the logic of relations.

I owe a great debt to Kentucky State University. My academic travel and scholarly research has been financially supported again and again, including work directly related to this project. A special thanks for a grant received from the Kentucky State University Faculty Research Fund Committee, chaired by my distinguished colleague, Dr. Louise Chawla. Most important, I received a sabbatical leave from regular administrative and teaching duties for the Fall Term 2001, which permitted the requisite time to refine and complete the entire manuscript. Thanks are also due my many colleagues in the Division of Literature, Languages, and Philosophy and in the Whitney M. Young Jr., College Honors and Integrative Studies Programs. Among the most intellectually talented persons I have encountered anywhere, these faculty communities have provided a most collegial, supportive, stimulating, and even fun environment in which to work. (Not enough people in academe can make these claims and this is no small matter to be taken for granted.) I must also thank my skilled administrative secretary, Millie Cummins, who not only deciphered and typed my red-inked and sometimes seemingly "hieroglyphic" manuscripts for grueling hours on end, but also offered some expert technical assistance on scanning and computer software issues.

I wish to thank all of the contributors for their enthusiastic support and their kind patience in waiting for the seemingly "forever" book. I also warmly thank Barry Whitney and the Editorial Board of *Process Studies* for the gracious permission to reprint or use material from the previous articles: some portions of chapter 1, 2, and 4 appeared in volume 25, while chapters 7 and 8 appeared in volume 27, numbers 3–4. I thank the *International Journal for Philosophy of Religion* for kind permission to reprint from volume 18 much of the material in chapter 10. I also thank Professor G. Olivetti, editor of *L'Archivo Filosophia*, for kind permission to reprint chapter 9. Moreover, I thank the *Southern Journal of Philosophy* for permission to reprint some portions of chapter 11 from volume 26, number 3.

Finally, I must thank SUNY Series in Philosophy Editor George R. Lucas Jr., for his helpful comments on earlier drafts as well as very helpful remarks from two SUNY Press referees, one who is anonymous and Daniel Dombrowski of Seattle University. The anonymous referee is to be thanked especially for the suggestion that I add brief editorial comments at the beginnings of chapters. I have done this for all but the first and last (the context of origin for the last chapter is explained immediately below). The purposes of these comments are to inform the reader on the origins or provenance of each essay, to point out the status as previously unpublished (where appropriate), and to continue the conversation of the introductory chapter by pointing out particular connections and complementaries between specific essays, thus hopefully enriching the interconnections for the reader. I have tried hard in this anthology to write about and to choose authors and essays that coherently fit the theme and address one another (even if not necessarily explicitly), thereby above all avoiding, in C. S. Peirce's apt expression, the "pitch fork full of articles."

A special word is in order regarding the collaboration between me and Donald Wayne Viney on the last chapter of this book, written especially for it, namely, chapter 11 on "The Logic of Future Contingents." Don and I first came to know each other in 1986 when the late George Nordgulen and I invited him to contribute a piece to the Eugene Peters *Festschrift*. Don and I learned quickly that our intellectual inclinations and interests were remarkably close and that in fact we had independently made essentially the same arguments in our dissertations on Harsthorne, both of which were conversant with analytic philosophy. Later we noticed similar strong affinities of interest as we were both publishing articles on issues concerning logic, freedom and contingency, and omniscience. It was thus only natural, with this SUNY Press opportunity at hand, that Don and I should attempt to put together what we hope is a consummate statement of Hartshorne's doctrine of futurity and its relation to contemporary analytic philosophy of time, modality, fate and omniscience.

Some unfortunate events and limitations of space prevented some prospective papers from appearing. I had phoned the University of Georgia Philosophy Department hoping to invite a contribution from Professor Bowman Clarke—perhaps the "dean" of analytic philosophy of process—only to learn of his untimely death. Given Bowman's special interest in the topic of this book, I thought it most appropriate that I dedicate it to his memory. Also, Dorothy Emmet kindly wrote back to me to decline her invitation because of poor health (she died several years later), but she expressed hearty enthusiasm for the project. I was glad that I was able to review at some length one of her last books (*The Passage of Nature*), which appeared in *Process Studies* (26, nos. 1–2 [1997]) just prior to her death. Also, I am sad to report that one of the contributors, the celebrated W. V. O. Quine, who answered my letter of invitation quite agreeably and with much dispatch, died recently. Finally, limitations of space prevented an invitation to David Griffin, who I discuss in the introductory chapter and whose quite interesting treatment of the epistemic theory of truth and antirealism in his very recent *Reenchantment Without Supernaturalism* (Ithaca: Cornell University Press, 2001) came to my attention too late for sufficient coverage. However, I am consoled by the fact that David is extraordinarily well published and well represented by SUNY Press.

In closing, I also dedicate this book to the memory of Charles Hartshorne, that "strange and alien greatness" (in the phrase of John Cobb), that great centenarian sage of American philosophy, who stated quite explicitly and publicly that he wished he had made clearer his own "sense of common ground" with the analytic tradition. I shall forever cherish his personally communicated reaction to my essay in the Peters *Festschrift* (entitled "Hartshorne and the Analytic Philosophical Tradition," see chapter 1, note 31): "I've read your essay. I see you have taken to defending me. With all these defenders around here [referring to me and some other invited participants at a 1988 University of Texas conference in his honor], I'm not sure I am needed anymore." What the world surely needs much more of—now more than ever—are the qualities of Charles's soul: a wisdom that seeks moderation combined with analytic rigor and clarity, high regard for the dignity of persons, high regard for the natural environment, high regard for aesthetic values, a thoughtful and tolerant piety, a generous heart.

> Tumult and peace, the darkness and the light—
> Were all like workings of one mind, the features
> Of the same face, blossoms upon one tree . . .
>
> —Wordsworth, cited in Hartshorne,
> *The Darkness and the Light*

Abbreviations

Alfred North Whitehead

AI	*Adventures of Ideas* (1933). New York: The Free Press, 1967.
CN	*The Concept of Nature*. Cambridge: Cambridge University Press, 1920.
ESP	*Essays in Science and Philosophy*. New York: The Philosophical Library, 1947.
FR	*The Function of Reason* (1929). Boston: Beacon Press, 1958.
MT	*Modes of Thought* (1938). New York: The Free Press, 1968.
PM	*Principia Mathematica*, 2nd ed. (with Bertrand Russell). Cambridge: Cambridge University Press, 1927.
PNK	*An Enquiry Concerning the Principles of Natural Knowledge*. Cambridge: Cambridge University Press, 1919.
PR	*Process and Reality*, corrected ed. (1929). Edited by David R. Griffin and Donald Sherburne. New York: The Free Press, 1978.
R	*The Principle of Relativity*. Cambridge: Cambridge University Press, 1922.
S	*Symbolism: Its Meaning and Effect*. New York: Macmillan, 1927.
SMW	*Science and the Modern World* (1925). New York: The Free Press, 1967.

Charles Hartshorne

AD	*Anselm's Discovery*. LaSalle, Ill.: Open Court, 1965
BH	*Beyond Humanism: Essays in the New Philosophy of Nature* (1937). Gloucester, Mass.: Peter Smith, 1975

CAP *Creativity in American Philosophy*. Albany: State University of New York Press, 1984

CSPM *Creative Synthesis and Philosophic Method*. La Salle, Ill.: Open Court, 1970.

DL *The Darkness and the Light: A Philosopher Looks at His Fortunate Career and Those Who Have Made It Possible*. Albany: State University of New York Press, 1990.

DR *The Divine Relativity: A Social Conception of God*. New Haven: Yale University Press, 1948.

IO *Insights and Oversights of Great Thinkers: An Evaluation of Western Philosophy*. Albany: State University of New York Press, 1983.

LP *The Logic of Perfection and Other Essays in Neoclassical Metaphysics*. La Salle, Ill.: Open Court, 1962.

MVG *Man's Vision of God and the Logic of Theism* (1941). Amden, Conn.: Archon Books, 1964.

NTOT *A Natural Theology for Our Time*. La Salle, Ill.: Open Court, 1967.

PCH *The Philosophy of Charles Hartshorne*. Library of Living Philosophers, Vol. 20. Edited by Lewis Hahn. La Salle, Ill.: Open Court, 1991.

PSG *Philosophers Speak of God* (with William L. Reese). Chicago: University of Chicago Press, 1953.

RSP *Reality as Social Process: Studies in Metaphysics and Religion*. Boston: Beacon Press, 1953.

WM *Wisdom as Moderation: A Philosophy of the Middle Way*. Albany: State University of New York Press, 1987.

WP *Whitehead's Philosophy: Selected Essays, 1935–1970*. Lincoln: University of Nebraska Press, 1970.

ZF *The Zero Fallacy and Other Essays in Neoclassical Philosophy*. Edited by Mohammed Valady. La Salle, Ill.: Open Court, 1997.

Part I

Overviews

Chapter 1

Introduction

On the Interface of Analytic and Process Philosophy

GEORGE W. SHIELDS

> The net result of these [Martin's] papers on Whitehead and Hartshorne is to show that their concerns are much closer to those of contemporary analytic philosophers than is commonly supposed.
>
> —R. M. Martin, *Whitehead's Categoreal Scheme and Other Papers*

> Now and then I have said, at least to myself, that had I been smarter, I would have made clear long ago how much common ground there is between my way of philosophizing and those more commonly regarded as analytic.
>
> —Charles Hartshorne, *Hartshorne, Process Philosophy and Theology*

> Whitehead himself was first and foremost a philosopher, as authentically so as Wilfrid Sellars, Willard Quine, Saul Kripke, Arthur Danto, Donald Davidson, or any other leading figure today. Even the slightest perusal of his writings will suggest this to the harshest and most suspicious critic.
>
> —George R. Lucas Jr., *The Rehabilitation of Whitehead*

This book is dedicated to exploring, in a variety of ways, the complex and largely neglected relationship between two twentieth century philosophical traditions, conventionally understood as "analytic" and "process" philosophy, which have been widely, but I think rather mistakenly, viewed as radically disparate and disconnected. I submit that such exploration is timely, contributes to an emerging sense of the relative continuity or seamlessness of contemporary philosophical developments among some historiographers of ideas, and most important, illustrates the very real potential for advancing a variety of research programs within both traditions.

The project envisioned here is timely for reasons connected with the emergence of a mood of self-reflection in both traditions. Recently, analytic philosophers have become increasingly self-reflective about the origins, historical trajectories, and status of the analytic philosophical tradition—a set of concerns that runs both implicitly and explicitly throughout this book. This is surely, in part, due to recent critiques of the analytic tradition from the hands of Alasdair MacIntyre, Richard Rorty, Stanley Rosen, Hao Wang, and others, as well as, indeed, the very emergence of such vocabulary as "postanalytic philosophy."[1] Perhaps of equal importance, however, has been the appearance of Michael Dumett's provocative essay on *The Origins of Analytic Philosophy*,[2] which has renewed the debate about the very nature of the analytic enterprise and about those who may be said to be properly engaged in its practice (see discussion of Dummett below). On the other hand, a number of contemporary process philosophers have recently turned explicit attention to the relationship between the two traditions. These efforts include contributor George R. Lucas Jr.'s *The Rehabilitation of Whitehead*, notably subtitled *An Analytic and Historical Assessment of Process Philosophy*, and Daniel Dombrowski's recent book on *Analytic Theism, Hartshorne, and the Concept of God*.[3] The present work continues with this self-reflective preoccupation, but does so by actually engaging a number of leading contemporary analytic as well as leading process philosophers in deliberation on philosophical topics of common interest.

Some recent work by historiographers of twentieth-century philosophy has been quietly dismantling the rather widespread notion that important contemporary philosophical movements have somehow emerged in compartmentalized, well-separated fashions. An important case in point resides in the recently published *Cambridge Companion to Husserl*, which asserts as its main unifying theme that "the so-called rift between analytic and continental philosophy emerges as an artificial construct."[4] The situation with the thought of A. N. Whitehead and various philosophical projects aligned with the "Peirce-Whitehead-Hartshorne axis" of process philosophy is, I submit, somewhat similar to that of Husserl and some members of the recent continental tradition vis-à-vis the analytic. While the entire anthology might be regarded as warrant for this point, I mention here two quick items favoring this contention to show its initial plausibility: (1) A careful examination of the formative period of Cambridge analytic philosophy, especially apparent in, say, the heyday of C. D. Broad's work in philosophy of science (circa 1914–1923), shows the indelible imprint of Whitehead's influence.[5] The English-speaking philosophical literature of this period abounds with references to "Extensive Abstraction," "Percipient Event," "Cogredience," and other Whiteheadian constructions. (2) Contributor John W. Lango has long argued that the Whitehead of "Mediterranean clarity" (Russell's term) found in *Principia Mathematica* is very much present in the mature speculative system of *Process and Reality*.[6] Apropos of Lango's thesis, it is often ignored that Russell himself eventually confessed that Whitehead was able to show him "at last" how a mathematical logician might make sense of a "vague and higgledy-piggledy world" of process.[7] In effect, from the point of view of detailed and cautious historiography, the emergence of major contemporary philosophical movements has been a far more *seamless* affair than the hastily generalized, diremptive perceptions of those movements would have us believe. The current project on *Process and Analysis* is dedicated to making contributions to this "seamless sensibility."

The plan for this introductory essay is to do the following things. First, I want to clarify the notions of process and analytic philosophy as frames of reference; second, I want to discuss each of the ensuing essays and some of the general literature that addresses the two traditions—in course, making connections and pointing out various "intersections" of concern; and, third, I want to address the notion of postanalytic philosophy with a particular view toward prospects for the *survival* of both the spirit of analytical inquiry and the quests of process metaphysics.

Notions of Analytic and Process Philosophy

In any purported comparison of philosophical traditions, it is helpful at the outset to get clear about the frame of reference for the traditions in question. This is easier to do for the notion of "process" philosophy than it is for the notion of "analytic" philosophy. By "process philosophy" I shall adopt Nicholas Rescher's broad definition: "Process philosophers . . . are those for whom temporality, activity, and change—of alteration, striving, passage, and novelty-emergence—are the *cardinal* factors in our understanding of the real." This means that process philosophy has a general *doctrinal* content in terms of which a given practitioner might be classified.[8] As such, and as Rescher further notes, process philosophy has a long, venerable history stretching back to Heraclitus, and, accordingly, transcends such important contemporary exemplars as A. N. Whitehead and Charles Hartshorne. Notwithstanding, the work of Whitehead and Hartshorne has been so deeply influential for contemporary thinkers concerned with the "processual nature of the real" that they merit pointed mention in any definition of the label "process philosophy." The very fact that Professor Rescher would need to caution his readers not to *identify* process philosophy with particular *thinkers* (i.e., Whitehead and Hartshorne) bears witness to their enormous influence. Thus, I have not hesitated to employ their names in the very title of this book. The situation is rather different in the case of analytic philosophy. Here it seems to me that any *doctrinal* criterion for the classification is immediately untenable. For "analytic" philosophers hold all sorts of metaphysical, antimetaphysical, epistemological, meta-ethical, ethical, and other views, covering an extremely wide spectrum of opinion. Even the notion of the analytic philosopher as one who embraces "the linguistic turn" is problematic, especially if this is defined in Dummett's way.

In Dummett's book on the origins of analysis, the thesis is put forth that the very essence of the analytic tradition is found in the idea (traced back to Frege) that philosophy's task is an account of thought, an account that must be and *can only* be given in terms of an account of language. All thought is mediated through language, and thus the philosophy of language is the fountain of all genuinely philosophical activity. If this be the criterion in terms of which a philosopher should be deemed "analytic," then it could be argued that a number of philosophers counted by nearly everyone as "paradigm case" analytic philosophers are in fact not so. Thus, it has been argued that Russell[9] hardly counts as an "analytic" philosopher on Dummett's criterion, for Russell's career-long interests were primarily ontological—he wished "to understand the world"—and the effect of his temporary conversion to the Tractarian Wittgenstein's view that logic and mathematics are at bottom *linguistic* phenomena was to give up the pursuit of logicomathematical philosophy as it, so conceived, offered no help in understanding the world. Morever, Dummett's criterion appears to entail that only philosophers of a nonrealist persuasion can be deemed "analytic" philosophers. Thus, not only Russell, but important philosophers such as William P. Alston, Alvin Plantinga, and John Searle (among numerous others)—universally regarded as analytic philosophers—ought not to be so regarded. This seems to be a plain *reductio* on Dummett's position. For these reasons (among others), I shall not adopt the Dummett criterion.

At the opposite end of the spectrum is Dagfinn Føllesdal's view (see RAP, chapter 1). Prof. Føllesdal argues that, not only is it mistaken to characterize analytic philosophy in terms of adherence to particular philosophical doctrines or even adherence to the linguistic turn, it is also mistaken to cast it as an essentially methodological movement concerned with techniques of logic, linguistic, or conceptual analysis. Even though philosophers regarded as quintessentially analytic have often been preoccupied with methodological technique, there is no uniform agreement on which methodologies are the really useful or sound ones. Instead, what characterizes all analytic philosophy is an *approach to philosophical problems that emphasizes justification and argument* (RAP 4–14). Thus, says Føllesdal, Aquinas and Husserl may be viewed as standing more or less in the analytic tradition, while, say, Heidegger and Derrida cannot be (RAP 12).

To some degree I am sympathetic to this point of view for it has the virtue of including philosophers who are caught up in the recognizable concerns of the analytic tradition and whose widespread exclusion from the conventional "canon" seems arbitrary. Why, for example, should the Husserl of the *Logische Untersuchungen*—a work so concerned with issues in the philosophy of logic that animated both Bolzano and Frege—be excluded or forgotten (as he is on occasion)? Moreover, Føllesdal's contention that any doctrinal, including and especially ontological claims, criterion will fail seems to me to be clearly correct (as suggested above). Consider just the case of Wittgenstein. While the Wittgenstein of the *Tractatus* can be reasonably interpreted as offering an atomistic ontology, what exactly are the "ontological claims" of the *Philosophical Investigations*? Certainly the conventional view is that Wittgenstein makes no such claims at all in the *Investigations*. And Henry Staten[10] has argued carefully for the interesting thesis that Wittgenstein's own linguistic *Ver-wendung* ("use" of language as a turning away from normal usage) and the "zigzag" structure of his writing in the *Investigations* can be viewed as "deconstructive syntax," closely aligned to Derrida's project of deconstructing the very idea of "the form of an entity," thus yielding a purported obliteration of ontology. In light of this, if we were to suggest some set of ontological claims as characteristic of the analytic tradition, then the later Wittgenstein stands outside that tradition, contrary to virtually universal presumption.

On the other hand, it would seem that Føllesdal's criterion is *too* broad. To exclude only Heidegger, Derrida, and a few other "radically subervisive" philosophers seems extreme. And even these few exclusions might be challenged (on Føllsdal's criterion), as I recently encountered, for example, a reviewer describing a new reading of Heidegger as so concerned with justification and the logic of his position in *Sein und Zeit* that he might be rightfully regarded as a virtual "Betrand Russell in *lederhosen*"![11]

In addition, it seems to me that Føllesdal's position suffers from a tacit conflation between prescriptive and descriptive notions of the analytic tradition. The prescriptive nature of his criterion is clearly betrayed when he states that, "whether one is an analytic philosopher depends on what importance one ascribes to argument and justification . . . Aristotle, Descartes, as well as a large number of other *truly great* philosophers are analytic philosophers. The way I have defined analytic philosophy, this is almost a tautology for me" (RAP 14, my italics). This forgets that the term "analytic philosophy" has its cultural meaning because of its actual historical usage. In other words, there ought to be some concern with the historically grounded descriptive sense of a term when considering questions of appropriate definition. I thus concur with P. M. S. Hacker when he states that, "If the term 'analytic philosophy' is to be a useful classificatory term, then it must do more work than merely to distinguish mainstream Western philosophy from the reflections of philosophical sages or prophets" (RAP 52).[12]

I think it wiser to view the notion of analytic philosophy as a "loose" or "soft" descriptive one, which must include both the concern with *argument and justification* and with a *variety* of logical, linguistic, and concept-analytic methodologies. Contrary to Føllesdal, it seems to me a rather plain historical fact that concern with philosophic method, linguistic, and logical tools has permeated this tradition from G. E. Moore's 1903 papers to its contemporary practice, and that this concern is the key, even if vague, organizing criterion exemplified in actual usage. One need not pick a particular analytic methodology as definitive if "analysis" be construed as a soft historical description.

With this soft criterion in mind, I want to suggest that analytic and process philosophy, especially as the latter has been developed by Whitehead, Hartshorne, and at least some of their followers, are not at all disjoined or disparate, but share some substantial common concerns, vocabulary, methodological predilections, and historical trajectories as well as profound differences. The relationship is in fact many-faceted and richly complex. *Indeed, the whole point of this anthology is to begin serious and urgently needed conversation about just this complexity, that is, the implicit and explicit commonalities and disaffections between the two traditions.*

Let me clarify my meaning by discussing a variety of rubrics under which the "interface" between the analytic and process traditions might be understood. These include the following: (1) analytic philosophers who have pursued ideas and theses of process philosophy, (2) implicit analytic themes in the philosophy of A. N. Whitehead, (3) explicit and implicit analytic themes in the philosophy of Charles Hartshorne, and (4) other process philosophers who have used methods or treated work of analytic philosophers. In course, I will provide the reader with a basic orientation to the ensuing essays, will draw various lines of connection, and will offer a general tour of the relevant literature. My aim is to be reasonably thorough in such a tour, which, to my knowledge, exists nowhere else in the critical literature.

Before I get to this task, however, I want to issue some important caveats that more properly contextualize the entire project. My own view of process philosophy is that it is attractive, in part, because it is an extremely global and accommodating perspective. Its purview is sweeping. As Nicholas Rescher has captured the point vividly in a recent essay:[13]

> The fact is that there is nothing inherently one-sided about process philosophy. On the contrary, it is very much of a broad church—a large-scale project that has affinities and involvements across the entire board of philosophical concerns.

Indeed, there is much in the continental philosophical tradition—obviously the work of Bergson, but Nietzsche, Husserl (especially *The Phenomenology of Internal Time Consciousness* and the later "existentialist turn" *Krisis*), Heidegger, and especially Berdyaev and Merleau-Ponty come to mind—which is congenial both doctrinally and methodologically to process thought along the Peirce-Whitehead-Hartshorne axis. There is in fact a bourgeoning literature on this comparative issue.[13] Moreover, there are at least two reasons why the constructive interface between the process and analytic traditions has been largely missed, and why therefore many have seen process thought as more akin to continental projects than analytic ones: First, for many, the broad scope of the analytic tradition has not been recognized or kept in mind, while, on the other hand, explicitly antimetaphysical "linguistic" philosophy of later Wittgensteinian inspiration has been more or less identified with analytic philosophy. On such assumptions, process and analytic philosophy have been glibly and superficially viewed as "oil and water." Second, as Rescher has pointed out,[15] some of the leading figures in the analytic tradition—F. P. Ramsey, Quine, and P. F. Strawson, for instance—have held "antiprocess" metaphysical views due in considerable measure to the influence of "tenseless" logical theory on their picture of the world. As the proceeding discussion in this Introduction and especially chapter 11 makes plain, however, any identification of anti-process logical theory and metaphysics with analytic philosophy is a much too restrictive view of that tradition as philosophers and logicians from Hintikka to A. N. Prior have held just the opposite set of convictions both in metaphysics and logical theory. At any rate, readers must be warned that in making a positive case for the confluence of the analytic and process traditions, I am neither asserting that process philosophy stands *against* the continental tradition in a predominant or clearly discernible fashion nor that process philosophers are never at odds with analytic colleagues (far be it the case!). Such views would seem to me to glibly generalize and grossly overlook the complexity of all the traditions in question. Rather, the emphasis here is to focus on that constructive confluence which has been almost completely ignored.

Analytic Philosophers on Process Thought

While I think it quite true to say that process philosophy has been marginalized, ignored, and/or misunderstood by a majority of analytic philosophers, it is by no means the case that it has been neglected by all. Some philosophers, whose methodological orientations are "analytic" by any standard and who have strong interests in formal and philosophical logic, have in fact taken a keen and sustained interest in the philosophies of Whitehead and Hartshorne. I have in mind such thinkers as the logicians Frederic Fitch, H. G. Hubbeling, and Richard M. Martin, and (Hartshorne's students) Bowman L. Clarke, Lucio Chiarviglio, and Norman M. Martin.[16] William P. Alston, also

Hartshorne's student (whose 1951 University of Chicago Ph.D. dissertation treated the topic of Whitehead and internal relations), has retained at least a measure of constructive interest as is evidenced by his important discussion of Hartshorne's philosophical theology in "Hartshorne and Aquinas: Toward a Via Media."[17] In addition, Hartshorne's defense of his famous modally formalized version of the ontological argument, as well as his enormous career long effort at thinking through the problems of philosophical theology with "exactitude, logical rigor" (MVG vii), has elicited wide discussion among analytic philosophers of religion (for bibliography see notes 16 and 30 in this Introduction and notes to chapters 9–11).

Still others have taken a serious and sympathetic interest in some basic *ideas and theses* of process philosophy (e.g., the objectivity of temporal change, theses of event ontology, etc.), accompanied by either lesser concern with adjudicating the writings of major process thinkers (such as Whitehead and Hartshorne) or considerable to extensive independence from such thinkers. Here I would include, among others, the distinguished philosophers R. M. Gale, Jaako Hintitkka, J. R. Lucas, Thomas Nagel, Karl Popper, A. N. Prior, Wilfrid Sellars, Robert Kane, and Nicholas Rescher.[18, 19] Moreover, it is important in this context to mention that G. H. von Wright has produced an interesting argument for quanta of temporal becoming in his Eddington Lecture on Time, Change and Contradiction. He has also come to agree explicitly with "the kinds of points" that Hartshorne has made against his earlier espousal of a Humean doctrine of external relations in *The Logical Problem of Induction* (for an explication of this critique see below), although he does not hold that the Whitehead-Hartshorne approach resolves the essentially epistemological quandry raised by the problem of induction.[20] And, in an important doctoral thesis, written under Rescher's guidance at the University of Pittsburgh entitled "Towards an Ontology of Process," Johanna Seibt has produced a protacted case for the logical incoherence of standard substance ontologies.[21]

Professor Rescher—the eminent logician, philosopher of science, analytic metaphysician and intellectual historian—has long held the notion that a process conceptuality, as contrasted with that of substance, has sweeping problem-solving utility. His published interest in process thought reaches as far back as an article on "The Revolt Against Process" and culminates in his sustained treatment recently published as *Process Metaphysics* (see previous references in note 18). I am privileged to have his kind permission to reprint here an essay on "The Promise of Process Philosophy,"[22] which presents much of what he does in the recent volume on process thought, but in a more compressed and panoramic form.

Note that this essay contains a section on Process Semantics. This represents a clear example of the sort of "thinking at the intersection" that this anthology is (in part) devoted to displaying and exploring. Rescher shows how a process conceptuality can be helpful in resolving some semantical difficulties generated by the standard subject-predicate or object-attribute logic (the classical logic of quantification found in the work of, say, Russell and Quine). To mention briefly just one advantage of process semantics, note that "action sentences" that contain conjunctions of predicates can be treated so that a *unit* of action can be properly characterized by *both* predicates. Thus, "Y spoke slowly and thoughtfully" does not become the disjointed "Y spoke slowly and Y spoke thoughtfully," as in classical logic, but rather, in the (partial) process rendition: (∃x) (x is an act of speaking and x is performed by Y and x is a slow action and x is a thoughtful action.) In this rendition, there is no unclarity about the fact that the *unit* of action in question is *both* slow and thoughtful. This kind of "intersection thinking" benefits both traditions. As indicated, it appears to resolve (or surely *helps* in resolving) a much-discussed problem among analytic philosophers, pointedly issued by Donald Davidson, concerning the standard logic-modeling of action sentences. On the other hand, it contributes to a more coherent philosophical package for the process conceptuality, since it avoids the embarrassment of conducting reasoning with a substance semantics that rubs against the grain of a process ontology.

In addition to Professor Rescher's essay, I am privileged to include his colleague Richard M. Gale's essay on "Disanalogies Between Space and Time." Perhaps nothing is more central to process thought than the thesis that the tensed modalities, that is, the notions of past, present, and future—McTaggart's A-Series—are both objectively and extralinguistically real. Professor Gale's classic treatise on *The Language of Time* put forth an important case for this "process" position. (Perhaps this is overstating, but at the least there is in this work a defense of a species of the so-called A-Theory of Time in which tensed language is to be regarded, with process philosophers, as semantically objective.) In course, he presented powerful objections to various arguments from "linguistic reduction" against the A-Theory championed by J. J. C. Smart and others.

This objection runs roughly as follows: For the linguistic reductionist, all tensed language is logically reducible to tenseless, token-reflexive or indexical expressions (expressions referring to themselves). This is purportedly shown by the fact that for any sentential formula involving tense, for example, "P is now an event of the past," we can substitute the "equivalent" expression "P is earlier than this utterance." Since we can always use the tense-neutral verb "*is*" while speaking of past, present, and future events, yet without employing the language of "past," "present," or "future," it seems that it is confused to say that an event changes with respect to pastness, presentness, and futurity, as if these were genuine (ontological) properties of events and not simply ways of referring to events. Gale argues, however, that such a *reduction* is confused because it ignores profound disanalogies between the spatial and temporal orders. Consider the following analysans for each A-series analysandum:

Analysandum	*Analysans*
X is now present.	X is simultaneous with this token.
X is now past.	X is earlier than this token.
X is now future.	X is later than this token.

Gale comments: "While it is correct to say that 'now' as well as 'this' in the *analysans* of the EP [Russell's egocentric particular] and TRI [token-reflexive] analyses, function as temporal indicators or demonstratives, it would be wrong to say that they pick out, select, or choose a moment of time."[23] In other words, it would be wrong for the linguistic reductionist to make such a claim because "this" is selective on the spatial order, but not on the temporal order. When we wish to point out something in the spatial field of vision we point to the intended object and say "this." And we could do so for any object within the visual spatial field, because things *coexist* on the spatial order. But there is no temporal field of vision analogous to the spatial order of coexistents. We cannot point to some distant future event and utter "this" with the same resulting clear-cut reference.

In his contribution to this volume, Gale continues with this general motif of temporal-spatial disanalogies, but takes it in new directions and provides interesting responses to new objections. Eschewing the naive (and absurd) concept of temporal becoming embodied in the notion that "now" can shift to a later time (a view not held by Whitehead or Hartshorne incidentally[24]), he aims to uncover commitments to modal disanalogies between temporal and spatial-indexical perspectives deeply embedded in our concepts of agency and objectivity.

While Gale's essay represents one important approach within the tradition of "analyzing our ordinary conceptual scheme"—and is thus aligned with P. F. Strawson's notion of descriptive metaphysics—the philosophy of celebrated contributor W. V. O. Quine represents by contrast an effort at revisionary metaphysics grounded in natural science and guided (or constrained) by the bound variables of quantificational logic. As interpreted by Leemon McHenry in his contribution on "Quine and Whitehead," there are important and neglected similarities between Quine's project and especially the A. N. Whitehead of the middle "philosophy of physics" period culminating in the *Enquiry Concerning the Principles of Natural Knowledge*: Both philosophers are revisionary metaphysicians of a decidedly naturalist bent who look to the empirical sciences as well as formal logic for construction of an ontology of *events*. While McHenry wonders at the outset whether Quine himself would find such a comparison "surprising," Quine responds with an extraordinary affirmation of the comparison: "McHenry ascribes to Whitehead a dualistic ontology of individuals and properties, and to me a monistic ontology of individuals, including classes. I protest that *my ontology is as dualistic as Whitehead's, and indeed is the same as his* except that classes have a clean-cut principle of individuation, namely, coextensiveness whereas properties have none" (my italics). Quine's guarded ontological requirement for individuation—"no entity without identity"—has moved him to reject the Whitehead-Russell notion of properties in favor of classes; a career-long rejection that he recalls as early as his undergraduate assimilation of *Principia Mathematica*. Nonetheless, the general connections with the "middle" Whitehead are striking, and, so far as I am aware, previously unnoticed.

Quine's relationship to Hartshorne's specific projects (and, by a large measure of implication, the later Whitehead's) is, of course, quite different. In important ways, Hartshorne's and Quine's views could not be more disagreeable. In a brief, but quite interesting, article on Quine in CAP, Hartshorne objects to the following doctrines, which are fundamental to Quine's philosophy: reductionist physicalism, a Humean doctrine of causality and external relations, the inclination toward determinism and a compatibilist notion of freedom, a timeless doctrine of truth (including *contingent* truth), holistic or unqualified empiricism (which Hartshorne suggests is itself a *reductio* on Quine's set theory), a concomitant *sharp* rejection of the *a priori*-empirical and analytic-synthetic distinction, agnosticism or atheism, and perhaps most key, a rejection of the intelligibility of *de re* modality. (This last item is the subject of an important essay in this volume by George L. Goodwin, which I discuss below.) Despite all this, it would be wrong to suggest that, regarding Quine and Hartshorne (and thus the later Whitehead in some considerable measure), "never the twain shall meet." Hartshorne himself recognizes this (CAP 245–246):

> Quine's realism, like Popper's, is congenial to a process philosopher. And his "qualified nominalism" is more congenial to my partly Peircean view of this issue than Whitehead's eternal-objects theory. Also, the rejection of an absolute mind-matter dualism is common ground with process philosophers generally.

Apropos of McHenry's contribution, I would add that Quine and Hartshorne are generally united in their acceptance of event ontology over an ontology of substances; indeed, Quine's bottom-line objection to Kripke's semantics for modal logic concerns its interpretation as entangled in "Aristotelian essentialism," an interpretation averted by Goodwin's suppliance of a Hartshornean event ontological underpinning.

Analytic Themes in the Philosophy of Whitehead

As the above discussion suggests, it is quite possible to see Whitehead's philosophy as containing (largely unrecognized) connections with specific contentions and projects of recent analytic philosophers. This represents George R. Lucas Jr.'s preoccupation in "Analytic and Post-Analytic Themes in Whitehead's Metaphysics" found in his *The Rehabilitation of Whitehead: An Analytic and Historical Assessment of Process Philosophy* (RW). As brief examples of these connections, consider the following: Lucas notes perceptively that Whitehead's position on logical consistency and his rejection of "Humean assumptions about the disconnectedness of discrete objects or formal descriptive principles, such as 'laws' of nature" (RW 142) leads precisely to Hilary Putnam's (1975) analysis of and distinction between "conceivability" and "logical possibility," and consequently to Putnam's treatment of related problems in modal logic and possible worlds semantics concerning essentialism and transworld identity.[25] Or consider the striking similarity between Whitehead's (dispersed) statements on the issue of personal identity over time and Derek Parfit's recent doctrine propounded in *Reasons and Persons*:[26] Personal identity is a matter of "sustained intentionality coordinated from moment to moment (and hence, both an on-going task and achievement of individual agency) rather than a simple substantial reference to the location, properties, and causal activity of the physical body alone" (RW 146).

In his specific contribution to this volume, Lucas makes the case for at least two interesting and substantive connections between Whitehead and Wittgenstein that, to my knowledge, have never been proposed previously:

(1) At a superficial level, it would seem that the cosmology of PR represents just the sort of "senseless" systematic theory "that most disciples of Wittgenstein would surely regard as an alien and unintelligible form of *Sprachspiel*." However, a deeper reading of Whitehead suggests that his elaborate categoreal scheme is not to be taken as a coarsely literal "representation" of reality (a *Vorstellung*), but is rather a heuristic model (a *bildlichen Darstellung*) that illustrates or shows aspects of the real which cannot be strictly "said." As such the scheme functions much like the theoretical physicist's heuristic "picture," for example, as in a quantum mechanical account of the atom, which is most useful for understanding atomic behavior, but certainly does not yield a "sensory image" that is to be taken as literal description. Lucas goes on to suggest that, in particular, Whitehead's "picture" of such matters as time, temporal process, and causality is far more illuminating and satisfying than alternative accounts, and may be regarded as a substantial gloss on Wittgenstein's rejection of the "passage of time" and his call for describing time lapse in terms of process (see *Tractatus* 6.361). (2) Lucas also

develops an interpretation of the mature Whitehead which puts him in the "ironic" and rather skeptical camp of the later Wittgenstein and G. E. Moore as contrasted with Frege and the early Whitehead and Russell of *Principia Mathematica*. Simply put, Whitehead rejects the central idea of "modernism," of *Aufklärung*, namely, that reason is entirely self-sufficient for the purposes of perfecting human knowledge and progress. There is no certainty for us, no bedrock logical foundation for mathematics, and no escape from final semantical ineffability. If this be thought implausible as an interpretation of Whitehead, think only of his (Whitehead's) crisp, starkly anti-Cartesian declarlation: "Philosophy has been misled by the example of mathematics" (PR 8).

Such a declaration should be taken, of course, in its intended *epistemic* context. Whitehead was attempting here to thwart any notion that philosophy can proceed in an arrogantly deductive manner which entertains the pretense of providing apodictic "proofs." However, he clearly did not intend to regard mathematics as providing no important clues to, on Lucas' reading, the best heuristic "picture"of which we are capable (among other sources on this score see "Mathematics and the Good," ESP, 97–113). The case for this is made by James Bradley in his quite original interpretive essay, which focuses on Whitehead's critical reflection on the Frege-Russell notion of the propositional function. Distinguishing between weak and strong theories of existence, Bradley argues that the Fregean propositional function analysis leads to the "weak" theoretical notion that "existence" ought to be exhaustively viewed as instantiation of a class: x exists if 'p of x' can be existentially quantified. This analysis, by definition, dismisses the search for the self-explanatory ultimate, which is the aim of speculative philosophy as exemplified by Whitehead. The strong theorist of existence is unsatisfied with the existentially quantified function and wants to ask, Why is there that which answers a description? According to Bradley, Whitehead takes up the cause of the strong theory by generalizing the modern Fregean concept of natural numbers into the serial connective $n + 1$. (That is to say, a natural number is that which exists necessarily in a series and is that which satisfies the function $n + 1$.) This "successor operator" $n + 1$ is the very model for creativity, and accordingly expresses the "category of the Ultimate," applicable to the entire domain of mathematical entities and in fact any entity whatsoever (including God). Note that all the key characteristics of Whiteheadian actual occasions are abstractly present in the serial function: uniqueness or novelty, intrinsic connection to others, cumulativeness, advance, and synthetic activity. In contrast to G. R. Lucas, however, Bradley's interpretation rejects the notion that Whiteheadian analysis leaves us with "semantical ineffability." Says Bradley, "The concrete, serial act or occasion is rationally and intelligibly describable through and through precisely because it is an ultimate and irreducible given which is intrinsically rule-governed." In the end, for Bradley, the great significance of

Whitehead's serial function analysis is that it represents a truly important effort at fusing the analytical tradition of functional analysis with the speculative effort of reaching intellectual satisfaction, and it does so without succumbing either to pan-rationalism or operationalism.

Yet another and quite distinctive connection between Whitehead and current issues in analytic metaphysics is made by John Lango. In the past decade or so, a number of analytic philosophers have been hard at work on the traditional metaphysical issue of universals and particulars (see footnote 1 of Lango's essay for a brief bibliography). Among these, Keith Campbell's 1990 treatise on *Abstract Particulars* has engendered considerable discussion and has re-opened the debate on the nature of properties, tropes, and relations. Of special interest to Lango is Campbell's argument to the effect that there can be no instances of relational particulars. Whitehead's metaphysics, cited but not pursued by Campbell at a couple of junctures, is especially relevant here as the basic notion of prehension can be interpreted as just such an example of a relational particular to which Campbell objects.

On Campbell's theory, a prehension can be viewed in such a way that it is no instance of a particular because a prehenson has a "foundation" in a nonrelational particular, namely, the prehending subject, for example, the actual occasion. In effect, the relation of prehension is *supervenient* on the actual occasion, and does not stand as a particular fact somehow outside the prehending subject and its objective datum. Just as we might say that two sheets of paper have the same color, namely, whiteness, and this relational fact of sameness is supervenient on the sheets, we can likewise say that the prehension-relation is a supervenient property of the prehending subject—it cannot be a prehensive subject and fail to have the prehensive relation. Ingeniously, Lango constructs a supervenience thwarting counterexample by analyzing a social series of Whiteheadian occasions where novelty is deficient (as in electronic occasions). Consider occasions A, B, C, and D, where A and B are contemporaries, C is subsequent to A and B, and D subsequent to C. It is logically possible that:

> D might have had a different simple physical feeling of C, but with exactly the same subjective forms. Here is how: Instead of feeling C's feeling of *A's* feeling of the defining characteristic, D might have felt B's feeling of it. But we have seen above that the subjective form of *B's* feeling is exactly the same as the subjective form of A's feeling, and thus that the subjective forms of C's two feelings are (by re-enaction) exactly the same. Now, if D were to have felt C's feeling of B's feeling of the defining characteristic, there would also have been the re-enaction of exactly the same subjective form. Therefore, the subjective form of this simple physical feeling that D *might*

> have had is exactly the same as the subjective form of the simple physical feeling that D *does* have.

The fact that D could have had an alternative physical feeling, that is, D's prehensions could have had alternative objective data (C's feeling of A or C's feeling of B), entails that the prehension-relation is *not* supervenient on D; the prehension-relation that D does have is thus a *particular* fact of relatedness. Thus, if this counterexample is correct, Whitehead's doctrine of prehension and social occasions provides a powerful challenge to any ontology of nonrelational particulars such as that proposed by Campbell.

There is indeed a rich mine of comparative philosophy here which has only begun to be explored. *If* given a fair hearing, efforts in this vein, such as Bradley's, Griffin's (see discussion below), Lango's, and Lucas's may well have obvious and profound benefits, including renewed interest in and access to bodies of philosophical literature once thought to be utterly removed from one another. In light of such thematic "connections" research, analytic philosophers might be more inclined to read Whitehead and to find surprising suggestions for new approaches to philosophic issues (Lango's case against the untenability of relational particulars is a perfect example). Likewise, process thinkers might be more inclined to consult analytic philosophers and to encounter new tools for the clarification, refinement, and criticism of process theses.

Analytic Themes in the Philosophy of Hartshorne

Whitehead's monumental *Process and Reality* was published just one year before Moritz Schlick's address on "The Future of Philosophy" before the 1930 World Congress of Philosophy at Oxford. Thus, Whitehead's mature philosophical ideas were being presented just as the era of antispeculative positivism was about to take center stage. By contrast, at roughly the same time, Charles Hartshorne's philosophical career was beginning its well-browned post-Ph.D. phase when he was appointed Assistant Professor of Philosophy at The University of Chicago in 1927. Unlike Whitehead, Hartshorne has thus lived through the gamut of the "age of analysis" in its Russell-Moore-Tractarian Wittgenstein, positivist, ordinary language/conceptual analysis, and now "pluralist" phases, and has done so with rather full cognizance, noting on a number of occasions his own sense of "common ground" with the analytic tradition (e.g., CSPM xiv). Thus, in Hartshorne's case, it is possible to draw on a number of *explicit* discussions of analytic philosophers from Russell and Moore to Ayer and Carnap to Wittgenstein, Strawson, Ryle, Quine, Sellars, and von Wright.[27] In an essay published in the Eugene Peters memorial *Festschrift*,[28] I attempted to chart and explicate Hartshorne's relation to various phases of the analytic tradition by working through his literary corpus with an eye toward published statements on analytic philosophers and issues of concern to analytic philosophers. My findings in that paper were that Hartshorne is "at the least a 'para-traveler' with the analytic tradition, who has employed its tools and some of its vocabulary, while keeping a critical distance, especially, for example, from any claims of methodological definitiveness on the part of some proponents of ordinary language philosophy and from certain dogmas such as verificationism and falsificationism."[29]

Just as G. R. Lucas and others have suggested that Whitehead's philosophy has significance for some recent projects in analytic philosophy, I would also submit that Hartshorne's work does as well. In addition to his much-discussed formalization of the ontological argument into modern modal logical notation (which has, for one, rather consciously inspired the defense of a closely similar modal version in the work of Robert Merrihew Adams[30]), Hartshorne has made some unique and still powerful technical contributions to such issues as the logic of future tense propositions, the logic of relations, genetic/strict identity theory, and metalogical considerations on operator semantics.[31] To give substance to these claims, let me briefly expand upon the first and last of these items (a more comprehensive discussion of the first item is found in the essay contributed to this volume by me and Donald Viney, while the third item is explored in George Goodwin's essay [chapter 9, section on "Individual Identity"]):

1. A good example of Hartshorne's skill at the logical analysis of language is afforded by his paper on "The Meaning of 'Is Going to Be,'" published in *Mind*,[32] a major forum for contemporary analytic philosophy. Here he provides a way of dismantling the logical argument for fatalism—defended by Bertrand Russell, Richard Taylor, Richard Montague, R. D. Bradley, and others—which is grounded on the Law of Excluded Middle. In one form of this argument given by Russell, the claim is that for any arbitrary future event x, our choices are exhaustively limited by the Law of Excluded Middle to the propositional schemas: "x will occur" or "x will not occur." In effect, since (allegedly) these schemas can be formally generalized into the tautologous sentential function X v~X, it is a truth of logic that the future will be one way and not another, that is, since one or the other of these alternatives must obtain on pain of denying the tautologous status of X v~X. Hartshorne observes that the assumption that "x will occur" and "x will not occur" is exhaustive begs the question of fatalism, since it assumes that, for *any* time t, there can simply *be* no indefiniteness with respect to x. Are not the alternatives in fact

a *triad* of statement forms such that "x will occur," "x will not occur," and "x may-or-may-not occur"? Further, the assumption that "x will occur" and "x will not occur" can be sententially formalized as X and ~X, respectively, represents a logical fallacy akin to assuming that (∀x)Px and (∀x)~Px exhaust the quantificational alternatives for a given variable-predicate function Px. Hartshorne holds that the logical status of "x will occur" and "x will not occur" is that of *contraries* as opposed to *strict contradictories*. Thus, if we sententially formalize "x will occur" as X, the strict contradictory ~X should represent "x *may not occur.*" Significantly, Hartshorne's suggested modal "square of alterns" approach to this issue (see chapter 11 for a full presentation) has a precise analogue in A. N. Prior's square of equipollence and opposition constructed for deontic logic as an extension of the logic of modality in his treatise on *Formal Logic.*[33] There Prior similarly observes that the strict contradictory of "A is obligatory" is "A is not-obligatory," rather than "Not-A is obligatory."

Hartshorne's original move here is to shift the focus from truth values attending propositions (on Hartshorne's approach we need only standard two-valued logic) to alternatives in predicate expression. This solution to the "logical problem of fatalism" has an elegant economy. No need here for Łukasiewicz's three-valued logic or perhaps tenuous distinctions between "analytic" and "synthetic" versions of the Law of Excluded Middle or outright abrogation of Excluded Middle. Nor, as will be argued in chapter 11, does Hartshorne preserve the Law of Excluded Middle at the cost of giving up the Law of Noncontradiction (as charged in Steven M. Cahn's reissued classic on *Fate, Logic, and Time*).[34]

2. Following Peirce's trail-blazing work on "illation" or "entailment" as logically primitive or fundamental, Hartshorne has developed an interesting explication of the idea that the logical syntax of standard propositional or truth-functional logic is such that "the defining power of propositional functions varies inversely with their symmetry" (CSPM 206). To illustrate this briefly, consider material entailment as contrasted with equivalence. Material entailment, as in A → B, is asymmetrical by virtue of the familiar rule that such entailment is not equivalent to its converse (thus, the formula [(A → B) ↔ [(A → B) • (B → A)]] has a contingent truth table). By contrast, equivalence, as in A ↔ B, is symmetrical by virtue of the familiar rule that such formula is equivalent to its converse (thus, [(A ↔ B) ↔ [(B ↔ A)] has a

> tautologous table). Hartshorne makes the significant observation that equivalence fails to yield truth tableaux completeness even when combined with negation, yet material entailment does so when combined with negation. Thus, (1) any conjunctive statement, say, (A • B), can be rewritten as ~(A → ~B), and (2) any disjunctive proposition, say, A v B, can be rewritten ~A → B. The equivalence case A ↔ B can be cast as the conjunction [(A → B) • (B → A)] and consequently by virtue of the conjunctive replacement rule of (1): (A ↔ B) ↔ ~[(A → B) → ~ (B → A)]. The *most* definitive of functions, the only functions capable of defining all others in singular fashion, are the Sheffer functions, which possess a triadic asymmetry that yet *includes* dyadic symmetry. We see this, Hartshorne notes, in their truth-tabular definitions—the Stroke = "false *iff* both propositional variables are true," and the Daggar = "true *iff* both propositional variables are false." In effect, the triadic relation, i.e., the product of the binary Sheffer construction A|B, which is itself dyadically symmetrical (A is true *and* B is true), stands as an asymmetry in terms of its truth value (false in relation to symmetrical truth). Hartshorne finds a metaphysically ultimate pattern here, namely, symmetry *within* an all-embracing asymmetry.

This is a powerful generalization of ideas that carries a devastating critique of some still prestigious philosophical contentions in the tradition of Hume. If directional or asymmetrical connectedness is a deep structure of possible worlds, as at least suggested by the above considerations on the most fundamental logical syntax, then G. H. von Wright's proposal that "There is no object which implies the existence of any other if we consider these objects in themselves," or more roughly in Hume's phrase, "what is distinguishable is separable," is false and necessarily so (as mentioned earlier von Wright has since conceded that the above proposal is deeply problematic). Contrary to Hume and von Wright, mutual separability of objects or events is not entailed by mere distinguishability. Says Hartshorne, "The letter *a* is distinguishable and separable from the letter pair *ab*; yet the pair is not separable from *a*."[35] In effect, a cumulative totality A • B entails its parts, say A, but A does not imply the totality A • B. In the case of entailment, then, the "conditioning" is asymmetrical and the order matters and this mirrors temporal inclusion and creativity. Yet, temporal inclusion or cumulativeness is found in this asymmetry *by virtue of temporally succeeding events which imply their past*, while the past events (or scope of events) do not do so conversely. "Dogs exist" does imply "mammals exist," while "mammals exist" does not imply that "dogs exist." *Differences in the historical or temporal scope* of terms comprising propositions has a connection to the semantics of propositions and thus their ordering as antecedent or consequent in the entailment expression. To object to this, as have Quine and von Wright, that such entailment examples as the above employ tense-neutral verbs is simply irrelevant if S. M. Cahn, A. N. Prior and others are correct (as I hold they are) in arguing that a shift of tense from verb to adverbial phrase such that the verb is rendered tenseless does not in fact eliminate tense without at the same time altering the semantic content of the proposition. Hartshorne is correct, it seems to me, in his central contention that tense can be an "uneliminable" aspect of the semantics of propositions.

Other Process Thinkers on Analytic Philosophy

A number of philosophers and theologians, whose main orientation is process thought, have given attention to issues in contemporary analytic philosophy or have employed methods of analytic philosophers.

(1) George L. Goodwin is perhaps the most significant figure within this group.[36] In an essay on Hartshorne's ontological argument included in this volume, he takes up the important question of Quine's attack on the intelligibility of *de re* modality at some length. While the whole project of Kripkean possible worlds semantics, upon which Goodwin's argument in part depends, is controversial, modal logic still has its able defenders, for example, Ruth Barcan.[37] Moreover, mathematicians are finding modal logic to be increasingly important to foundational issues (see, for instance, Geoffrey Hellman's intriguing work on *Mathematics Without Numbers: Towards a Modal Structural Interpretation*[38]). Thus, Goodwin's project *contra* Quine remains significant for the contemporary scene. For the uninitiated, let me provide a very brief account of the essential problem and Goodwin's treatment of it:

Quine has objected to the idea of *de re* modality, since it involves quantification across modal operators, for example, as in (∃x) (necessarily, x is greater than seven), which he regards as logically illicit. Quine points out that we cannot existentially generalize from the "licit" *de dicto* formulation:

(a) Necessarily, nine is greater than seven

to

(b) (∃x) (necessarily, x is greater than seven)

This is because "nine" in sentence (a) is referentially opaque, that is, it fails to denote in a singular way, and thus opens the door to counterexamples in the generalized sentence (b). For instance, Quine holds that "nine" can mean "the number of planets," but surely it is not a property of "the number of planets" that it is necessarily greater than seven. The thrust of this is that, because of referential opacity in quantified modal logic, we do not know what it *means* to introduce propositions of the form (∃x) N (x > 7). However, Hartshorne is clearly committed, in his ontological argument,[37] to such forms as:

(c) (∃x) (Necessarily, x is perfect)

And, if Quine is right, we do not know what (c) means any more than we know what (b) means.

Consequently, an effective Hartshornean response to Quine's critique of *de re* modality requires an intelligible semantics for modal logic. At this juncture Kripke's celebrated, "Semantical Considerations on Modal Logic,"[40] comes to bear effectively on the issue. On the terms of Kripke's semantics, we *can* get an intelligible notion of sentences having the form of "(∃x) N (x > 7)." Such sentences say:[41]

> that there is some object, x, in this world which has the property, greater-than-seven, in this world and in every possible world in which x exists. In other words, x exists in this world and at least some possible worlds accessible from this world, and x falls under the extension of the predicate, greater-than-seven, in every world in which it exists.

However, while Kripke semantics thus resolves the issue of providing a *formal* semantics for sentences involving quantification into modal contexts, the very terms of this semantics raise the further question of what it means for an individual to exist in various possible worlds. This problem has come to be known as the Problem of Transworld Identity. Quine has challenged Kripke further by arguing that his solution to the problem of referential opacity issues in a semantics involving the notoriously difficult idea of "essential properties." For instance, must C. S. Peirce be a philosopher in every possible world in which he exists in order to be C. S. Peirce in those possible worlds? Could he be a seventeenth-century sea captain in some possible worlds, and yet still be C. S. Peirce? It is just here, Goodwin argues, that Hartshorne's ontology of temporal process can be employed, providing Kripke with intelligible criteria for making "transworld" identifications. The Problem of Transworld Identity seems perplexing and insoluble when employing, to use Quine's phrase, "Aristotelian essentialism," in which essential properties inhere in substances and require no reference to temporality. Hartshorne's event ontology places the search for a criterion for transworld identity in the much wider matrix of successive and causally efficacious temporal units of becoming. "Temporal inheritance" becomes the *essential* factor in determining identity, and thus more readily settles the above questions: C. S. Peirce might well exist as a literary critic in some possible world, since he might have been one in this actual world, that is, since there was a time in the "history" of Peirce in which he was not a philosopher, and he could have been subjected at that time to different influences. But most certainly he could not be—in any possible world—a seventeenth century sea captain, since this would have *nothing* in common with his succession of temporal events. Thus, to put it cautiously, if Hartshorne's ontological criteria do not "resolve" the Problem of Transworld Identity, it seems clear that they simplify it.

(2) David Ray Griffin has engaged in dialogue and debate with a number of analytic philosophers of religion and philosophers of mind. This dialogue has taken place largely in two recent books (a very recent third work, *Reenchantment Without Supernaturalism*, deals with analytic philosophy of language and epistemology, but is discussed briefly in the section on "Postanalytic Philosophy" below):

A. Most famously, he has attacked the classical notion of omnipotence, a notion defended by certain analytic theists, on grounds that it is logically incoherent; consequently, his notions of I-omnipotence (I for "incoherent") and C-omnipotence (C for "coherent") have become somewhat commonplace (even if contentious) vocabulary in the field of philosophy of religion. His 1991 work on theodicy—*Evil Revisited*[42]—contains two chapter length discussions of critiques of process theology's so-called social view of omnipotence as issued by Nelson Pike and Bruce Reichenbach. One important bone of contention here is the so-called Premise X, the notion that it is logically possible for an agent A to determine all of the properties (including any activities) of a distinct entity B. Griffin denies X and provides (in my view) a rather impressive point by point counterargument to, in particular, Pike's efforts at defense of X (implicit in the classical doctrine of omnipotence). Briefly consider an example: Pike introduces a "strengthened version" of X, which he takes to be immune to the process critic who envisions X as a version of the "monopolistic" fallacy:[43]

> ["Strengthened" Premise X] It is possible for A to completely determine all of the activities of B *even in the case where B is making whatever effort it can to determine its own activities for itself.*

Griffin quickly sees that this revision is a semantical ruse. Says Griffin perceptively:[46]

> Although Pike is right that I would consider his "strengthened" version of premise X to be logically false, showing its inherently problematic nature does not require the introduction of Principle P or any other outside principle. His premise is *contradictory* all by itself—that is, it is *self*-contradictory. If A is *completely* determining *all* of B's activities, then B cannot be making *any* "effort of its own" to determine its own activities for itself. Any *effort* B exerted would be part of its *activities* and would therefore by hypothesis be completely

> determined by A. Pike has again failed to realize that the choices, desires, and efforts of the individual are its central "activities."

The work Griffin has produced in *Evil Revisited* offers yet another example of the benefits of process-analytic exchange. For in having to respond to the criticisms of Madden, Hare, Basinger, Plantinga, Pike, and Reichenbach, he has been pressed to clarify in a significant way crucial process theological notions of types of causal agency, absolute and relative coercion, modes of persuasion, and so on.

B. An important recent event in the history of the process-analytic interface is the appearance in 1998 of Griffin's remarkable treatise *Unsnarling the World-Knot: Consciousness, Freedom, and the Mind-Body Problem* (UWK). Here Professor Griffin gives a detailed and careful review of the current situation in analytic philosophy of mind as found in such writers as Keith Campbell, Daniel Dennett, William Lycan, Colin McGinn, Thomas Nagel, John Searle, Galen and P. F. Strawson, and especially Jaegwon Kim. Through numerous channels of evidence and argument, Griffin shows that contemporary dualist and materialist research programs have reached an intractable dead end in the quest for a unified, scientifically acceptable position which preserves *all* of our "hard core" or "deep" or "pragmatically ineluctable" common sense intuitions about the existence of consciousness and freedom—a point conceded in various ways by many of the above mentioned authors. Indeed, the whole situation seems to cry out for some novel "radical alternative" conceptuality, especially one geared to providing, in Galen Strawson's words, "an adequate grasp of the fundamental nature of matter at some crucial *general* level of understanding."[45]

This alternative conceptuality, argues Griffin, is what he calls "physicalist panexperientialism" as developed systematically in the philosophies of A. N. Whitehead and Charles Hartshorne. This view is *physicalist* in that it rejects the Cartesian notion that mental phenomena are necessarily or universally nonextended in phenomenal space; instead, it holds that *every* actual occasion of experience has a physical or extensional aspect. It is also *panexperientialist* in that every genuine individual is constituted by actual occasions that have some degree of "openness to their environment," some degree of "interiority," and are partially self-creative syntheses of antecedent occasions—syntheses which necessarily involve a grasping or prehending of other, that is, past occasions. In Whitehead's famous summary dictum, "the many *become* one and are increased by one."

Among analytic philosophers, Thomas Nagel has long suggested (albeit, with important worries and qualifications) a similar move to panexperientialism or "ontological idealism," although his version lacks the systematic metaphysical motivations and nuanced development of Whitehead's PR or

Hartshorne's still powerful essay on "The Compound Individual" (WP, chapter 4). Notwithstanding, Nagel sees that this move has a chief advantage in avoiding the whole problem of the *arbitrariness* of the emergence of sentience and/or consciousness within the biological continuum—indeed, he sees the "emergence" of psychological phenomena as impossible on a materialist ontology.[46] Moreover, William Seager, who has treated these issues with care, agrees that the panexperientialist alternative fares well on the score of overall theoretical parsimony.[47] In an impressive recent treatise on consciousness, David F. Chalmers has also recognized some advantages of a "panpsychist" theory.[48]

However, among analytic philosophers, it is Jaegwon Kim who has responded to Griffin most appreciatively.[49] Indeed, Griffin seems to get at the primary trouble spot in Kim's "supervenience" project as follows: Kim wants to preserve both physicalism and the common sense notion of mental causation (as do process philosophers with the caveat that *materialist* physicalism is not wanted). In order to achieve this he has proposed a "mereological supervenience" model of the mind-body relation in which mental causation is viewed as a kind of supervenient causation. In Kim's analysis, mental phenomena do not directly cause other mental phenomena to occur; rather, they do so only in the sense of being supervenient on a physical state which in turn causes another physical state on which is a supervenient mental state. Thus, the mind-body relation is roughly analyzed as follows (SM 106):

> A: "when a mental event M causes a physical event P, this is so because M is supervenient upon a physical event, P*, and P* causes P"
>
> A[1]: "when a mental event M causes another mental event M*, this is so because M supervenes on a physical state P, and similarly M* on P*, and P causes P*"

The analyses A and A[1] make it clear that the exercise of casual agency really takes place at the physical level (in A, P* causes P, and in A[1], P causes P*), while the mental events function as macrolevel descriptions of whole sets of microphysical events, sets labeled collectively as P and P* (and this is just one way of defining "supervenience"). But, as Griffin argues (UWK 219–227) and as Kim himself has more recently suggested, this whole approach seems to dissolve into epiphenomenalism. Kim has changed the *vocabulary* of the epiphenomenalist model (i.e., Kim speaks of a mental event as being supervenient upon the physical event rather than of a physical event causing a mental event), but the point remains that there is no direct casual role played by mental events. Thus, in Kim's own words, "any 'physicalistically correct' account of mental causation must . . . expos[e] itself to the charge of epiphenomenalism" (SM 360; cited by Griffin, UWK 225). This is a serious flaw as epiphenomenalism presents mental events as lacking causal efficacy and thus implies that our notion of *intentional* action is entirely illusory. Contrary to Kim's own laudable desire to build our philosophical theories around the best of current scientific theory and practice, epiphenomenalism is an inherently antievolutionary perspective as it suggests that animals and humans evolved with persistent natural selection of entirely superfluous mental entities. Physicalist panexperientialism, by definition, has no such problem.

(3) Although this has not been explicitly emphasized, it is a commonplace that contemporary process philosophy clearly has had its greatest impact so far on the fields of philosophy of religion and theology. Since analytic philosophy has also shaped these disciplines in significant ways, it is not surprising that a large part of the confluence of the analytic and process traditions has taken place in the context of debates in the philosophy of religion. Note that Hartshorne's work in modal logic, theory of modality, and theistic arguments has inspired, not only new research on the ontological argument, but constructive efforts at revisioning other arguments for the existence of God. Contributor Billy Joe Lucas, a specialist in symbolic logic whose dissertation committee at the University of Texas at Austin included Hartshorne, presents an example in his essay on "The Second Epistemic Way." Developed within the framework of a Brouwerian modal logic (Quantified B Minus, first described in Lucas's 1981 Ph.D. dissertation on "The Logic of Omniscience"), Lucas argues that three basic premises about omniscience logically entail that an omniscient being must actually exist if one is so much as logically possible. In effect, the presumption of the truth of these three premises:

1. Necessarily, for any x, if x is epistemically unsurpassable, then it is not possible for there be a true proposition which x does not know.
2. For any x, if x knows all true propositions, then x is an omniscient being.
3. It is logically possible that there exists an x such that x is an epistemically unsurpassable being.

logically implies that an omniscient being *does* exist. This is close, although not identical, to Hartshorne's suggested epistemic argument at LP 70–73, first formalized by Nasser and Brown[50] ; thus, Lucas's title of the *second* epistemic way.

It should be observed that a successful epistemic argument for omniscience is of crucial importance to Hartshorne's project for neoclassical natural theology. This is because the attribute of omniscience is "the key," as it were, to other generic traits of deity (PSG 22–24). For example: It is arguable that, if the neoclassical description of God is to be religiously adequate, then "if x is God, then x is maximally benevolent" is a required meaning postulate of neoclassical theism.[51] But, Hartshorne argues, unsurpassable benevolence is analytic of the idea of omniscience. The issues invoked here are complex and broad ranging and thus cannot be treated adequately in an introduction, but the rough or basic idea is this—Plato's intuition about the coextensiviness of knowledge and moral virtue is correct (DR 126):

> The reason that in us knowledge is not identical with virtue is only that we mean by knowing not necessarily the actual, concrete awareness of things, but the virtual or abstract awareness of them. Thus a man may know that his acts will have harmful consequences in the sense that, if asked, he would give the right answer to questions; but it does not follow that in the precise moment of decision he has these matters present to his mind with any concreteness and correctness. However, the divine or adequate awareness cannot in this way escape the identity of knowing and valuing. While virtual and abstract knowledge has little of the values of concrete reality, actual and concrete knowledge has all the values, and cannot fail to respond; for the ability to be aware and the ability to respond are identical.

In effect, the claim is that an omniscient being's eminent sympathetic participation in the experience of others removes the very *sine qûa non* for any negative motivations such as hatred, indifference, envy, etc., which undergird malevolence.

The above is just one of numerous examples which could be adduced to show that, far from depending on the ontological argument alone for the rational support of theistic belief, Hartshorne presents a systematic, cumulative web of arguments that are "mutually supportive," and of which the ontological is only a part, albeit, an important one. If sound, the epistemic argument supports not only the fundamental claim of any religiously adequate theism that "God is omniscient or perfect in knowledge," but that "God is personal and benevolent." It also buttresses Hartshorne's version of the design argument as it supports the plausibility of asserting that there is an eminent cosmic ordering agent (who deliberates fundamental nomological order) when there are independent grounds for belief in a mind of cosmic scale. Thus, efforts like Lucas's are both interesting in their own right and of great interest to those attracted to Hartshorne's natural theological project.

(4) Finally, there is a host of dispersed articles in the literature authored by process thinkers which bear on the process-analytic interface. I include some of these with brief annotations in a footnote.[52]

Postanalytic Philosophy

Perhaps a number of readers are convinced at this point that there are indeed intersections at which both analytic and process philosophers have been and can be engaged in mutually helpful research and criticism. However, "post-modernists" of Richard Rorty's ilk will no doubt raise disconcerting questions about whether this *rapprochement*, if it exists at all, amounts to naught.[53] What difference does it make, especially to the wider culture, if it can be shown that there is some substantial common ground between analytic and process philosophy, when yet both modes of philosophizing are in fact "dead" (because argumentative philosophy of whatever stripe is dead)? Too little and too late to join hands with practitioners of analytic methods (or be perceived as doing such), since analytic methods have produced little other than continuous disagreement, forcing their practitioners to retreat into small enclosures dedicated to utterly idiosyncratic concerns. Analytic (or any other) philosophy in the realist tradition is a "myth" anyway since the "meaning" of any text or object is an unstable affair, always subject to deconstruction.

There is much to be said about this topic and I will have space here merely to make a few hopefully plausible remarks in response to the spectre (some would, of course, say the reality) of a "postanalytic," or stronger still, a "postphilosophical" culture.

First of all, the antirealist point of view which is part and parcel of Rorty's perspective and of deconstructive postmodernism generally can be directly challenged in important and complementary ways. I have in mind at least two such ways, one provided by John Searle and another provided by contemporary process philosophy:

I find John Searle's effort in "Does the Real World Exist?, Parts I and II," in his *The Construction of Social Reality* to be effective (CSR, chapters 7 and 8). Searle argues that there is simply no problem created for external realism—that is, the notion presupposed in our public cognitive discourse that there exists a reality independent of our representations of it—by *any* kind of conceptual, social, or linguistic relativism. For instance, consider Nelson Goodman's conceptual relativism. It is perfectly possible to agree with Goodman's point that the question, How many objects are there in a given perceptual field?, can be answered in any number of ways *depending on the pragmatic interests of the persons answering the question,* and yet, at the same time, we can affirm the proposition that there is an external reality which exists independently of any of our ways of so-called world making (to employ Goodman's vocabulary). Indeed, argues Searle, "world making" is precisely wrongheaded. The conflation between world and description which is embodied in Goodman's vocabulary is just the root of the *appearance* of an inconsistency between conceptual relativism and external realism. For in fact we do not make worlds, we make *descriptions* which either do or do not apply to the world. Consider Searle's example (CSR 162): Given three separate circles labeled A, B, and C in a given perceptual field, why not just say that the field *really* has three objects under the criterion of Carnap arithmetic and *really* has seven objects (A, B, C, A + B, B + C, A + C and A + B + C) under a criterion of mereological-sum logic? There are at least two considerations that bolster an affirmative answer: (1) the perceptual field remains fixed in terms of its being the basis or source for variant conceptual schematizations, and (2) the field provides *constraints* for the kinds of conceptual schematizations which might be applied to it; in other words, while the field admits of variant descriptive schemas, it does not at all follow that *just any* descriptive schema will apply. While the above two descriptions of the perceptual field seem intelligible enough, a description such as "the field contains a million octagons" does not seem intelligible as a description, and to argue for its inclusion as a viable description simply seems to engage in what Umberto Eco has aptly called "overinterpretation."[54] Indeed, it may even be the case, as C. S. Peirce seems to suggest, that the "interpretations" of any given object, text, or perceptual field are nondenumerable, are given to "unlimited semeiosis," but this is a far cry from "hermetic drift" or "anything goes."[55]

Searle's point about the non sequitur fallacy is perhaps most clearly made in a footnote discussion of Putnam's attack on so-called Metaphysical Realism (CSR 164). According to Searle, Putnam conflates external realism and what might be called the thesis of the privileged conceptual scheme in his definition of Metaphysical Realism (MR). If we let ER = "Reality exists independently of our representations of it," let PS = "Reality is correctly described by exactly one conceptual scheme," and let CR = "All representations of reality are made relative to some pragmatically or arbitrarily selected set of concepts," then Putnam's critique of MR runs as follows:[56]

1. MR *iff* (ER and PS).
2. CR logically entails ~ PS.
3. CR is the case.
4. By *modus ponens* from 2 and 3: ~ PS.
5. By virtue of '*iff*' in premise 1 and simplification: MR logically entails (ER and PS).
6. By inference from 4), i.e., ~PS logically entails ~ (ER and PS): ~ (ER and PS)

   ∴ *By modus tollens* from 5 and 6: ~ MR

But the problem here is that ER and PS are logically independent of one another, and thus the first premise is suspect. If our example above about the perceptual field of circles is correct, it would follow that it is clearly possible for ER to obtain without there being just *one* conceptual description which applies. Thus, the fact that Putnam has shown correctly that CR entails that ~PS is utterly irrelevant as to whether or not ER obtains. For, (ER and PS), ~PS, ∴ ~ER, is an invalid conjunctive syllogism indeed.

Contemporary process philosophy has its own distinctive voice to add to the debate over antirealism, a voice that complements Searle's position sketched above, and which, I suggest, if sound can accommodate the later Wittgenstein and Derrida's emphasis on the indeterminateness of language as well as postmodern rhetoric about the "myth of the given." The Whitehead-Hartshorne view is that "external" reality is always a given as an *initial presupposition* of all interpretation, judgement, and linguistic formation. The whole point of Whitehead's distinction between perception in the mode of causal efficacy and in the mode of presentational immediacy is to assert that, *contra* Hume, sensations and other high-level psychological phenomena such as ideation are the *end* result of a complex process of construction which *begins* with the prehension of actualities outside the prehending subject. *Physical* prehensions must be present for any conceptual-linguistic experience to arise in the first place. And it is difficult to see how it could be otherwise if we accept the doctrine of prehensions. Could experience be coherently conceived as the interpretation of somehow *already* interpreted data? Why then not an infinite regress of interpretations? As Hartshorne once put the point while commenting on Husserl's *Ideen* I and *Cartesian Meditations*, the way to capture the phenomenologically evident intentionality of consciousness without succumbing to solipsism is to see that a full account of "experience *of* " requires the positing of a *content* of the experience which is really independent of the experience. Says Hartshorne, "No experience is merely 'of' that very experience, nor even merely of an earlier moment in the same stream of experiences [it would then be indistinguishable from that earlier moment], nor can merely 'intending' an object that may not exist constitute the 'of ' in 'experience of ' [because the projection of possibilities is grounded *somehow* in actual objects of experience] (IO 275). However, the role of the given in the cognitive situation is, for process theory, not to provide unfettered and absolutely incorrigible access to external reality, for this is impossible since experience *is* also conceptually and linguistically filtered. Rather, in consonance with Searle's point of view, *the given provides direction and constraint to all interpretation* and is a logical precondition for the very possibility of genuine revision in conceptual and linguistic formation.

Moreover, as David Griffin has recently emphasized,[57] the Whitehead-Hartshorne position distinguishes between propositions and *linguistic formations* of propositions. Properly speaking, a proposition *is* a state of affairs capable of being true or false, rather than a verbal statement of a state of affairs. Such a definition helps to liberate us from the muddled conflation between epistemic conceptions of truth (which problematically equate the *meaning* of truth with how we determine truth) and the transcendental conception embodied in our ordinary intentions when we utter "that is true" and where we are attempting to point to that which *makes* something true. (Note that independent support for this position resides in the important recent attacks on epistemic conceptions of truth issued by Alston, Davidson, and Horwich.[58]) Under this distinction, it is perfectly possible for there to be the extraordinary variation in linguistic formations of propositions as emphasized by deconstruction. Whitehead was in fact much concerned with linguistic variability and this led him to speak of the "hopeless ambiguity" and "vagueness" of language (PR 193, 196). Such a definition of propositions also allows us to see how Whitehead himself could rail against the naively realistic view of science as offering up un-interpreted "facts" or "data." Whitehead accepted nothing like what Wilfrid Sellars has described as the "myth of the given."[59] At the same time, his (Whitehead's) doctrine of primal physical prehensions explodes any notion of the absolute isolation of the subject from external reality or any absolute denial of the given.

While the discussion here is quite compressed, I submit that enough has been said to indicate that process "minimalist" and "critical" realism is hardly naive, and is mindful in its own way of the points being made in the postmodern critique of the given and postmodern sensibilities about language.

The import of the above discussion is as follows: If *either* a minimal external realism of Searle's sort *or* a process minimalist realism as sketched above is strongly plausible (inclusive disjunction), then the way is prepared for the following perspective wherein neither critically realistic analytic philosophy nor critically realistic systematic metaphysical inquiry of the sort represented by Whitehead and Hartshorne are subject to demise:

First, if we can agree that argument and inquiry are indispensable human activities (and even Rorty has attempted to *argue* in the standard sense for the view that philosophical argument is dead),[60] then analytic philosophy will remain a useful and perhaps even essential, albeit, clearly insufficient, intellectual resource. As noted earlier, analytic philosophy is in fact best understood, not as a set of material doctrines subject to partisan dispute, but as a spirit of rigor and a method(s) of inquiry. Broadly speaking, the spirit of the analytic philosophical enterprise is present whenever philosophers have recognized and attended to the inescapably logical, semantical, and linguistic components of philosophical issues (this includes the "distrust" of language and demarcation of the limits of language and formal logic). Moreover, in spite of wide disagreement on final matters of conviction, there just stubbornly *is* a certain sort of publically accessible, scientific achievement in the deliberations of philosophers at work on analytic tasks. Good evidence for this arises, I submit, whenever our colleagues or students are surprised to find just how radically altered their understanding of a particular position or argument becomes once it is very carefully analyzed and, where appropriate, logically formalized. Such results of linguistic and logical analysis are indismissable. While surely not definitive in forming our final convictions if we come to such, they yet *demand* a rational response in terms of the refinement, qualification, revision or even abandonment of a position or argument. Thus, I cannot see that any *wholesale* rejection of the quest for logical, semantical, and linguistic elucidation and criticism of argumentative discourse is a viable option for us, unless we take the most radical step of Rorty, Derrida and some others in abandoning the very notion of argument. I and no doubt others cannot take that step, because, if for no other reason, ethical, political, and religious *praxis* are unavoidably entangled at *some* level with "argument"—not in the sense of mere confrontations of "incommensurable vocabularies"[61]—but in the usual sense of marshaling some kind of accessible evidence in relevant and logically coherent ways. Indeed, it seems to me that the deep paradox about Rortyean "neopragmatic" postmodernism is to be found precisely in its lack of *pragmatic* value! "Where do we go from here?" if no one *can* in principle give a publically accessible argument? Why write for a public audience or speak publically at all? Even Rorty's own appeal to the pragmatic efficacy of literature is undermined by any robust application of deconstructive antirealism to the literary text, since "efficacy"—*a fortiori* "social efficacy"—presupposes at least some basic measure of shared interpretation resisted by deconstruction. To allude to one of Rorty's own examples, Dickens' *Bleak House* spoke to the nineteenth-century English-speaking public precisely because the basic meaning and affective impact of Dickens' narrative was in fact sufficiently publically accessible and shared.

Having said all this, I wish to issue caveats aplenty: To admit the above is not to assert that the postmodernist "revolt" against analytic philosophy has failed to make an important and healthy point. The arrogance of many practitioners of analytic philosophy to the effect that no other methods or perspectives have much value—an arrogance which is rather effectively ridiculed by Rorty in his *The Consequences of Pragmatism*—is surely wrongheaded. It is wrongheaded because, even after the most sophisticated conceptual, logical, and linguistic analysis of a position or argument has been carried on at a tolerably sufficient length, all sorts of relevant issues remain, issues that arguably can be helped along only by appeals to phenomenological description, imaginative analogy, and/or our aesthetic sensibilities. The title of an anthology spearheaded by British philosopher H. D. Lewis makes the point here: clarity is not *enough*. Moreover, none of the above means that analysis or any other mode of philosophizing will somehow create massive public agreement on philosophic issues. For among other reasons, such issues are a many-sided labyrinth, we can and sometimes do miscommunicate, and we sometimes just "intuit" differently. Nor does any of this mean that philosophers are free from the grip of rhetoric, patterns of social construction, and/or passion. Indeed, I concur with the postmodernist reading of intellectual history, which asserts that the history of philosophy *is* a history of passion, certainly at least in part. The anecdotal evidence alone surely supports this. Virtually every philosopher I have known is quite visibly passionate about ideas.

However, by issuing these caveats and at once accepting the pragmatic indispensability of rational argument that is attentive to widely accepted canons of analytic and critical thinking, the following question is raised acutely: How ought we to *weight* the respective elements of reason, sociohistorical conditioning, and pathos in assessing the activity of philosophy? This question seems to me not to be clearly answerable at present. Thus, the immediate future seems set upon a difficult agenda of defining and articulating some *via media* between implausible and unwanted metaphilosophical extremes, namely, the extreme of vainly hoping in the power of argument to sway wholesale public agreement, and the extreme of utter despairing resignation from the traditional visionary-investigative-argumentative tasks of philosophy.

Despite the difficulty of the search for such a *via media*, the general attitude toward the status of analytic philosophy that I want to advance and that undergirds my efforts in organizing and editing this anthology is tolerably clear and might be put this way: The very vocabulary of *post*analytic philosophy, especially as it is often rhetorically employed by deconstructive postmodernists, suggests a dismissal, a throwing away of tools thought to be no longer useful. Ironically, this stands in tension with the spirit of inclusion and the rejection of marginalization that is so valued (I think rightly) by deconstructive postmodernists. Instead of dismissal, I suggest that the tools of analytic philosophy ought to be continuously cultivated and refined, while at the same time their limitations and the need for and philosophical significance of other approaches ought to be clearly recognized. This, shall I say, "transcending-yet-including"—a "*supra*analytic" rather than postanalytic—stance is expressed with admirable clarity and forthrightness by Robert Nozick when asked about his own relationship to analytic philosophy during his philosophical development:[62]

> I just wanted to think about questions, and here [in analytic thought] were tools that I could use to think about them. I always thought that analytic philosophy wasn't large enough to contain everything I wanted to say. *I wanted to be a philosopher who drew on analytic philosophy, and anything else that would be helpful in advancing understanding.*

This seems to me to set the right tone and to represent the ideal which ought to inform process and other philosophers about the status and uses of analytic philosophy.

Second, as suggested presciently by George R. Lucas, Jr.,[63] Whitehead in particular may well be rejuvenated for the wider philosophical community without any particular efforts on the part of process philosophers or theologians. The rejuvenation may well come either from the renewed interest in all manner of historical figures or the emerging intellectual ascendancy of grand cosmological inquiry found in the likes of Barrow, Bohm, Hawking, Linde, Polkinghorne, Tipler, and others. (It is not without interest in this context that Bohm, Barrow and Tipler have all taken an explicit published interest in Whitehead's philosophy.[64])Yet even if Whitehead's own specific cosmological views may prove not to hold much credence in the wake of future (some would say current) developments, the sort of systematic, large-scale, integrative, speculative cosmology and metaphysics his work exemplifies is, by definition, bound to remain alive and well in an intellectual environment which values global cosmological projects. As such, the exhortation to and defense of speculative philosophy in PR, chapter 1, may stand as one of Whitehead's most enduring legacies. As viewed in this anthology (chapters 3 and 6 are of special relevance here), analytic philosophy can well serve as handmaiden to such global speculative projects, rather than as sheer detractor.

If I am right about the above matters, then both analytic and process philosophy have a future, a future perhaps marked by greater dialogue, cooperation, and sympathetic criticism. To this end, the ensuing essays are dedicated.

Notes

Works frequently cited have been identified by the following abbreviations:

CSR John Searle. *The Construction of Social Reality*. New York: Macmillan—The Free Press, 1995.

RAP Hans Glock, ed. *The Rise of Analytic Philosophy.* Oxford: Basil Blackwell, 1996.

RW George R. Lucas Jr. *The Rehabilitation of Whitehead: An Analytic and Historical Assessment of Process Philosophy*. Albany: State University of New York Press, 1989.

SM Jaegwon Kim. *Supervenience and Mind: Selected Philosophical Essays*. Cambridge: Cambridge University Press, 1993.

UWK David R. Griffin. *Unsnarling the World Knot: Consciousness, Freedom, and the Mind-Body Problem.* Berkeley: University of California Press, 1998.

1. See A. MacIntyre, *After Virtue* (South Bend: University of Notre Dame Press, 1985); J. Rajchman and C. West, eds., *Post-Analytic Philosophy* (New York: Columbia University Press, 1985); R. Rorty, *Philosophy and the Mirror of Nature* (Princeton: Princeton University Press, 1979), *Contingency, Irony, and Solidarity* (Cambridge: Cambridge University Press, 1988), and R. Rorty, *The Consequences of Pragmatism* (Minneapolis: University of Minnesota Press, 1982); S. Rosen, *The Limits of Analysis* (New York: Basic Books, 1980); Hao Wang, *Beyond Analytic Philosophy: Doing Justice to What We Know* (Cambridge, Mass: MIT Press, 1988).
2. M. Dummett, *The Origins of Analytic Philosophy* (London: Duckworth Press, 1993).
3. D. Dombrowski, *Analytic Theism, Hartshorne, and the Concept of God* (Albany: State University of New York Press, 1997).
4. Barry Smith and David W. Smith, eds., *The Cambridge Companion to Husserl* (Cambridge: Cambridge University Press, 1995), p. 3 and liner notes.
5. Cf. RW, chapters 7–8.
6. J. W. Lango, *Whitehead's Ontology* (Albany: State University of New York Press, 1972).
7. B. Russell, *Portraits from Memory* (New York: Colliers, 1956), p. 41.
8. By generally characterizing process thought in doctrinal terms and analytic philosophy in methodological ones, I am not thereby suggesting that process thinkers have no vested interests in methodological issues. (I here respond to the comment of an anonymous referee.) Hartshorne has been especially preoccupied with philosophic method as the title of his formidable *Creative Synthesis and Philosophic Method* makes plain. Indeed, in my view, one of Hartshorne's strengths is the way in which he has integrated wide-ranging methodological influences—use of the doctrinal matrix via Peirce diagrams, use of criteria derived from modern formal logic (including intensional as well as extensional systems à la C. I. Lewis and Carnap), use of phenomenlogical description, appeals to the evidences of ordinary language and the analysis of ordinary language, appeals to pragmatic criteria, and so on and so forth—into an arguably coherent and balanced methodological package. However, process thinkers clearly have differences in methodological approach and emphasis. That this is so is evidenced by a special issue of *Process Studies* devoted to "Methodological Alternatives in Process Theology." (Such methodological approaches are here delineated into three basics types: "empirical," "speculative ," and "rational" [see 19, no. 2 (Summer 1990), especially the introductory essay by Sheila Greve Davaney and

Delwin Brown].) The point I want to make here is that, while process thinkers recognize themselves *as* process thinkers despite their differences in methodogical emphasis or approach, there simply are no process thinkers who have little or no interest in the "processual nature of the real" as described in Rescher's definition. Thus, a doctrinal, not methodological, definition should serve for a *general* characterization of process philosophy.

9. For this slant on Russell I am indebted to Ray Monk's interesting essay, "Was Russell an Analytic Philosopher?" in RAP, chapter 3. I should add that the early G. E. Moore, who was perhaps the first to use the term "analysis" as a label for a type of philosophizing in his 1903 *Principia Ethica* and classic article on "The Refutation of Idealism," clearly did not have in mind the Fregean project of "analysis of language." The early Moore's "analysis" was directed at concepts, which, for him, had a Platonic status as objective constituents of reality. Some concepts are simple and unanalyzable, while others can be decomposed into constituent concepts whose combination is semantically equivalent to the original *analysandum*. The simple concepts come, as it were, before the "mind's eye," and may be understood without linguistic elucidation. On Moore's Platonism, see T. Baldwin, *G. E. Moore* (London: Routledge, 1990).
10. H. Staten, *Wittgenstein and Derrida* (Lincoln and London: University of Nebraska Press, 1984), see esp. "Wittgenstein Deconstructs," chapter 2.
11. Charles Bambach, "Sacred Sophist: A Review of Herman Philipse's *Heidegger's Philosophy of Being*," *Boston Book Review* 6, no. 5 (June 1999): 20.
12. Hacker adds, "and from the obscurities of speculative metaphysicians, such as Hegel, Bradley or Heidegger." The later Whitehead will be regarded by many as belonging to this group of obscurantists. Indeed, Whitehead's employment of neologisms and sweeping abstractions were major factors in his largely negative reception in the Anglo-American philosophical scene of the 30s and 40s (cf. Wolfe Mays, *The Philosophy of Whitehead* [London: Macmillan, 1959] and L. Susan Stebbing, "Review of A. N. Whitehead, *Process and Reality*," *Mind* 39, New Series [1930]: 466–475). However, I am convinced that the "obscurantism" is largely apparent only. A studied, reasonably sympathetic, and deeper reading of PR reveals a thinker informed by his profound learning in logic, mathematics, and the exact sciences, who exhibits historical sensitivity, generalizing power, and originality. Much of this anthology is devoted to showing that neither the middle nor late Whitehead is to be lightly dismissed on impatient, prejudiced, and/or superficial readings. For a similar appraisal of the later Whitehead vis-à-vis his

early reception see George R. Lucas Jr., "Whitehead and Russell," RW, chapter 7.

13. N. Rescher, "On Situating Process Philosophy," *Process Studies* 28, nos. 1–2 (1999): 40.
14. Among the more recent essays, cf. D. Dombrowski, "Hartshorne on Heidegger," *Process Studies* 25 (1996), and William S. Hamrick, "A Process View of the Flesh: Whitehead and Merleau-Ponty," *Process Studies* 28, nos. 1–2 (1999).
15. Rescher, "On Situating Process Philosophy," p. 40.
16. Frederic B. Fitch, "Combinatory Logic and Whitehead's Theory of Prehensions," *Philosophy of Science* 24 (1957) and his "The Perfection of Perfection" in *Process and Divinity: The Hartshorne Festschrift*, ed. Eugene Freeman (La Salle, Ill.: Open Court, 1964), chapter 28. R. M. Martin, *Whitehead's Categorial Scheme*, see chapters I–V: "An Approximative Logical Structure for Whitehead's Categorial Scheme," "On Hartshorne's *Creative Synthesis* and Event Logic," "On the Whiteheadian God," "On Coordinate Divisions in the Theory of Extensive Connection," and "On Abstractive Hierarchies"; also chapter VII: "On Mathematics and the Good," which treats Frederic Fitch's logistical analysis of Whiteheadian themes in theology, the doctrine of coordinate division and real number theory. Also see Martin's "On the Organization of Thought: Whitehead" and "On Universal Algebra and the Whiteheadian Cosmology," in *Mind, Modality, Meaning and Method* (Albany: State University of New York Press, 1980), and his "Ontology, Category-Words and Modal Logic" in *Process and Divinity*, chapter 14. Especially important is Martin's at once sympathetic and severely critical essay "On the Language of Theology: Hartshorne and Quine" in *Existence and Actuality: Conversations with Charles Hartshorne*, ed. John B. Cobb Jr., and Franklin I. Gamwell (Chicago: University of Chicago Press, 1984), chapter 3. For a discussion of Martin, see William L. Power, "Philosophical Logic and Process Theology: The Work of R. M. Martin," *Process Studies* 5, no. 3 (Fall 1975); for a development of semiotics influenced by Martin, see Power's "Peircean Semiotics, Theology, and Religious Realism," in *New Essays in Religious Naturalism*, ed. C. Peden and L. Axel (Macon, GA: Mercer University Press, 1994). H. G. Hubbeling, "Hartshorne and the Ontological Argument" in PCH, chapter 18, and his *Logic, Language and Criterion: A Defense of Non-Positivistic Logical Empiricism* (Born N.V., 1971). (Interestingly enough, Hubbeling describes Hartshorne as a philosopher "who combines Wittgensteinian analysis with Whitehead's philosophy," *Logic, Language and Criterion,* p. 92.) Some important relevant work by Bowman L. Clarke includes: *Language and Natural Theology* (The Hague: Mouton,

1966); "Language and Whitehead's Conception of Speculative Philosophy," in *Process and Divinity,* chapter 12; "God and Time in Whitehead," *Journal of the American Academy of Religion* 48, no. 4 (1980); "Hartshorne on God and Physical Prehensions," *Tulane Studies in Philosophy: Hartshorne's Neoclassical Theology,* ed. Forrest Wood Jr. and Michael DeArmy, 34 (1986); "Two Process Views of God," *International Journal for Philosophy of Religion* 38, nos. 1–3 (1995); and for discussions of Clarke's contributions to formal and philosophical logic, process metaphysics and other topics, see *Logic, God and Metaphysics: The Bowman Clarke Festschrift,* ed. James F. Harris (Dordrecht: Kluwer, 1992). Lucio Chiarviglio, "Extension and Abstraction," in *Process and Divinity*, chapter 11, and "Hartshorne's Aesthetic Theory of Intelligence," in PCH, chapter 3. Norman M. Martin, "Taking Creativity Seriously: Some Observations on the Logical Structure of Hartshorne's Philosophy" in PCH, chapter 17. Relevant work by Dorothy Emmet includes her *The Effectiveness of Causes* (Albany: State University of New York Press, 1986) and *The Passage of Nature* (Philadelphia: Temple University Press, 1992). Both of these works are highly conversant with recent analytic discussions of events, causation, and time, in D. H. Mellor, L. B. Lombard, Derek Parfit, Quine, and P. F. Strawson; also see my "Review of Dorothy Emmet, *The Passage of Nature,*" *Process Studies* 26, nos. 1–2 (1997). For a discussion of Davidson, Quine, Strawson and Whitehead on event theory, see Leemon McHenry, "Descriptive and Revisionary Theories of Events," *Process Studies* 25 (1996).

17. William P. Alston, "Hartshorne and Aquinas: Toward a *Via Media*" in *Existence and Actuality*, chapter 4, followed by Hartshorne's reply. Alston's relation to Hartshorne here has been treated rather thoroughly in Dombrowski's *Analytic Theism, Hartshorne and the Concept of God*, chapter 4. For a sympathetic treatment of Alston's "The Elucidation of Religious Statements" in *Process and Divinity*, chapter 23, connecting it with Hartshorne's theory of formal and material predication in religious discourse, see my "The Semantics of Perfection," Ph.D. Dissertation, The University of Chicago, 1981, section 3.4 on "Meaning and Analogical Predication," pp. 110–115.
18. R. M. Gale, *The Language of Time* (London: Routledge & Kegan Paul, 1968); Jaakko Hintikka, *Time and Necessity* (Oxford: Oxford University Press, 1973); J. R. Lucas, *The Future: An Essay on God, Temporality and Truth* (Oxford: Basil Blackwell, 1989); Thomas Nagel, *Mortal Questions* (Cambridge: Cambridge University Press, 1979) and his *The View from Nowhere* (Oxford: Oxford University Press, 1986). (I include Nagel because of his qualified defense of "panpsychism." On

this see D. Dombrowski, "Nagel as a Process Philosopher," *American Journal of Theology and Philosophy* 15, no. 2 [May 1994]). Karl Popper, *The Open Universe: An Argument for Indeterminism* (Totowa, NJ: Rowan & Littlefield, 1982); A. N. Prior, *Papers on Time and Tense* (Oxford: Oxford University Press, 1968) and *Time and Modality* (Oxford: Oxford University Press, 1957); Wilfrid Sellars, "Foundations of a Metaphysics of Pure Process," *The Monist* 64 (1987); Robert Kane, "The Modal Ontological Argument," *Mind* 93 (1984), "Free Will, Determinism and Creativity in Hartshorne's Thought," in PCH, chapter 6, and Robert Kane and S. H. Phillips, eds., *Hartshorne, Process Philosophy, and Theology*, see here esp. Kane's "Transcendence, Temporality and Personal Identity: A Response to Ford"; Nicholas Rescher, "The Revolt Against Process," *The Journal of Philosophy* 59 (1962) and his *Process Metaphysics: An Introduction to Process Philosophy* (Albany: State University of New York Press, 1996).

19. The logician and semiotician D. S. Clarke Jr. has contributed the only essay in *Process Studies* (prior to my own editorship of volume 25) that directly addresses "Whitehead and Contemporary Analytic Philosophy" (16, no. 1 [Spring 1987]). This essay is interesting and deserves at least brief comment. Clarke holds that historically Whitehead has been neglected by analytic philosophers for two basic reasons: (1) The rise of positivism at the time of the very birth of *Process and Reality* caused Whitehead to be received as the advocate of grand but "cognitively meaningless" systematic metaphysics. (2) After the collapse of positivism on grounds of its own violation of the verifiability criterion and Quine's attack on the analytic-synthetic distinction, linguistic analysis emerged. Here the methods of psychological introspection employed by Whitehead ran against the grain of the "linguistic turn" wherein "no adequate account of our mental operations can ignore their linguistic base." In addition, Whitehead attempted to generalize the notion of experience to non-language bearing entities, and this, seemingly by definition, is metaphysics outside the lense of language. But Clarke attempts to sketch a way in which Whitehead's own resources in *Symbolism: Its Meaning and Effect* can be employed to extend features of language analogically to nonhuman organisms. This is through Whitehead's "first" version of the "functioning of sense presentations as types of symbols." Here "natural signs or symbols" can be viewed as sensa which have as their meaning the signification of experiences capable of altering the actions of organisms. In effect, there is a kind of *semiotic* activity in subhuman organisms which is sufficiently analogous to the use and interpretation of language in humans. Thus, Whiteheadean "panpsychism" can assimilate the "linguistic turn" through the path of

semiotics. While Clarke does not suggest this, I see no obvious reason why such a semiotic approach could not be applied "all the way down" the levels of nature by connecting it to information-theoretic models of quantum theory wherein elemental entities actively process information more akin to "semantic content" than "syntactic-bit" information (on this see William Seager's discussion of quantum mechanics in "Consciousness, Information, and Panpsychism," *The Journal of Consciousness Studies* 2, no. 3 [1995]: 272–288). On the other hand, while Clarke's proposal may well hold promise for making sense out of Whiteheadean doctrine from the point of view of those analytic philosophers committed to the linguistic turn, the point of my rejection of Dummett's reading of the analytic tradition is to suggest that that tradition is in fact larger than commitment to the linguistic turn. Thus, process philosophy may well exhibit other connections to the analytic tradition.

20. G. H. von Wright, *Time, Change, and Contradiction* (Cambridge: Cambridge University Press, 1969). Von Wright may be said to offer an argument for quanta of becoming only in the provisional sense that such quanta or temporal units follow from a rigorous adherence to the Law of Noncontradiction and from a rejection of the notion of instantaneous states. (Von Wright does say that he finds "instantaneous change" problematic, "but hardly more so than the concept of continuous change." See his "Reply to Dalla Chiara on Time, Change and Contradiction," in *The Philosophy of G. H. von Wright*, vol. 19, Library of Living Philosophers Series, ed. Lewis E. Hahn [La Salle, IL: Open Court, 1989], p. 864.) Clearly, however, continuous change involves contradiction: "For then, in any second, for any S and some p there is both p and not-p, and the same with any other fraction of time" (Hartshorne, *The Philosophy of G. H. von Wright*, p. 74). However, while von Wright *permits* such assumptions and thus we could draw out of his lecture Hartshorne's manner of running the argument, it is clear that von Wright is in fact mainly interested in suggesting other alternatives. His Logic of Temporal Division would allow for the possibility of a contradiction "for short intervals." To employ some of Chiara's notation, von Wright is suggesting that for some given time interval $\triangle t_i$ a change from state a to ~a could occur within a *region of* $\triangle t_i$, but this would not entail that $\triangle t_i$ could be characterized as exhibiting contradictory predicates *as a whole*. Under the conditions of such a "dialectical logic," the theorem ~N~ (a $\wedge$ ~a) may well hold. While I do not have the space to develop this here and now, the dialectical logic of change of the von Wright/Chiara genre bristles with potential connections to Whitehead's genetic analysis of phases within the concrescence of actual

occasions. See Maria Luisa Dalla Chiara, "Von Wright on Time, Change and Contradiction," in *The Philosophy of G. H. von Wright*, chapter 27. Hartshorne and von Wright have exchanged views in *The Philosophy of G. H. von Wright*: see Hartshorne's "Von Wright and 'Hume's Axiom'" and von Wright's "Replies to My Critics: Induction and Probability-Hartshorne." The agreement cited is found at p. 734. For a brief discussion of this exchange see my abstract of these two pieces in *Process Studies* 20, no. 2 (1991).

21. Johanna Seibt, "Towards an Ontology of Process," Ph.D. Dissertation, The University of Pittsburgh, 1990; also see her *Properties as Processes: A Synoptic Study of Wilfrid Sellars' Nominalism* (Atascadero, Calif.: Ridgeview Publishing Co., 1990).
22. N. Rescher, "The Promise of Process Philosophy," in *Frontiers in American Philosophy*, vol. 1, ed. Hermann Saatkamp and Robert W. Burch (College Station: Texas A & M University Press, 1992).
23. R. M. Gale, *The Language of Time*, p. 201.
24. Whitehead and Hartshorne view each actual occasion as unique and unrepeatable. Whether we identify the "now" (or the "now-here") with an occasion in its nascent condition or as the just completed occasion, such "now" cannot "shift" by virtue of its unrepeatability.
25. H. Putnam, "The Meaning of Meaning," in his *Philosophical Papers*, vol. 7 (Cambridge: Cambridge University Press, 1975), p. 233.
26. D. Parfit, *Reasons and Persons* (Oxford: Oxford University Press, 1984).
27. "Three Strata of Meaning in Theistic Discourse," LP, chapter 4; "Reflections on Wittgenstein," IO, chapter 25; "Wittgenstein and Tillich: Reflections on Metaphysics and Language" in CSPM, chapter 7 (parts of which appeared originally in *Foundations of Language*, vol. 2 [1961]: 20–32); "Mind and Matter in Ryle, Ayer and Croce," IO, chapter 24; "The Structure of Metaphysics: A Criticism of Lazerowitz's Theory," *Philosophy and Phenomenological Research* 19, no. 2 (1958): 226–240; "John Wisdom on Gods: Two Views of the Logic of Theism," LP, chapter 5. On Carnap: It is little known that Hartshorne was partly instrumental in procuring Carnap's appointment at Chicago. (Hartshorne had also supported the ultimately denied request to appoint Hans Reichenbach in addition.) Carnap worked rather closely with Hartshorne on a number of projects, including the "Appendix to Chapter II-Relativity and Logical Entailment," in DR 95–113. Carnap was reportedly intrigued by Hartshorne's formalized reduction to absurdity against St. Thomas's doctrine of God (DR 12–15), and Hartshorne's doctrine that all contingent propositions require at least one empirical concept in their formulation. See DL 230–233. Also see Hartshorne's prescient and

technically competent critique of positivism in his "Logical Positivism and the Method of Philosophy," BH, chapter 16. Hartshorne's critique of P. F. Strawson is found at CSPM 186–189. On Wilfrid Sellars and W. V. Quine see CAP, chapters 21–22.

28. G. W. Shields, "Hartshorne and the Analytic Philosophical Tradition" in *Faith and Creativity: Essays in Honor of Eugene H. Peters*, ed. by G. Nordgulen and G. W. Shields (St. Louis: CBP Press, 1987), pp. 197–228. I was delighted by Hartshorne's kind personal comments to me about this paper at the conference in his honor held at the University of Texas-Austin in February 1988.
29. *Faith and Creativity*, p. 197.
30. R. M. Adams, "The Logical Structure of Anselm's Argument," in his *The Virtue of Faith and Other Essays in Philosophical Theology* (Oxford: Oxford University Press, 1987), esp. p. 233; J. Hick, "A Critique of the 'Second Argument,'" in *The Many-Faced Argument*, eds. J. Hicks and A. C. McGill (London: Macmillan, 1967) and Hartshorne's response, "John Hick on Logical and Ontological Necessity," *Religious Studies* 13, no. 2 (1977); Tomis Kapitan, "Perfection and Modality: Hartshorne's Ontological Proof," *International Journal for Philosophy of Religion* 7 (1976); R. L. Purtill, "Hartshorne's Modal Proof," *The Journal of Philosophy* 63, no. 14 (1966).
31. On the logic of relations, see DR 95–113 and Hartshorne's "The Neglect of Relative Predicates in Modern Philosophy," *American Philosophical Quarterly* 14, no. 4 (1977). On genetic and strict identity, see Hartshorne's "Strict and Genetic Identity: An Illustration of the Relations of Logic to Metaphysics," in *Method and Meaning: Essays in Honor of H. M. Sheffer*, ed. P. Henle et al (New York: Liberal Arts Press, 1951).
32. *Mind* 74 (1965).
33. A. N. Prior, *Formal Logic* (Oxford: Oxford University Press, 1973), see esp. "The Logic of Modality: Sec. 6-Deontic Logic," pp. 220–229.
34. Also see G. W. Shields, "Fate and Logic: Cahn on Hartshorne Revisited," *The Southern Journal of Philosophy* 26, no. 3 (1988). Michael Clark has presented a rather detailed critique and analytic discussion of Hartshorne's 1965 *Mind* essay in "Discourse about the Future," in *Knowledge and Necessity*, Royal Institute of Philosophy Series: vol. III, ed. by G. N. A. Vesey (London: Macmillan and St. Martin's Press, 1970). For a brief discussion of Clark, see Shields and Viney, chapter 11, in this volume.
35. *The Philosophy of G. H. von Wright*, p. 59.
36. See his *The Ontological Argument of Charles Hartshorne* (Missoula: Scholars Press, 1978).

37. See Ruth Barcan Marcus's classic and still much discussed essays: "Interpreting Quantification," *Inquiry* 5 (1962) and "Essential Attribution," *The Journal of Philosophy* 68 (1971). A clear discussion of the main issues is to be found in K. Konyndyk, "Quantified Modal Logic," in his *Introductory Modal Logic* (South Bend: Notre Dame University Press, 1986), chapter 4.
38. G. Hellman, *Mathematics Without Numbers* (Oxford: Oxford University Press, 1989).
39. While Hartshorne has never explicitly employed a formula which quantifies across modal operators, Goodwin has argued, and Hartshorne has apparently endorsed the view, that his whole theory of modal correspondence commits him to quantification across modal operators. See Hartshorne's "Foreword" and Goodwin, *The Ontological Argument of Charles Hartshorne*, pp. 95–97.
40. S. Kripke, "Semantical Considerations on Modal Logic," in *Reference and Modality*, ed. L. Linsky (Oxford: Oxford University Press, 1971).
41. Goodwin, *The Ontological Argument of Charles Hartshorne*, p. 100.
42. D. R. Griffin, *Evil Revisited: Responses and Reconsiderations* (Albany: State University of New York Press, 1991).
43. Griffin, *Evil Revisited*, p. 130.
44. Griffin, *Evil Revisited*, p. 131.
45. Galen Strawson, *Mental Reality* (Cambridge, Mass.: MIT Press, 1994), p. 105.
46. T. Nagel, *Mortal Questions* (Cambridge: Cambridge University Press, 1979), pp. 180–181.
47. W. Seager, "Consciousness, Information, and Panpsychism," p. 286.
48. David F. Chalmers, *The Conscious Mind: In Search of a Fundamental Theory* (Oxford: Oxford University Press, 1996), see esp. "Is Experience Ubiquitous?," pp. 293–301. Chalmers's suggested "panpsychism" at first appears to be classical identist panpsychism, but he qualifies himself ("It may be better to say that a rock *contains* systems that are conscious," p. 297). He does not in the end prefer panpsychism, but he states that it ought to be taken "seriously," for there are "no knockdown arguments against the view, and there are various positive reasons why one might embrace it," p. 299.
49. Jaegwon Kim, "Physicalism and Panexperientialism: Response to David Ray Griffin," *Process Studies* 28, Nos. 1-2 (Spring-Summer 1999). Kim says that "Griffin's essay [a synopsis of relevant portions of UWK to which Kim is responding] poses serious challenges to contemporary physicalism" and he thanks Griffin for "his important service in bringing the Whiteheadian perspective to bear on current debates in analytical philosophy of mind and showing how the two approaches can be

relevant to each other," p. 34. This does not mean that Kim embraces panexperientialism (he does not), but his openness and frank appreciation of the perspective is noteworthy. For an overview of panexperientialism which discusses objections issued by J. Kim, Colin McGinn and Karl Popper as well as Bryant Keeling's "Wittgensteinian" critique, see my "Physicalist Panexperientialism and the Mind-Body Problem," *American Journal of Theology and Philosophy* 21, no. 2 (May 2001).

50. A. G. Nasser and P. Brown, "Discussion Note," *The Australian Journal of Philosophy* 47 (1969): 61–64.

51. My dissertation involved the construction of a "meaning postulate" semantics for neoclassical theism as suggested by Bowman Clarke's modification of Carnap's meaning postulate procedure. The mentioned postulate is discussed in detail in "The Semantics of Perfection," pp. 87–90, 315–318.

52. L. Bryant Keeling, *God-Language and Metaphysics*, Ph.D. Dissertation, The University of Chicago, 1971, and my critique in *Faith and Creativity*, pp. 215–218. Also see Keeling's "Feelings as a Metaphysical Category: Hartshorne from an Analytical Point of View," *Process Studies* 6, no. 1 (1976). Dan Dombrowski, "Must a Perfect Being Be Immutable?," in *Hartshorne, Process Philosophy and Theology*, chapter 5. Jan van der Veken, "From Modal Language to Model Language: Hartshorne and Linguistic Analysis," in *Hartshorne, Process Philosophy and Theology*, chapter 2. For an excellent discussion of contemporary analytic philosophy of omniscience, see Donald Wayne Viney's "God Only Knows? Hartshorne and the Mechanics of Omniscience," in *Hartshorne, Process Philosophy and Theology*, chapter 4. Also see John W. Lango, *Whitehead's Ontology* (Albany: State University of New York Press, 1972). In addition to "Hartshorne and the Analytic Philosophical Tradition" and "Fate and Logic" (see notes 31 and 37), some of my own published work which is relevant here includes the following: G. W. Shields, "Davies, Eternity and the Cosmological Argument," *International Journal for Philosophy of Religion* 21, no. 1 (1987); "Is the Past Finite? On Craig's Kalām Argument," *Process Studies* 14, no. 1 (1984); "Infinitesimals and Hartshorne's Set-Theoretic Platonism," *The Modern Schoolman* 59, no. 2 (1992); "Hartshorne and Creel on Impassibility," *Process Studies* 21, No. 1 (1992); "Ultimate Explanations: From PSR_1 to PSR_5," unpublished paper presented at the Philosophy of Religion Session of the annual meeting of the American Academy of Religion, Boston, December 1987 (this paper's modally formalized *reductio* against the Strong PSR, inspired by Peter van Inwagen, is published in my "Design, Chance and Necessity," in *Facets of Faith and Science*, vol. IV, ed. J. van der Meer [Lanham and London: University Press of

America, 1996]); a review of *The Philosophy of Charles Hartshorne* treating papers by Kane, Hubbeling and N. M. Martin appears in *International Journal for Philosophy of Religion* 36, no. 4 (1994); "God, Modality and Incoherence," *Encounter* 44, No. 1 (1983); two reviews of Goodwin appear in *Journal of Religion* 60, no. 3 (1980) and *Religious Studies Review* 11, no. 1 (1985); and "Review of Nicholas Rescher's *Process Metaphysics*," *Process Studies* 25 (1996). Some relevant work on topics in the philosophy of physics can be found in my "The Semantics of Perfection," pp. 197–222, and in "The Wider Design Argument and the New Physics," in *Science, Technology and Religious Ideas*, ed. by M. Shale and G. W. Shields (Lanham, Md. and London: University Press of America, 1994)—where I address Many-Worlds quantum theory and the Hartle-Hawking universal wave-function. For a discussion of Hartshorne's ontological argument and some aspects of my dissertation, see Edgar A. Towne, "Logic, Semantics, and Dipolar Theism," *Process Studies* 28, nos. 3–4 (1999): 231–254.

53. Cf. R. Rorty, *Contingency, Irony and Solidarity* (Cambridge: Cambridge University Press, 1988). For some important criticisms and appreciations of Rorty's views see *Reading Rorty*, ed. Alan Malachowski and Jo Burrows (Oxford: Basil Blackwell, 1990).
54. Cf. U. Eco, *Interpretation and Overinterpretation*, ed. by S. Collini (Cambridge: Cambridge University Press, 1992).
55. U. Eco, "Unlimited Semeiosis and Drift: Pragmaticism *vs.* Pragmatism," in *Peirce and Contemporary Thought*, ed. K. Ketner (Cambridge, Mass.: Harvard University Press, 1995).
56. ER for External Realism; PS for the Privileged Scheme thesis; CR for Conceptual Relativism and MR for Metaphysical Realism. The logical formalization presented here represents my reading of Searle's discussion of Putnam and is not found explicitly in his text.
57. D. R. Griffin, *Reenchantment Without Supernaturalism: A Process Philosophy of Religion* (Ithaca: Cornell University Press, 2001), chapter 9: "Religious Truth and Language," see esp. pp. 324–326.
58. William P. Alston, *A Realist Conception of Truth* (Ithaca: Cornell University Press, 1996), pp. 189–190; Donald Davidson, "The Structure and Content of Truth," *Journal of Philosophy* 87, no. 6 (1990): 302; Paul Horwich, *Truth* (Oxford: Oxford University Press, 1990), pp. 89–93.
59. Note Whitehead's assertion at PR 15: "Every scientific memoir in its record of the 'facts' is shot through and through with interpretation."
60. In his most radical moments, Rorty appears to regard all "cognitive" discourse as fantasy, thus aligning himself with Derrida's notion of discourse as play. But Derrida's project of deconstruction is most vulnerable with respect to its explicit rejection of standard canons of critical

thinking and basic logical principles (e.g., Noncontradiction). On this score, and on the topic of deconstruction of the very notion of argument in the standard sense, I find John M. Ellis's "Analysis, Logic and Argument in Theoretical Discussion," in his *Against Deconstruction* (Princeton: Princeton University Press, 1989) to be pointedly on target: Deconstruction has framed its "projects" such that skepticism or critical questioning about them is disallowed; Derrida's "tone of aggrievement" in his famous critical encounter with John Searle is disturbingly out of place if Derrida is serious about the notion that he has no "position" to be attacked; proponents of deconstruction describe their "point of view" as ineffable, except when under attack, at which point there are claims of "mischaracterization"; proponents of deconstruction make the claim that Derrida is employing an "other" logic, but do not provide nonrhetorical working models of what this logic could be—in fact, in practice (as Ellis illustrates with numerous examples), they appeal to the very standard of noncontradiction they are purportedly deconstructing.

Before the above comments are rejected out of hand as Rorty or Derrida "bashing," please note that I certainly think there are important insights in the work of both of these thinkers, and I am by no means dismissing them. Derrida is right to hold that linguistic formations of "meanings" are unstable—surely at least sometimes and perhaps often (Whitehead would say "often"). He is only wrong, it seems to me, to hold or imply that this is the all-pervasive condition of human discourse and inquiry. (I suspect that his extreme form of linguistic holism taken over from Saussure's now much contested idea that a single alteration in a linguistic system changes the entire system is in part responsible here.) As Hartshorne himself once said to me in conversation while leaving a philosophical meeting in his honor at the University of Texas: "The deconstructionists aren't entirely wrong, you know. Communication *is* the big problem in philosophy." Moreover, Rorty is to be congratulated for calling our attention to both the importance of historical "timing" in philosophical and scientific work and of philosophical vocabulary in terms of eliciting attention and effectively communicating in philosophical subcultures. For a sympathetic assessment of Rorty that yet has affinities for process thought, see Brian Hendley, "The Conversation Continues: Rorty and Dewey," *Process Studies* 20, no. 2 (Spring 1991). Also see contributor James Bradley's extremely interesting meditation on Whitehead and the postmodernism of the later Heidegger in his "Whitehead, Heidegger, and the Paradoxes of the New," *Process Studies* 20, No. 3 (Fall 1991).

61. Rorty appears to leave us with the simple dichotomy: either two philosophers employ incommensurable vocabularies or they do not.

What about the notion of *degrees* of incommensurability? Much comparative and historical philosophical scholarship is devoted to showing that, despite superficial appearances to the contrary, philosophers are sometimes in substantial agreement, and that alternative vocabularies are sometimes intertranslatable (or roughly so). I think Rorty in general overestimates the extent to which philosophers ultimately disagree.

62. Giovanna Borradori, *The American Philosopher* (Chicago: University of Chicago Press, 1991), chapter 4: "Anarchy at Harvard: Robert Nozick," p. 78. My italics.
63. George R. Lucas Jr., "The Seventh Seal—On the Fate of Whitehead's Proposed Rehabilitation," *Process Studies* 25 (1996): 115–116.
64. David Bohm, "Response to Conference Papers," and David Griffin, "Bohm and Whitehead on Wholeness, Freedom, Causality, and Time," *Zygon* 20, no. 2 (1985); J. Barrow and F. Tipler, *The Anthropic Cosmological Principle* (Oxford: Oxford University Press, 1986) contains surprisingly lengthy comments on process philosophers, including Bergson, Alexander, Whitehead, Hartshorne, and Teilhard at pp. 121–122, 185–205.

Chapter 2

The Promise of Process Philosophy

NICHOLAS RESCHER

Editor's Comment: This opening essay is particularly appropriate to the aims of this book, as it represents a direct counterexample to the superficial assumption that analytic and process thinkers are far removed from one another; for Rescher is himself an esteemed and widely recognized analytic philosopher ("analytic" by anyone's standards or definitions) who is yet intensely interested in the problem-solving import of the idea of process. Just as important, this chapter represents a direct counterexample to the common association of analytic philosophy with antiprocess logical theory and related "eternalist" metaphysical doctrines. In this respect, the essay complements and connects with points made later in the essay by Gale (chapter 4), Goodwin's essay (chapter 9, section IV), and in the essay by Shields and Viney (chapter 11 on future contingents) While many of the studies in this volume are directly concerned with either Whitehead or Hartshorne or both, Rescher's is distinctive in setting his discussion of process philosophy in a much wider historical context, ranging from considerations of Heraclitus to Descartes, Leibnitz, and Hume to Bergson and Whitehead (thus its appropriate placement in part I: "Overviews"). With characteristic dimunition and caution, Rescher not only argues for the theoretical economy of the process versus substance conceptuality, but insists that process philosophy as developed so far is as yet only a "program" for philosophical research, albeit, one that inspires confidence. Rescher would thus concur with the conclusion of chapter 1 that process philosophy indeed has a future, but for the somewhat different reason that it has much unfinished business to pursue.

Introduction

In recent years, "process philosophy" has virtually become a code word for the doctrines of Alfred North Whitehead and his followers. But of course, this cannot really be what process philosophy is ultimately about: If there indeed is a "philosophy" of process, it must pivot not on a *thinker* but on a *theory*. What is at issue must, in the end, be a philosophical position that has a life of its own. Whitehead himself fixed on "process" as a central category of his philosophy because he viewed time and change as salient metaphysical issues. Invoking the name of Bergson, he adopted "Nature is a process" as a leading principle and saw temporality, change, and passage as fundamental facts to be reckoned with in our understanding of the world.[1] This view was underpinned by Whitehead's appreciation of Leibnizian *appetition*—the striving through which all things endeavor to bring new features to realization.[2] And in back of this lay the Heracleitean doctrine that "all things flow," and the rejection of a Parmenidean/atomistic view that nature consists in the changeable interrelations among stable, unchanging units of existence.[3]

As Whitehead himself thus emphasized, process philosophy does not represent the doctrine of a particular thinker, but reflects a major tendency or line of thought that traces back through the history of philosophy to the days of the pre-Socratics. Its leading exponents were Heracleitus, Leibniz, Bergson, Peirce, and William James, and it ultimately moved on to include Whitehead and his school (Charles Hartshorne and Paul Weiss, as well as Andrew Paul Ushenko), and also others such as Samuel Alexander and C. Lloyd Morgan.

As is often the case in philosophy, the position at issue is best understood in terms of what it opposes. From the time of Aristotle, Western metaphysics has had a marked bias in favor of *things.* Aristotle's insistence on the metaphysical centrality of ostensively indictable objects (with *tode ti* as a pointable-at *this)* has made an enduring and far-reaching impact. The Aristotelian primacy of substance and its ramifications (see *Metaphysics* IV, 2; 10003b, 6–11)—with its focus on midsize physical objects on the order of a rock, a tree, a cat, or a human being—has proved decisive for much of Western philosophy. However, another line of thought was also current. After all, the concentration on perduring physical *things* as existents in nature slights the equally good claims of another ontological category, namely processes, events, occurrences—items better indicated by verbs than nouns. Clearly, storms and heat waves are every bit as real as dogs and oranges. Even on the surface of it, verb-entities have as good a claim to reality as noun-entities. For process theorists, *becoming* is no less important than being—but rather the reverse. The phenomenology of change is stressed precisely because the difference between a museum and the real world is seen as crucial to our understanding of reality. Moreover, processes are not in general a matter of the doings of things. The fire's heat causes the water to boil. But it is clearly not a *thing.* To be sure, some events and processes relate to the doings or undergoings of things (the collapse of a bridge) or of people (Smith's breaking a leg). And other events and processes relate to the coordinated doings of things (an eclipse of the sun) or of people (a morning rush hour). But many events and processes are patently subjectless in that they do not consist of the doings of one or more personal or impersonal agents (a frost, for example, or a magnetic field). At work in these self-subsistent or subjectless processes are not "agents" but "forces."

The progenitor of this rival tradition was Heracleitus. For him reality is not a constellation of things at all, but one of processes. The fundamental "stuff" is not material substance but process, namely "fire," and all things are products of its workings *(puros tropai).* Process is fundamental: the river is not an *object,* but a continuing flow, the sun is not a *thing*, but an enduring fire. Everything is a matter of process, of activity, of change (*panta rhei*)! Not stable things but fundamental forces and the fluctuating processes they produce constitute the world. We must at all costs avoid the fallacy that Bergson characterized as "spatializing time."

The principal standard bearer of this line of thought into the domain of modern philosophy was Leibniz, who maintained that all of the "things" that figure in our experience (animals alone grudgingly excepted) are mere phenomena and not really things at all. The world in fact consists of clusters of processes he calls "monads" (units), which are "centers of force" or "bundles of activity." For Leibniz, processes rather than things furnish the basic materials of ontology.

Against this historical background, it seems sensible to understand "process philosophy" as a doctrine committed to, or at any rate inclined towards certain basic propositions:

1. That time and change are among the principal categories of metaphysical understanding.
2. That process is a principal category of ontological description.
3. That processes are more fundamental, or at any rate not less fundamental, than things for the purposes of ontological theory.
4. That several of the major elements of the ontological repertoire (God, nature-as-a-whole, persons, material substances) are best understood in process terms.
5. That contingency, emergence, novelty, and creativity are among the fundamental categories of metaphysical understanding.

Process philosophers, then, are those for whom temporality, activity, and change—of alteration, striving, passage, and novelty-emergence—are the cardinal factors in our understanding of the real. Ultimately it is a question of priority. Process philosophers view the time-oriented aspects of the real as constituting its most characteristic and significant features. For them, process has priority over product—both ontologically and epistemically.

This general process-oriented approach is historically too pervasive and systematically too significant to be restricted in its bearing to one particular philosopher and his school. Indeed, one important task for the partisans of process at this historical juncture is to prevent the idea of "process philosophy" from being marginalized through a limitation of its bearing to the work and influence of one single individual or movement.

Process Ontology

To be sure, one perfectly plausible way of downgrading processes is to question not their reality, but rather their fundamentality. On this approach, it is conceded that nature is indeed replete with many and varied activities and processes, but insisted that they are simply the doings of a substantial agent.

Every verb must have a subject, and every event or occurrence is a matter of the agency of things. Denying the ontological autonomy of processes, this process-reducibility doctrine insists that all there is in the world are things and their properties and actions. This perspective reasserts an orthodoxy that maintains the ontological substance-bias of Western philosophy.

But in fact it represents a rather problematic position. The world is full of processes that do not represent the actions of things (save on a rather naive and obsolescent atomist/materialist model of nature). When water freezes or evaporates, it is not a "thing" (or collection thereof) that is active in producing this result. The freshening of the wind, the forming of waves in the water, the pounding of the surf, the erosion of the shoreline are all processes that are not really the machinations of identifiable "things."

Consider such a process as "a fluctuation in the earth's magnetic field" or "a weakening of the sun's gravitational field." Clearly such processes will make an impact on things (magnetic needles, for example). But by no stretch of the imagination are these processes themselves the doings/activities of things/substances. There is not a thing, "a magnetic field" or "a gravitational field," that *does* something or performs certain actions. The idea that processes *can* be the doings of things represents a plain truth. But the idea that processes *must* be the doings of things is nothing but an unhelpful prejudice. Where is the thing that is being active when we have a fall in barometric pressure? For process philosophers, the classical principle *operari sequitur esse* is reversed: their motto is *esse sequitur operari,* since being follows from operation because what there is in the final analysis is the product of processes.

But can processes really get on without things to give them existential embodiment? Traditional metaphysics sees processes (such as the rod's snapping under the strain when bent sufficiently) as the manifestation of dispositions (fragility), which must themselves be rooted in the stable properties of things. It takes processes to manifest dispositions that are themselves products of the categorical (nondispositional) features of things. Process metaphysics involves an inversion of this perspective. It takes the line that the categorical properties of things are simply stable clusters of process-engendering dispositions.

But can these process-dispositions avoid the need for rooting in the categorical properties of things? Is the dispositional realm autonomous—that is, can dispositions be self-activating? After all, dispositions are matters of if-then. If this is all we have, can we then ever move to the categorical sphere?

The answer is affirmative. We can do this provided we have *nested* dispositions. If all we have are dispositions of the form

When and where p, there q

then of course we would need a categorical input (namely p) to have a categorical output. But with nested dispositions of the form

When and where (when and where p, there q), there r

we can in fact get a categorical output from hypothetical inputs. Where dispositions are sufficiently complex (i.e., nested), a transition from the dispositional to the categorical sector is possible. Mere dispositions can combine to engender categorical actualities. And so processes (rod-snappings) can occur in the framework of a process ontology that has no recourse to processual substances with categorical properties that underwrite the dispositions (such as rod-fragility) that processes actualize. In this connection, an important asymmetry is often lost from sight. Processes can make do without things. As the example of "it is getting colder" shows, there can be "subjectless" processes—processes which to all appearances are not, like sneezing or dissolving, encompassed in the activities of things. On the other hand, no workable substance ontology can operate without a heavy reliance on processes. A substance, after all, is determined (individuated) as such by its properties, and there are just two major types here, namely, the dispositional and the absolute (nondispositional, categorical). But the dispositional ones are crucial—at any rate from an epistemic point of view. For all that we can ever *observe* about a substance is what it does—what sorts of impacts (changes, effects) it produces in interaction with others—that is, what sorts of processes it engenders. The absolute (nondispositional) properties that we attribute to things are always the product of a theory-bound conjecture—features imputed to things to provide a causal explanation for their impacts upon others. As Leibniz insisted, a substance is primarily a center of force, a bundle of dispositions to exert impacts of various sorts on the others. Substances can come on the stage of consideration only through the mediation of processes.

One must not forget that even on the basis of an ontology of substance and property, dispositional properties are *epistemologically* fundamental. Without them, a thing is inert, undetectable, disconnected from the world's causal commerce, and inherently unknowable. Our only epistemic access to the absolute properties of things is through inferential triangulation from their dispositional properties—or better, from the processes through which these manifest themselves. Accordingly, a substance ontologist cannot get by without processes. If things are totally inert—if they do nothing—they are pointless. For without processes there is no access to dispositions, and without dispositional properties, substances lie outside our cognitive reach. One can only observe what things do, via their discernible effects—what they *are*, over and above this, is a matter of theory projected on this basis.

A process ontology simplifies matters. Instead of a two-tier reality that combines things and the inevitable processes, it settles for a one-tier ontology of process alone. It sees things not just as *the products* of processes (as one cannot avoid doing) but also as the *manifestations* of processes—as complex bundles of coordinated processes. It replaces the troublesome ontological dualism of *thing and activity* with a monism of activities of varying sorts. In its sight, things simply *are* what they do. Even as thought itself is a cognitive process, we cannot understand its products without seeing them too as products of processes.

Process and "The Problem of Universals"

Let us now turn from particulars to universals. Recourse to process is also a helpful device for dealing with the classical problem of universals. We are surrounded on all sides by instances of types more easily conceived of as being processes rather than substantial things, not physical items like a magnetic field or an aurora borealis, but also conceptual artifacts like words or letters of the alphabet, let alone songs, plays, or poems.

Processes can, do, and must have patterns and periodicities that render them in principle repeatable. After all, to say that an item (be it a thing or a process) has a *structure* of some sort is to attribute something to it that other items can in principle have.[4] But of course, structure, though repeatable ("abstractable"), is itself not an abstraction—it is something that a concrete item concretely has.

Classically, there are three rival theories of "universals," which see them, respectively, as: (1) *made by minds* (nominalism), that is, imputed to things by minds in virtue of their (the minds') operation; (2) *found (by minds) in things* (Platonic realism), that is, perceived by minds in preexisting aspects of things; (3) *generated in mind-thing interaction* (conceptualism). Now a substance ontology, which is bound to see universals as simply being the properties of things (Aristotelian secondary substances), encounters difficulties here. For on its basis one is driven inexorably towards Platonism. We want universals to be objective, but can only secure this status for them on the basis of a Platonic realism. And when we look more closely at the sorts of things at issue—letters of the alphabet, say, or poems—this does not really seem to be such an attractive option.

But with process universals (processual structures) there are fewer difficulties. Processes are inherently universal and repeatable—to be a process is to be a process of a certain sort, a certain specifiable makeup. What concretizes processes is simply their spatiotemporal emplacement, their positioning in reality. And so a process as such is by its very nature a concrete universal—any actual process is *at once* concrete and universal. There is, presumably, little or no problem about process types because these can be accounted for in terms of a commonality of structure.

In particular, colors, say, or numbers or poems lend themselves naturally to a process account. Take phenomenal colors, for example. A *mental* process such as perceiving or imagining a certain shade of red is simply a way of perceiving redly or imagining redly (in a certain particular way). That putative universal—the shade of phenomenal red—ceases to be a mysterious *object* of some sort and becomes a specifiable feature of familiar processes (perceivings, imaginings). How distinct minds can perceive the same universal is now no more mysterious than how distinct walkers can share the same limp. Otherwise mysterious-seeming universals such as odors or fears are simply shared structural features of mental processes. Universals are pulled down from the Platonic realm, to become structural features of the ways in which we concretely conduct the business of thinking. Recourse to a process approach is once again a useful problem-solving device.

Process Philosophy of Nature

Let us move on from matters of ontology to some issues in the process philosophy of nature.

A classical atomism whose ontology consists only of atoms and the void is the ultimate contrary to a process philosophy. A physics of fields and forces that operate on their own, without an embedding in things, is the quintessence of a process philosophy of nature. But wherein lies the appeal of such a view?

A substance ontologist is committed to seeing the physical world (nature) as a collection of *things or objects*. And on this basis, he/she immediately faces the problem of accounting for *laws* that coordinate the behavior of things. (How do all hydrogen atoms learn how to behave like hydrogen atoms?)

But by seeing the world as a matrix of processes—by viewing nature as the substantiation of a family of operative principles (taken in their all inclusive systemic totality)—we secure straightaway a coherent conceptualization of nature in a way that removes such difficulties. For the idea of law is inherent in the very concept of a process. And we can *understand* the world's processes precisely because we ourselves are a party to them, seeing that we ourselves, in our own makeup and being, participate in the operation of nature.

A process approach thus simplifies greatly the problem of securing a coherent view of nature. Modern physics teaches us that at the level of the very small, there are no ongoing *things* (substances, objects) at all in nature—no particulars with a continuing descriptive identity of their own—there are only patterns of process that exhibit stabilities. (The orbit-jump of an "electron" is not the mysterious transit of a well-defined physical object at all.) Only those stability waves of continuous process provide for any sort of continuity of existence. The development of stable "things" begins at the subsubmicroscopic level of the buzzing proliferation of "events" that have no fixed nature in themselves but only exist in reciprocal interaction with each other, and which have no stable characteristics in and of themselves, but only exhibit stable aspects at the level of statistical aggregates.

It was unfortunate for them that the founders of process philosophy did not witness the rise of the quantum theory. The classical conception of an atom was subject to the principle that "by definition, atoms cannot be cut up or broken into smaller parts," so that "atom splitting" was a *contradiction in terms.* The demise of classical atomism brought on by the dematerialization of physical matter brings much aid and comfort to a process-oriented metaphysics. Matter in the small, as contemporary physics concerns it, is not a Rutherfordian planetary system of particlelike objects, but a collection of fluctuating processes organized into stable structures (insofar as there is indeed stability at all) by statistical regularities—that is, by regularities of comportment at the level of aggregate phenomena. Twentieth-century physics has thus turned the tables on classical atomism. Instead of very small *things* (atoms) combining to produce standard processes (windstorms and such), modern physics envisions very small processes (quantum phenomena) combining to produce standard things (ordinary macro-objects) as a result of their *modus operandi.*

The quantum view of reality throws classical atomism on the trash heap, for it holds that, at the microlevel, what was usually deemed a physical *thing, a* stably perduring object, is itself no more than a statistical pattern—a stability wave in a surging sea of process. Those so-called enduring "things" come about through the compilation of stabilities in statistical fluctuations, much like gusts of wind. Processes are not the machinations of stable things; things are the stability patterns of variable processes. All such perspectives of modern physics at the level of fundamentals dovetail smoothly into the traditional process approach.

Neither the logic of object and predicate nor even the grammar of subject and verb prevail in the language of nature, but the language of differential equations, the language of process. In this regard as in so many others, Leibniz had insight far beyond his time. Important though logic and language are (and he stresses that they are very important), it is the mathematical language of process—of transformation functions and differential equations—that is of the greatest help in depicting the world's physical realities. (This is something of which Whitehead, himself a first-rate mathematician, was keenly aware.)

Process Psychology: Difficulties of the Self

Next, let us briefly consider the utility of the process approach in philosophical psychology. The self or ego has always been a stumbling block for Western philosophy because of its recalcitrance to accommodation within its favored framework of substance ontology. The idea that "the self" is a *thing* (substance), and that whatever occurs in relation to "my mind" and "my thoughts" is a matter of the activity of a thing of a certain sort (a "mind" substance) is no more than a rather blatant sort of fiction, a somewhat desperate effort to apply the thing paradigm to a range of phenomena that it just does not fit.

It is, after all, rather repugnant to conceptualize people (persons) as *things* (substances)—oneself above all. Aristotle already bears witness to this difficulty of accommodating the self or soul into a substance metaphysics. It is, he tells us, the "substantial form," the entelechy of the body. But this accommodation strategy raises more problems than it solves, because the self or soul is so profoundly unlike the other sorts of entelechy examples that Aristotle is able to provide.

People instinctively resist being described in thing-classificatory terms. As Sartre said, a wrongdoer may say "I did this or that act"[5] but will resist saying "I am a thief," "I am a murderer." Such attributions indicate a fixed nature that we naturally see as repugnant to ourselves. People tend to see themselves and their doings in processual terms as sources of teleological, agency-purposive activities geared to the satisfaction of needs and wants as they appear in the circumstances of the moment. In application to ourselves, at any rate, static thing-classifiers are naturally distasteful to us.

If one is committed to conceiving of a *person* within the framework of a classical thing-metaphysic, then one is going to be impelled inexorably towards the materialist view that the definitive facet of a person is the body and its doings. For of everything that appertains to us, it is clearly one's *body* that is most readily assimilated to the substance paradigm. Think here of David Hume's ventures into self-apprehension:

> From what (experiential) impression could this idea (of *self*) be derived? This question is impossible to answer without a manifest contradiction and absurdity; and yet it is a question which must necessarily be answered, if we would have the idea of self pass for clear and intelligible. . . . For my part, when I enter most intimately into what I *call myself*, I always stumble on some particular perception or other, of heat or cold, light or shade, love or hatred, pain or pleasure. I never can catch *myself* at any time without a perception, and never can observe anything but the perception.[6]

Here Hume is perfectly right. Any such quest for *observational* confrontation with a personal core substance, a self or ego that constitutes the particular person that one is, is destined to end in failure. The only "thing" about ourselves we can get hold of *observationally* is the body and its activities.

However, from the angle of a process metaphysics the situation has a rather different look. We have difficulties apprehending what we *are* but have no difficulty experiencing what we do. Our bodily and mental activities lie open to experiential apprehension. There is no problem with experiential access to the processes and patterns of process that characterize us personally: our doings and undergoings, either individually or patterned into talents, skills, capabilities, traits, dispositions, habits, inclinations, and tendencies to action and inaction are, after all, what characteristically define a person as the individual he or she is. What makes my experience mine is not some peculiar qualitative character that it exhibits but simply its forming part of the overall ongoing process that defines and institutes my life.

Once we conceptualize the core "self" of a person as a bundle of actual and potential processes—of action and capacities, tendencies, and dispositions to action (both physical and psychical)—then we have a concept of personhood that renders the self or ego experientially accessible, seeing that experiencing itself simply *consists* of the exercise of such processes. In a process-oriented approach, the self or ego (the constituting core of a person as such, that is, as the particular person he or she is) is simply a megaprocess—*a structured system of processes,* a cohesive and (relatively) stable center of agency. The crux of this approach is the shift in orientation from substance to process—from a unity of hardware, of physical machinery, to a unity of software, of programming or mode of functioning.

Miguel de Unamuno says that Descartes got it backwards, that instead of *cogito, ergo sum res cogitans* it should be: *sum res cogitans, ergo cogito.*[7] But this is not so. Descartes's reversal of scholasticism's traditional substantialist perspective is perfectly in order, based on the sound idea that activity comes first (*Im Anfang war die Tat*)—that what we do defines what we are. The fundamentality of psychic process for the constitution of a self was put on the agenda of modern philosophy in Descartes.

Leibniz went even further in generalizing the view that agency defines the agent. Along Cartesian lines, he saw the unity of the self as a unity of process, taking its individuality to consist in a unified characteristic mode of acting (of perceiving the world). But in this regard the self was, for Leibniz, paradigmatic for substance in general. In effect, Leibniz's monadology took the Cartesian process approach to the personal self and *universalized* it to encompass substance in general. A substance, like a self, is just so much a "thing" as a center of action.

The salient advantage of this process-geared view of the self as an internally complex process of "leading a life (of a certain sort)"—with its natural division into a varied manifold of constituent subprocesses—is that it does away with the need for a mysterious and experientially inaccessible unifying substantial *object* (on the lines of Kant's "transcendental ego") to constitute a self out of the variety of its experiences. The unity of self comes to be seen as a unity of process—of one large megaprocess that encompasses many smaller ones in its makeup. We arrive at a view of mind that dispenses with the

Cartesian "ghost in the machine" and looks to the unity of mind as a unity of functioning—of *operation* rather than *operator.* A "self" is viewed not as a *thing* but as an integrated process.

On this basis, the Humean complaint—"One experiences feeling this and doing that, but one never experiences *oneself* "—is much like the complaint of the person who says, "I see him picking up that brick, and mixing that batch of mortar, and troweling that brick into place, but I never see him building a wall." Even as "building the wall" just exactly is a complex process that is *composed* of those various activities, so—from the process point of view—one's self just is a complex process *composed* of those various physical and psychic experiences and actions in their systemic interrelationship.

The process-based approach in philosophical psychology doubtless has difficulties of its own. But they pale into nothingness compared to those of the traditional substantival approach.

Process Theology

Let us now move on to another theme, process theology.[8] The neo-Platonic sympathies of the church fathers impelled the theology of the Western monotheistic religions to the orthodox philosophical stance that to see God as existent we must conceive of God as a being, a *substance* of some (presumably very nonstandard) sort. And to the pleasure of philosophers and the vexation of theologians, this has opened up a host of theoretical difficulties. For example: (1) On the classical conception of the matter, a substance must always originate from substances. Q: Whence God? A: From him- or herself, God is *causa sui.* (2) Substances standardly have contingent properties. Q: Does God? A: No; God is in all respects (self-) necessitated. (3) Substances standardly have spatiotemporal emplacement. Q: Does God? A: No; He, unlike standard substances, exists altogether outside place and time. And so on. No sooner has Western theology made God a substance in order to satisfy its ontological predilections than it has to break all the rules for substances, and take away with one hand what it seemed to give us with the other.

But in conceptualizing God in terms of *process*—as a characteristically unified family or system of transcendent processes bearing *ab extra* on humankind and world—we overcome many such difficulties at one blow. For it now becomes far easier to understand how God can be and be operative. To be sure, conceiving of God in process terms involves recourse to various processes of a very special kind. But extraordinary (or even supranatural) *processes* pose far fewer difficulties than extraordinary (or let alone supranatural) *substances.* After all, many sorts of processes are in their own way unique—or, at any rate, very radically different from all others. It is not all that hard to see that processes like the creation of a world or the inauguration of its nomic structure are by their very nature bound to be unusual. But in the world of processes, that is not all that strange.

Moreover—crucially—God is a *person*. And so, once we have an account of personhood in process terms as a systemic complex of characteristic activities, it is no longer strange to see God in these terms as well. If we "processify" the human person, then we can more readily conceive of the divine person in process terms as well. God is now understood as a complex system of characterized processes that creates and sustains the world and endows it with law, beauty (harmony and order), value, and meaning.

The process approach accordingly affords a framework for the conceptualization of God that not only removes many of the difficulties inherent in the thing-oriented, substantival approach of traditional metaphysics, but also makes it vastly easier to provide a philosophical rationale for the leading conceptions of Judeo-Christian religiosity.

The Agenda for Process Philosophy

As these deliberations indicate, the process approach has many assets. But it has some significant liabilities as well. For it is by no means unfair to the historical situation to say that process philosophy at present remains no more than a glint in the mind's eye of certain philosophers. All that we have so far are suggestions, sketches, and expressions of confidence. The work of developing the process doctrine to the point where it can be compared with other major philosophical projects like materialism or absolute idealism still remains to be done. Many writers have hinted at a process philosophy, but nobody has yet developed one—not even Whitehead, though he has perhaps gone further in this direction than anyone else.

Take an example. What is it that makes "*this* typing of *AND*" and "*that* typing of and" two instances of the same process? Obviously it is not the sameness of the product—identical *ands* can in principle be produced in very different ways by very different processes. Rather it is that the two concrete processes invoked are simply two different spatiotemporal instances of the same generic procedure—that exactly the same recipe is followed in either case. Clearly the theory of process individuation and reidentification needs to be carefully worked out. The issue is complicated. For processes are sometimes collected together not through processual sameness but merely a sameness of product. Take Aristotle's example of "building a house." Clearly, house building is not really a single sort of process at all but a family of processes linked only by a sameness of product. What this sort of complexity is needs to be worked out carefully.

Moreover, we need a more detailed theoretical analysis of the interrelationships of processes. It is clear, for example, that two such relationships are fundamental: (1) The process/subprocess relation that makes one process into a subsidiary component or constituent of another. (2) The concrete-process/process-type relationship that renders two given concrete processes instances of a common type—presumably under the aegis of a principle of commonality of structure. The character and connection between these modes of process relationship is something that very much needs to be clarified.

To develop an adequate groundwork for process philosophy we need:

- An analysis of the conception of process in its various manifestations and an explanation of which of its features have primary importance for metaphysical purposes;
- A survey of the major sorts of processes that bear importantly in metaphysical issues;
- A thoroughgoing examination of the nature of emergence, novelty, innovation, and creativity;
- A clear scheme for distinguishing the salient features of diverse processes: living versus inert, conscious versus unconscious;
- A classifying taxonomy of processes of various sorts;
- Provision of a cogently developed line of argument for the primacy of process;
- An integrated and coordinated presentation of the scientific and philosophical ideas relating to processes;
- A systematic survey of the pivotal issues from a process point of view to show how the process approach can avert difficulties; and
- A reasoned schema for distinguishing and characterizing natural processes in a hierarchical format (proto-physical, physical, chemical, biological, social), suitably distinguishing each level from and yet relating it to the next.

This list is only the starting point. To provide an adequate account of process philosophy we need cogent and integrated series of well-developed expositions and arguments to articulate and substantiate the central theses of this position. A great deal of work remains to be done before process philosophy becomes anything like a well-defined philosophical doctrine. Perhaps, as Andrew J. Reck has shrewdly noted, "the unfinished and never-to-be-finished quality of [processual] flux has seduced many adherents to the metaphysics of process away from systematic theory-building."[9] Be this as it may, the fact remains that at this state of the historical dialectic, process philosophy is not a developed *doctrine* but a projected *program*. All that can be said at this time—though said with a considerable degree of confidence—is that this program is well worth pursuing. On all indications—and there are a good many of them—the process approach to philosophical issues offers good promise of engendering a substantial philosophical doctrine that has much interest in itself and can overcome various serious defects of the available alternatives. But we stand at the frontier here precisely because there is still so much to be done.[10] Let me take one final stab at showing how it can overcome some serious defects of alternative approaches, namely, in this case substance semantics.

Process Semantics

The idea of *nonexistent individuals* has long troubled subject-predicate theorists. How can there possibly be a nameable individual—such as the winged horse Pegasus—that does not actually exist?[11] In standard logic, after all, ". . . a . . ." is equivalent to "(∃x)(x = a & . . . x . . .)." But how are we then to avert the awkward consequence that the truistic premise

winged horse (Pegasus)
does not yield the patently false conclusion:
(∃x) x is a winged horse?

Bertrand Russell's well-known theory of descriptions endeavored to resolve the issue within the framework of subject-predicate logic, but ran into various difficulties which need not be rehearsed here.

In the middle years of this century, W. V. O. Quine suggested the interesting idea of dispensing with named individuals altogether in semantical theory, replacing them with suitable "adjectives."[12] Dismissing the substantive *Pegasus,* we are to resort to the object-description *pegasizes.* For Quine's approach we are to rephrase the equation "x = a" as a predication where "= a" is taken as a general term, so that "Pegasus is a winged horse" becomes the harmless truism: "Whatever pegasizes (i.e., nothing) is a winged horse." In such cases the singular term or name "comes to play the role of the 'F' in 'Fa' and ceases to play that of the 'a.'"[13] In this vein, Quine speaks of an "artificial and trivial-seeming device (which creates) the *ex hypothesi* unanalyzable, irreducible attribute of *being Pegasus.* . . . The noun 'Pegasus' itself could then be treated as derivative, and identified after all with a description: "'the thing that is-Pegasus,' 'the thing that pegasizes.'"[14] The singular term for a nonexistent such as Pegasus is thus switched to a predicative position, so as to become a general term. We trade that noun in for a less problematic adjective. Pegasus simply vanishes as a "nonexistent individual."

But Quine is left standing in an anomalous position. For his elimination of singular terms in favor of adjectives does not, as he himself recognizes, involve the actual elimination of objects to which the *ex hypothesi* noninstantiated predicate is (nominally) attributed: "the objects stay on as values of the variables though the singular terms be swept away."[15]

This uncomfortable halfway house can be abandoned, however, if we shift to a process semantics. On such an approach, one would look at "pegasizing" not as a characteristic attribute that represents *a property of individuals,* but as *a process* that can transpire at coordinate positions.[16] There is now a shift from *adjectives to verbs.* Pegasizing is now a very particular sort of process, and the object neutral conception of "it pegasizes" is analogous to "it rains" or "it is hot." The (false) statement "Pegasus exists" will be glossed as

$(\exists p)$(pegasizing at p)

and the (true) statement "Pegasus does not exist" would be glossed as its denial

$(\forall p) \neg$ (pegasizing at p)

where "p" is a *positional* variable in a space-time framework. After all, what concretizes a particular instance of a physical process of a certain generic sort as a part of the world's activities is precisely its locatability in the space-time framework. It is particularized through the operation of a certain sort of process of location placement (be it ostensive or descriptive in terms of a locational system such as coordinates). Every particular physical process conjoins a "positional" placement aspect with a "structural" type-classification aspect: it is both a *this* and a *what.* (Note: "adding 2 and 2" is not a physical process, but Smith's adding 2 and 2 here and now is.)

This approach, which dispenses with singular object/substance terms altogether and uses quantification as a merely positional device, can be carried over uniformly to existents as well. By parity of reasoning one eliminates not only nonexistents such as Pegasus as (mysterious) objects, but Quine's object descriptions as well. For, in this approach, one goes beyond seeing pegasizing as *an adjective to* insisting on seeing it as a genuinely process-indicative verb.

But now a process semanticist can carry the preceding idea one step further. For one can proceed to adopt a uniform approach to existents and nonexistents, putting quining ("to quine") along with pegasizing ("to pegasize"). There is no longer any need for a shadowy variable-range of nonnameable individuals because one can straightforwardly operate with instances of verb-application. "It quines here" does duty for "Quine is here," and "it quines somewhere" replaces "Quine exists." "Quine is a philosopher"—that is, "Quine sometimes philosophizes"—does not now represent the subject-predicate claim:

philosopher (Quine)

but rather the process-relating claim that Quine sometimes philosophizes, namely:

some philosophizings are (parts or aspects of) quinings

or more fully

$(\exists p)$(it philosophizes at p & it quines at p & (it philosophizes at p @ it quines at p)).

Here @ represents *containment or inclusion* among processes. Accordingly, the process semanticist treats *nonexistent* particulars and *actual* particulars alike—both are reflected in processes that may or may not be realized at coordinate reference positions.

In general, a process semantics must accomplish with verbs and adverbs what a semantics of individuals accomplishes with properties and relations. When the one says "X has the property F" the other says "X functions F-ly" for some suitably F-corresponding process. (Thus "X is triangular" becomes "X disports itself triangularly.") And where the one says "X bears the rotation R to Y," the other says "X functions R-ly toward Y." (Thus "X is north of Y" becomes "X locates itself to-the-north-of Y-ly.")

Further refinements suggest themselves. For example, one can now also introduce process/action variables. For this purpose we might as well use the convenient *x, y, z* . . . , now freed from their previous role as individual-object variables. And we shall further adopt the notation "T(x)" for "the process x is of type T," as a mechanism of process-description in the place of object-characterization.

This variant semantics makes it possible to overcome some well-known difficulties that affect the standard thing-property semantics.

Consider, for example, Donald Davidson's well-known complaint that standard subject-predicate logic has difficulty in coming to terms with:

1. X buttered the toast slowly and deliberately.

As he sees it, the closest one can come to formulate this by standard means is:

2. X buttered the toast slowly and X buttered the toast deliberately.

And Davidson now objects: "The trouble is that we have nothing here we would ordinarily recognize as a singular term. Another sip that we have not caught the logical form of the sentence is that in this last version there is no implication that any *one* act was both slow and deliberate."[17] But recourse to a semantics of processes serves to avert these difficulties. To render (1) we first move to:

3. (∃y)(y is an action of buttering toast & y is an X-performed action & y is a careful action & y is a deliberate action).

The final step in the rendition is to gloss that individual-object reference to X processually by making use of the equivalence:

y is an X-performed action = (∃p)(it y's at p & it X's at p & (it y's at p @ it X's at p)).

We then arrive at:

4. (∃y)((toast buttering (y) & (∃p)((it y's at p & it X's at p) & (it y's at p @ it X's at p)) & deliberate action (y) & slow action (y))).

Observe (a) that there is now indeed something in this statement that "we would ordinarily recognize as a singular term," namely, "a (certain particular) toast buttering," and (b) that the formulation of (4) makes it transparently clear that a single action is at issue throughout. Thus in the language of processes, the formalization of (1) presents no great problems. Its truth-conditions can be formulated more effectively in terms of processes and their relations than in terms of things and their properties.

As this brief sketch indicates, a semantics of processes is a useful resource that affords means for overcoming some of the characteristic limitations, problems, and difficulties of a semantics of objects-and-attributes.

Notes

1. A. N. Whitehead, CN, chapter 3.
2. PR 12, 47.
3. PR 318, 471.
4. The events which constitute a process must be temporally coordinated. But they need not be causally connected. The king's morning toilette is a process. He arises, and then brushes his teeth, and so on. The unifying linkage of this complex process is "and then." But there is no causal connection. (He does not brush his teeth *because* he has washed.) In consequence, specifically causal processes constitute a particular sort of process.
5. "Bad Faith," in *Being and Nothingness*, trans. Hazel Barnes (New York: Pocket Books, 1966), p. 107ff.
6. David Hume, *A Treatise of Human Nature*, book II, part IV, section 6, "Of Personal Identity." In the "Appendix," Hume further elaborates: 'When I turn my reflection on *myself* I never can perceive this self without some one or more perceptions; nor can I ever perceive anything but the perceptions. It is the composition of these, therefore, which forms the SELF."
7. Miguel de Unamuno, *Del sentimiento tiágico de la vida*, ed. P. Felix Garcia (Madrid: 1982), p. 52.
8. For a useful anthology on the topic, see *Process Theology: Basic Writings*, ed. Ewert H. Cousins (New York: Macmillan, 1971), which seeks to integrate the tradition of Whitehead with that of Teilhard de Chardin.
9. Andrew J. Reck, "Process Philosophy: A Categorical Analysis," in *Studies in Process Philosophy* II ed. R. C. Whittemore, *Tulane Studies in Philososophy* 24 (New Orleans: Tulane University Press, 1975), p. 59.
10. I am indebted to Johanna Seibt and David Carey for constructive comments on a draft of this paper.

11. On the history of the issue see "The Concept of Nonexistent Possibles," in Nicholas Rescher, *Essays in Philosophical Analysis* (Pittsburgh: University of Pittsburgh Press, 1969), pp. 73–109.
12. W. V. Quine, "On What There Is," in *From a Logical Point of View* (Cambridge, Mass.: Harvard University Press, 1980) p. 179, section 37.
13. W. V. Quine, *Word and Object* (Cambridge, Mass.: Harvard University Press, 1980), p. 179, section 37.
14. Quine, "On What There Is," p. 8.
15. Quine, *Word and Object*, Sect. 40, p. 192, n. 1.
16. On the logic of position see chapter 13, "Topological Logic," in Nicholas Rescher, *Topics in Philosophical Logic* (Dordrecht: D. Reidel, 1968), pp. 229–249.
17. Donald Davidson, "The Logical Form of Action Sentences," in *The Logic of Decision and Action*, ed. Nicholas Rescher (Pittsburgh: University of Pittsburgh Press, 1967), p. 81.

Chapter 3

Whitehead and Wittgenstein

The Critique of Enlightenment and the Question Concerning Metaphysics

GEORGE R. LUCAS JR.

Editor's Comment: As mentioned at the very outset of this chapter, an earlier draft of this essay was presented as a plenary address at the Seventeenth International Wittgenstein Congress, but it is here published for the first time in its entirety and as substantially revised. Professor Lucas's contribution is distinctive in presenting a revisionist reading of Whitehead's categoreal scheme as heuristic scheme, a reading that aligns the later Whitehead as a "postanalytic" thinker of a certain sort (as epistemically wary but without the stark anti-realism). Perhaps more precisely, in Lucas's apt expression, Whitehead is seen here as "broadly analytic," a phrase more attuned to the enlarged notion of "supra-analytic" philosophy discussed and advocated in chapter 1.

Introductory Remarks

In the summer of 1994, I was privileged to deliver the closing plenary address for the Seventeenth Annual Symposium of the International Wittgenstein Congress, meeting just outside Vienna. The theme of the congress was "Ludwig Wittgenstein and the British Tradition in Philosophy." Other distinguished plenary speakers, from Martha Nussbaum to R. M. Hare and Jaakko Hintikka, commented on Bertrand Russell, G. E. Moore, and even R. G. Collingwood in relation to the development of Wittgenstein's thought. I was asked to comment on Alfred North Whitehead, on whose work in the philosophy of science and in speculative metaphysics I had concentrated for most of my own professional career. Mine promised at first to be an exceedingly brief closing address, since there was so little material with which to work. I chose to present my own view of Whitehead as a mathematical and analytic philosopher, unafraid of the speculative turn but not so given to metaphysics and philosophical theology as the vast majority of his subsequent followers. The focus of those remarks was to comment on a peculiar tendency among the pivotal founders of analytic philosophy to turn their backs on the principle tenets of that philosophical tradition in their later work. This tendency is well documented in the case of Whitehead, but constitutes a surprising comment upon the work of the later Wittgenstein.

Within the British tradition of philosophy itself, Bertrand Russell, G. E. Moore, and A. N. Whitehead certainly rank as the foremost figures in the twentieth century. Together they represented the "great trinity" of British philosophy at Trinity College, Cambridge, early in this century, whose work largely defined English-language philosophy during a period just prior to World War I, when Wittgenstein first came to Cambridge to study philosophy with Whitehead's pupil and colleague, Russell. Without intending blasphemy, however, it is readily apparent in hindsight that Wittgenstein completely transcended this trinity, and is now regarded by a vast majority of scholars as the most important figure in philosophy in any language and in any country during this century.[1]

Scarcely twenty years have elapsed, however, since English-language readers were confronted with the possibility that Wittgenstein could no longer be understood adequately as a part of this "British tradition" in philosophy. In their 1973 landmark study, *Wittgenstein's Vienna*, Stephen Toulmin and Allan Janik argued that "the preconceptions with which his English hearers approached [Wittgenstein] debarred them almost entirely from understanding the point of what he was saying."[2] Their striking cultural observation in turn adds depth and documentation to earlier startling suggestions by one of my own professors, Eric Heller, in his essay on Wittgenstein in his magisterial work, *The Artist's Journey into the Interior.*[3] Heller there argued that the cultural antecedents of Wittgenstein's thought were to be found in the work of Austrian predecessors and contemporaries, specifically citing Otto Weininger, Adolf Loos, Karl Kraus, Franz Kafka, and Robert Musil, and Heller suggested that Wittgenstein himself exhibited far more intellectual affinity with Rilke, Pascal, and Nietzsche than with Frege, let alone any analytic British philosopher.

Heller notwithstanding, it remained the case that, prior to the appearance of the Toulmin/Janik study, the so-called logical interpretation of Wittgenstein prevailed relatively unchallenged. This conventional interpretation portrays Wittgenstein as an English-speaking genius who had refined the logical and analytical techniques of Russell and Frege to a degree unimagined by either of them. Toulmin and Janik argued, by contrast, for the primacy of the Viennese "ethical" (one might also say, "aesthetic") interpretation of Wittgenstein's work. They dramatically portray him as, first and foremost, an expatriate genius whose philosophical outlook was framed by the intellectual foment of *fin-de-siecle* Vienna, whose *Tractatus* owed as much to Hertz and Boltzmann as to Russell or Frege, and was itself more comparable to Arnold Schönberg's

Harmonielehre than to Whitehead and Russell's *Principia Mathematica.*[4] So intellectually profound and engaging are the images they recollect of the cultural world inhabited by the likes of Brückner, Mahler, Max Plank, and Sigmund Freud, that one begins to wonder what ever could have induced Wittgenstein to leave it!

Yet Wittgenstein did leave the complex and fascinating intellectual world of early twentieth century Vienna, and he did decide to come to Cambridge; after a time, moreover, he returned; and finally he remained. To his friend David Pinsent he once described coming to Cambridge to study with Russell as "my salvation." English-language philosophy, and Anglo-American analytic philosophers, have doubtless erred in stressing too one-sidedly and for too long the contributions of Wittgenstein as judged exclusively from the perspective of their own philosophical orientation, ignoring the deeper roots of Wittgenstein's own beliefs about the connection of logic and ethics—connections widely discussed among leading intellectuals in Vienna. A great deal of the personal anguish of Wittgenstein the man certainly stemmed from his having found himself divided between two radically incommensurable cultural worlds, at home in neither.[5] It may not really be possible to appreciate him apart from appreciating both of those worlds from which he was alike both alienated and attracted.

Whitehead's Place in Twentieth Century Philosophy

It is not my intention to comment, however, solely upon Wittgenstein, but upon what, if anything can or needs to be said about Wittgenstein in conjunction with Whitehead. In order to develop the comparisons I shall wish to draw, I need first to say something about my own, rather unconventional understanding of Whitehead himself. For, of the various representatives of British philosophy in the early twentieth century (during which Wittgenstein was drawn to Cambridge to study, and later to teach) Whitehead, perhaps alongside R. G. Collingwood, is the most difficult to categorize. Despite his reputation for odd metaphysical views, several philosophers during the past decades have been drawn to study Whitehead on account of his scientific and mathematical interests, and his desire to understand the implications for philosophy (broadly speaking) of the profound changes in the sciences wrought by revolutionary thinkers from Darwin, Maxwell, and Poincaré through Einstein, Plank, and Schrödinger.[6] Whitehead was one of the earliest English-language philosophers to portray "Newtonianism" as a historical artifact and a modern, Western cultural ideology. He explicitly desired both to understand the origins of Newtonianism in this fashion, and also to suggest alternatives for what he took to be its necessary reconstruction in light of the work of these other major figures of science and philosophy, past and present. Whitehead viewed Newtonianism and its alternatives in a sense quite similar to that in which Ernst Mach, another critic of Newtonianism, viewed scientific theories: that is, as complex assemblages of facts and interpretations which are intended to be descriptive of, rather than judgments on, experience (sensations).

Metaphysics, as Whitehead practiced it, is surprisingly similar to Mach's approach to science: namely, both thought that theories should aim to save experience, and should be routinely purged of abstract theoretical entities or constructs which were not grounded in or inferred from those experiences. Mach called such abstractions "metaphysical"; Whitehead did not aim his criticism at "metaphysics" per se, but condemned specific "metaphysical" entities in Newtonianism as examples of a "Fallacy of Misplaced Concreteness." Like Wittgenstein, Whitehead held that the business of philosophy was therapeutic: in Whitehead's case, this involved diagnosing cultural incoherence—the sense in which the conceptual underpinnings of Newtonianism were increasingly at odds with other cultural tendencies more closely tied to experience, and how Newtonianism was even at odds with ongoing scientific discoveries—leading to confusion and philosophical conundrums. The therapy lay in uncovering the artifacts of "misplaced concreteness" that resulted in the underlying incoherence of worldview, and healing these anomalies by addressing and surgically removing the incoherencies in that predominant worldview. Philosophy would have succeeded in its task when these sources of confused incoherence—creating what Wittgenstein sometimes called "bewitchment"—were set right, causing the anomalies and conundrums themselves simply to disappear. It certainly bears mention that Collingwood developed a similar, though much more detailed and sophisticated, conception of metaphysics as a therapeutic critique of tacit cultural presuppositions (what Collingwood termed "absolute presuppositions"), which is one reason he found Whitehead's thought so congenial.[7]

Born the son of an Anglican minister at Ramsgate, England, in 1861, Alfred North Whitehead attended mathematics lectures at Cambridge. Along with Moore and the renowned idealist philosopher, J. M. E. McTaggart, he was a member of the famous but secretive "Cambridge Apostles" club, which he credited for a good deal of his philosophical education.[8]

Whitehead subsequently taught mathematics, mathematical physics, and logic, first as a Fellow at Trinity College (until 1910), and afterward in the Imperial College of Science and Technology at the University of London (1910–1924). While at the University of London, he coauthored the monumental, three-volume *Principia Mathematica* with his student and friend, Bertrand Russell. He published, in addition, a version of general relativity theory in 1922, which still stands to this day as an alternative to Einstein's fundamental philosophical assumptions—one that nonetheless appears to yield both mathematically and empirically equivalent testable outcomes. Despite Einstein's own mystified response to this challenge, and despite occasional examination, analysis, and discussion by a series of leading relativity theorists down through the years, this alternative of Whitehead's has never been disproved or successfully dismissed as a legitimate challenge to Einstein.[9] During this period Whitehead also published several works that are considered classics in the foundations of algebra, geometry, and the philosophy of science, all of which earned for Whitehead the reputation as a leading figure in the early development of what came to be called "Cambridge analytic philosophy."

Whitehead subsequently retired from the University of London and accepted an offer to come to the United States to serve as Professor of Philosophy at Harvard University. Apart from delivering the Gifford Lectures at Edinburgh during the academic year 1927–1928, he did not return to his native land, but remained in America as a naturalized citizen and active scholar until his death in 1947.

Whitehead was sixty-three when, in 1924, he assumed his position at Harvard with an inaugural series of lectures, revised and published early the next year under the title, *Science and the Modern World*.[10] This, one cannot help but note, was the same age at which Kant published the first edition of his *Kritik der reinen Vernunft*. But this comparison with Kant, with whose influence on philosophy Whitehead had become so thoroughly disillusioned, must end at this point. For there is no dispute whatever among scholars about the importance of Kant's mature "critical" work, beginning at age sixty-three. In marked contrast to Kant, Whitehead at this relatively advanced age in effect began a second career that, depending upon one's intellectual commitments, must be regarded either as the blossoming of broad and productive philosophical interests, or else as a regrettable and inexplicable disaster.

What Whitehead did at this critical juncture was to turn his attention from an exclusive (some might say narrow) focus on logic and technical problems in science and in the philosophy of science, to a wider preoccupation with the history of science—including the history of scientific revolutions and a historical approach to the logic of scientific discovery—as well as to philosophy of culture, philosophy of history, philosophy of religion, and most characteristically, to problems in speculative metaphysics and cosmology. His grand work of this period, *Process and Reality*[11] (based on the decidedly unsuccessful Gifford Lectures at Edinburgh),[12] represents an attempt to sketch a detailed cosmological foundation for twentieth-century physics intended to replace the cosmology of Newtonianism.

His wide and varied interests during this period earned a large audience in America, by no means limited to philosophers, and prompted comparisons of his work with that of grand systematic philosophers like Hegel, Leibniz, and Aristotle. It is still true even today that Whitehead remains one of the most frequently quoted and cited authors in commencement addresses and other academic ceremonial occasions in the United States: he appears to be a useful resource whenever a university rector or president wishes to appear wise.[13] In Great Britain, by contrast, only R. G. Collingwood followed and approved of Whitehead's "speculative turn," and for many decades his work was almost unknown on the European continent.

As with Wittgenstein, it remains a matter of serious dispute how deep, in fact, is this alleged "divide" between the early and the later Whitehead. At the time and since, and in the cultural context of Anglo-American analytic philosophy, Whitehead's later thought was regarded by nondisciples as an anomaly—as a throwback, in essence, to the worst unrestrained excesses of nineteenth century speculative thought. It is said that the Harvard philosophy faculty had first hoped to persuade Bertrand Russell to join their department, and failing this, they turned to Whitehead as a suitable alternative. Although the department included at least one unreconstructed and unashamed metaphysician (William E. Hocking), the majority of the faculty were repelled by metaphysics, and so regarded Whitehead's surprising philosophical metamorphosis on coming to America with profound dismay. While politely received and well thought of as a colleague, Whitehead found himself quietly isolated and largely without intellectual influence among his mainstream philosophical colleagues.[14] Ever since, philosophers from Reichenbach to Rorty have expressed profound disrespect and disaffection for this "later Whitehead."

It is possible, however, to portray Whitehead's interests during this period as a fairly consistent extension of earlier work and interests, enriched by reflection drawn from the extraphilosophical resources and influences—including his lifelong interest and immersion in literature, especially Romantic poetry, and history—that had constituted an essential part of his preparatory school training and intellectual background. Some scholars have also attributed these extraphilosophical interests to Alfred and Evelyn Whitehead's participation, for a time, in the Bloomsbury circle.[15] Whitehead's later thought surely seems characteristic of what we now recognize as a legitimate alternative "style" of philosophy to the analytic—namely, "Continental" or "postanalytic" philosophy. It remains to be seen whether this work by Whitehead was a "throwback" to outdated or inadequate modes of thought, or whether he will come to be seen as one of the earliest harbingers of a radically revised, broadly analytic philosophy, of which we have numerous more recent advocates today, ranging from Hilary Putnam and Richard Rorty to Whitehead's one-time pupil, the late Willard V. A. Quine,[16] whose own remarks on Whitehead and on Leemon McHenry's discussion of descriptive and revisionist metaphysics grace this volume as among the last of Quine's writings prior to his death in 2000.

What is the evidence for this "continental" interpretation of Whitehead? When we examine a work like *Process and Reality*, for example, we find that Whitehead—in a manner somewhat analogous to the approach of Heidegger, Gadamer, or Derrida—is engaged in a kind of dialogue or discussion with the great European philosophers of the past, and is likewise engaged in an exegesis of many of the important philosophical texts of that European tradition. In addition to Plato's *Timaeus*, Whitehead discusses at great length in these Gifford Lectures many of the central works of Locke, Descartes, Spinoza, Hume, and Kant, and engages in a thoughtful and critical reconstruction of the currents of thought giving rise to the modernist worldview. I shall wish, in my conclusion, to return to this "critique of modernism" that can be found in these works. For now I simply note that, like Jacques Derrida in particular, Whitehead is especially prone to offer interpretations of traditional texts and figures that strike many of his readers as unusual, unorthodox, and sometimes even unjustifiable. For example, Whitehead is quite fascinated by a brief comment of John Locke, that the passage of time is constituted by a "perpetual perishing."[17] Despite the fact that this text is hardly mentioned by other commentators, Whitehead uses this interesting and suggestive phrase of Locke's as the centerpiece of his own reinterpretation of the philosophy of being and of time.

It is principally this historical, etymological, exegetical, and even literary approach to a body of texts—what Heidegger liked to call "the tradition," and Cambridge philosopher Michael Oakeshott termed "the practical past"—that distinguishes European or "Continental" philosophical method from the largely nonhistorical, analytic, and empirical approach to specific problem-solving characteristic of American and British philosophy in the twentieth century. Russell wrote an interesting book on Leibniz as well as his infamous *History of Western Philosophy*. But he and Moore always regarded philosophical problems, like scientific problems, as entirely separable from the history of their discussion—most previous examples of which Russell thought to represent serious mistakes. Certainly the flowery, wide-ranging, and detailed literary and historical essays of Whitehead stand in sharp contrast to the largely ahistorical aphorisms of Wittgenstein, often taken as paradigmatic rhetorical expression for analytic philosophy. Despite his English and American roots, then, Whitehead seems to fit more comfortably within this Continental European tradition than he does within the logical-analytic tradition in which he began his career. There is this odd and somewhat ironic comparison with Wittgenstein, namely, that Whitehead perpetually seems strangely "out of context," and so, I would maintain, subject to perennial misunderstanding and misinterpretation on that account. Whitehead and Collingwood somehow "do not *belong*" to their culture, while Wittgenstein found himself "between" cultures and hence a member of none.

A Sketch of Whitehead's Metaphysical Views

I mentioned the discussion of time and temporality in Whitehead's scientific and metaphysical writings, for which he is justifiably well known. These afford us an excellent brief illustration of his later metaphysical theories. Indeed, because of this emphasis on time, Whitehead is often associated with philosophers like Henri Bergson and nonanalytic or preanalytic British philosophers like Samuel Alexander, who (in Alexander's phrase) "take time seriously"—either by placing primary emphasis on the subjective experience of flux and becoming, or by defending the notion of "pure becoming" and temporal passage as real rather than illusory.

These traditional associations are somewhat misleading. Like Einstein, and wholly unlike Bergson, Whitehead is first and foremost a philosopher of space rather than of time. He devotes a significant portion of *Process and Reality*, his most important work, to a complex discussion of the geometrical relations comprising what he termed the "extensive continuum," the geometry of space-time that he proposed as a linear and well-ordered alternative to the nonlinear space-time of Einstein. This, in turn, continues a discussion of "logical space" in the *Principia*, and of the "extensive continuum" and geometrization of physical space that pervade other works of this "early" period.

Specifically, Whitehead does *not* (as did Bergson and Alexander) rhapsodize on time, or portray time itself as something primordial, existing prior to and independent of discrete entities themselves. Neither, however, does Whitehead's focus on space and geometrical relations lead him to follow the example of those like Einstein and Reichenbach, who deny the reality of the apparent asymmetry in the present-past and present-future relationships, and who accordingly attempt to reduce temporality and the experience of temporal passage and becoming merely to a set of spacelike relations. Both such familiar approaches represent, for Whitehead, the unjustifiable departure of metaphysical theorizing from its ground in experience.

In *Process and Reality*, Whitehead frequently uses the aforementioned phrase borrowed from John Locke to describe time as "[a] perpetual perishing." Uniquely in Whitehead's thought, temporality, passage, and what the British astronomer Arthur Eddington famously described as the "arrow of time" arise as a consequence of a more fundamental fact of nature: the becoming and the "perishing" of episodic events or discrete occasions of experience. The genesis of, and the transition between, these "quanta" of experience define what Whitehead termed an "epochal theory" (i.e., a quantized theory) of time.

Borrowing traditional Latin terminology from Descartes, Whitehead labels these quantized episodes or events *res verae*, thereby indicating that these epochal events are the fundamental or foundational actualities from which all else derives. These *res verae* or "actual entities," are "actual" in two possible senses. Each event is "actual" in a primary sense of being *active* and actively self-relating, coming-to-be by constituting itself as a subject out of elements (or "objective data") drawn from its past. Whitehead describes this primary activity as the "*concrescence* of an actual occasion." Once fully constituted and determinate, an event "perishes": that is, it *ceases* to be active or to experience its own subjective immediacy.

In contrast to the views of most of his interpreters and disciples, however, Whitehead did not hold that this fully constituted event then disappears or evaporates into oblivion. Rather, each no-longer-active "actual entity" remains "actual" in a secondary, but equally important sense: that is, as *efficacious*. Each determinate entity now, in its turn, serves as an objective datum or element for inclusion within the self-constitution of *subsequent* (present) active occasions of experience.

This process of the becoming of actual entities, and of their subsequent "perishing" (i.e., their transition from a state of active, subjective immediacy to one of fixed, passive, unchanging objective determinateness) defines a "flux of becoming" and gives rise to the experience of temporal passage. Concrescence defines the present, the event as subject. The perishing of subjectivity, the no-longer-active event serving as object, defines the past. Each actual entity, at different phases in its career, functions as both subject and object: constituting itself out of its own past, and, in turn, serving as an objective datum in the past of subsequent (present) active occasions. This ongoing and perpetual transition from present subjectivity to past objectivity thus defines the "arrow" or asymmetrical vector-quality of temporal passage.[18]

This "two-career" doctrine of activity, in turn, comprises Whitehead's "Reformed Subjectivist Principle."[19] He defines this central principle of his own metaphysical position in direct contrast to what he termed the "Subjectivist Principle" of Descartes, a principle which, Whitehead argued, characterizes all of modern science and philosophy up until the beginnings of the twentieth century. The Cartesian "Subjectivist Principle" distinguishes sharply between what is subject and what is object, between mental "thinking substance" and material "extended substance." To this Whitehead contrasted his own, Spinozistic doctrine of one substantial, underlying activity, "epochalized," or quantized. Each "quantum of experience" functions at different phases in its career as "subject" and as "object." This "reformed" subjectivist principle is, quite obviously, a fundamental redefinition of objectivity and subjectivity in terms of temporal passage.[20]

A noted American philosopher and authority on Whitehead, Professor George L. Kline, perceptively notes that Whitehead's concept may be helpfully illustrated in comparison with J. M. E. McTaggart's well-known analysis of time.[21] In Whitehead's case, the past objectified events literally serve as the "material cause" (in Aristotle's sense) of present activity. Hence his "actual entities" can thus be ordered, in analogy with McTaggart's "B" series, as "earlier" and "later": earlier entities are those which serve as objectified data in the constitution of the later. This causal relationship of past to present is further asymmetrical, in that the relations of present (or "later") entities to their past (or "earlier") antecedents are always *internal* (or constitutive); while the relations of past entities to subsequent (present) entities are always *external* to (i.e., nonconstitutive and unaffected by) their inclusion in the self-constitution of some later event.

This ontology of present (subjective) and past (objective) events gives rise, however, to a dramatic departure from McTaggart. In Whitehead's case there can be no such thing as a determinate "future" event.

In contrast to "the present" as locus of activity, and "the past" as locus of determinate potentiality, "the future," on Whitehead's account, is merely the locus of unrealized possibilities that may or may not come to be actualized in any of a variety of ways. A present moment is (to use an awkward phrase) "as far forward into time" as one can go, since there is nothing "further on or beyond" the present activity of the self-constitution or concrescence of actual occasions. In contrast to McTaggart, the Whiteheadian "B-series," the asymmetrical causal relation of earlier to later events, thus does *not* entail that there are "future events" of some determinate sort, moving steadily ever closer to, and finally "sliding into the shining present," and then moving out the "other end" of the present and receding ever farther into the past.

There is nothing in Whitehead's account, then, analogous to McTaggart's "A-series" of events, unrolling like fixed images on a spool of motion-picture film and giving rise to the illusion of future-present-past time as a "moving image of eternity." If one were to press this image in Whitehead's case: instead of "unrolling" an already-produced picture film, the passage of time would be like the actual ongoing manufacturing of each successive frame of the not-yet-completed film. Each successive present moment would consist of composing yet another new "frame" (episode or quantum of experience) as a unique synthesis of elements found in the preceding frames, and adding this new one on to the front of the ever-lengthening film strip.

No matter how incomplete the metaphors one employs, the important point to be borne in mind is that Whitehead's event ontology is intended to provide an account of time that squares with common experience without rendering that experience illusory or reducing it to something utterly unlike it, as Einstein and positivist philosophers like Hans Reichenbach and Adolf Grünbaum have proposed. Whitehead also avoids the troublesome proposals from Bergson and Alexander to elevate time itself to the status of some mysterious metaphysical abstraction "within which" our temporal experiences somehow occur.

Whitehead and Wittgenstein: the Question of Metaphysics

The foregoing account admittedly portrays Whitehead as far more deeply embedded in the context and conversation of early-twentieth-century British analytic philosophy than is customarily recognized. But what of his relationship to, or influence on, Wittgenstein?

Of the three members of "the Cambridge trinity," Whitehead had the least influence on the formative education, let alone on the later substantive views, of Wittgenstein. Beyond a few polite invitations to dine at the Whitehead's while he was a young student at Cambridge, there is no historical evidence that Wittgenstein spent much time with, paid much attention to, or absorbed much influence from Whitehead while the latter was a teaching Fellow at Cambridge. Whitehead is mentioned briefly in a few terse sections of the *Tractatus*,[22] where Wittgenstein modifies or challenges certain hidden or faulty presuppositions in the *Principia*. But it is Russell who dominates in this work. Wittgenstein never turns his attention to Whitehead in the manner in which he studied Moore, for example, in *On Certainty*. By the same token, there is no evidence that Whitehead read the *Tractatus*; in fact, by the time Wittgenstein returned to Cambridge for the second time in the 1930s, Whitehead had already long since departed for his appointment at Harvard, and frankly was, by this time, too advanced both in years and in career to have taken much notice of the philosophy of the later Wittgenstein emanating by word of mouth from Cambridge, England to Cambridge, Massachusetts in the 1930s and 1940s.

Indeed, it is entirely in accord with convention to describe Whitehead as a philosopher stubbornly engaged during his Harvard years in continuing to try to do the very things that both the earlier *and* the later Wittgenstein said could not be done and should not be done. Though I mean to question this conventional wisdom, it is certainly apparent that Whitehead *was*, as we have noted, primarily interested in accounting for time, causality, unity and plurality, and in characterizing "Nature" as such and "the World" as such, and even in assessing the nature of God and of the relationship of God and the World in his mature cosmology. Yet, Wittgenstein remarks famously[23] that "the World" is the totality of facts; and so is not itself a fact; hence, phrases like "the World" and "Nature" name nothing of which there can be meaningful discourse.[24]

Later, in the *Philosophical Investigations*, Wittgenstein writes:[25] "What *we* do is to bring words back from their metaphysical to their everyday use." Whitehead, like Russell, however, mistrusted this "everyday use" of words, and so could be said to have been engaged in precisely the opposite task of taking words *from* their everyday use and refining them for metaphysical "precision." In Whitehead's case, this resulted in a technical vocabulary and categorial structure for metaphysics that is difficult, arcane, and frequently off-putting, quite apart from the disincentive that his later metaphysical themes themselves seem to arouse among a great many philosophers.

Whatever else he repudiated during his later period, Wittgenstein never abandoned the view that philosophy must tolerate *nothing* metaphysical, that the correct method in philosophy would be (as he concludes the *Tractatus*) that "whenever someone wanted to say something metaphysical, to show him that he had given no meaning to certain signs in his sentences" (6.53). The later Wittgenstein describes the task of philosophy as clarification and description, not theorizing, and never "explanation" (cf. *Investigations*, section 109). Metaphysics, on this view, as Joachim Schulte remarks, "is a formal, systematic theory imitating natural science but (unlike natural science) necessarily mired in senselessness because of its language and theme."[26] Once again, based on the sample of Whitehead I have offered—his "theory of time and temporality"—it must surely seem that Whitehead's later philosophy represents just such a systematic theory, imitating natural science. Just as surely, the elaborate cosmology of his great work, *Process and Reality*, setting forth an alternative cosmology to Newtonianism, describing the geometry of space-time, and commenting on the Primordial and Consequent natures of God, must seem like a grand, speculative metaphysical theory of the sort that Wittgenstein did not regard as the proper domain of philosophy, and that many members of this Congress will surely regard as the most alien and unintelligible form of *Sprachspiel*.[27] (Or, what Wittgenstein himself might have labeled "gassing"!)

We need not, of course, simply grant the young Wittgenstein without argument his exceedingly restrictive view of philosophy in the *Tractatus*, nor must we simply accept as apodictic his rather conventional (for the period) antimetaphysical rhetoric. If we set that aside and simply ask about the quality of the philosophy involved, I cannot escape the feeling (and it is only that) that Whitehead's account of time and temporality, and his elaborate description of the problem of causality (which I analyze in detail elsewhere[28]) present a fundamentally sound picture or working model of what is meant when we speak of time, or of what is meant when we speak of causality in the natural world. Wittgenstein himself writes:

> We cannot compare a process with 'the passage of time'—there is no such thing—but only with another process (such as the working of a chronometer). Hence we can describe the lapse of time only by relying on some other process. (*Tractatus*, 6.3611)

It would not be the least bit misleading to describe Whitehead's work as providing a detailed gloss, and a fuller and more adequate commentary, on just what this terse comment might actually entail.

On the whole, the particulars of Whitehead's "picture" seem to me more in keeping with what must finally be correct than do alternatives proposed that seem to me wholly intuitive, unverifiable, and often even wildly counterfactual. Many alternative accounts of time, moreover, are put forward by philosophers who in other respects hold themselves exemplars of exact, antimetaphysical philosophy, or by physicists who nevertheless rest their case on not one single shred of empirical detail either placed in evidence or conceivably so placed! The tendency to ungrounded speculation, it seems, runs deep in Western culture, and is especially pronounced among modal logicians and theoretical physicists. Perhaps we should politely say that Whitehead is firmly rooted in a long-standing tradition of grand speculative metaphysics emanating from Cambridge University, spanning the period from Isaac Newton to Stephen Hawking!

But such remarks merely divert attention from what Heidegger calls "the *question* concerning metaphysics." My own approach has been to regard the elaborate categorial scheme put forth by Whitehead, not as a literal account or as a "theory of nature" in the usual realist sense, but as a heuristic device designed to suggest—by implication, analogy, and the use of metaphorical language—aspects of the real that we must grasp. As such, an account of time or causality like Whitehead's is—like an account of the Bohr hydrogen atom, or a description of the "tunneling effect" in quantum mechanics—not a *Vorstellung*, not a literal mental picture or representation—but rather a *bildliche Darstellung*, a public model or representation in the sense described by Wittgenstein's Viennese predecessors, Hertz and Boltzmann.[29] These are meant to be models that show publicly what is the best account we can give of experience, not to substitute as the literal truth of experience. And anyone who has had the interesting experience of trying to teach a first course on quantum theory to students thoroughly enmeshed in a Newtonian classical worldview knows full well that such models can only *show* what cannot be *said*.[30]

We need not rely on physics alone for examples of the kind of modeling I have in mind. The much debated reliance on so-called folk psychology in cognitive science—including the description of human and animal actions in terms of levels of intentionality by Daniel Dennett[31]—provide further illustrations of a much criticized, but apparently indispensable reliance on some form of modeling to develop economical accounts of what is the case. In all of these instances, models, drawings, analogies, and diagrams invariably are meant to illustrate, to tease out aspects of the real, without attempting to provide the literal one-to-one correspondence between the logical structures of descriptions and of the facts themselves that the early Wittgenstein required of propositions. Instead, like the propositions of the *Tractatus* itself, such models—including Whitehead's models and metaphors of temporal passage and causality—aim to picture, portray, or *show* (but do not say) what must be the case.

In sharp distinction to most other process philosophers, I have long argued that Whitehead never meant his metaphysical categories to be taken literally. Rather, he seems to take for granted the modern physicist's belief that he is merely providing heuristic models—*bildlichen Darstellungen*—that would aid readers in the interpretation and understanding of experience itself.[32]

If this is basically correct, then the disagreement with Wittgenstein is portrayed much differently.

The young Wittgenstein did not believe that such *Darstellungen* could be given for issues like values, ethics, or religious belief. One approaches these matters by defining the limits of descriptive discourse; distinguishing what can be said from what can merely be shown. Some of what Whitehead was interested in saying could, according to the early Wittgenstein, only be shown. Once the strict, univocal view of language and logic in the *Tractatus* is abandoned, however, it is no longer clear that Wittgenstein is entitled to draw so clear a distinction between what can be shown or said, or indeed, regarding what might be "shown" precisely by being (in a heuristic or metaphorical sense) "said."[33] In any case, much of Whitehead's interest in physical cosmology, the major portion of his so-called metaphysics, is more of a piece with those accounts of objects and states of affairs that *can* be given, or else consists of accounts of principles (like those of the *Tractatus* itself, or else like Hertz's underlying principles of physical "economy," mathematical elegance, and least action) which are heuristic in the sense that they can be indicated through pseudopropositions that, once understood, can be discarded.[34]

Whitehead, Wittgenstein, and the Critique of Enlightenment

Such considerations notwithstanding, however, there is simply no evidence that Whitehead, apart from his participation with Russell in the *Tractatus* project, ever exerted any meaningful influence on the development of Wittgenstein's thought; nor did Whitehead seem to take much notice of Wittgenstein in his own later philosophy. Surprisingly, however, there are a number of parallels: some of these are merely interesting curiosities; others seem quite significant.

We may notice that both philosophers were, for substantial portions of their productive lives, expatriates. I commented at the outset on the obvious but routinely overlooked importance of this "metaxalogical" condition[35]—this "cultural between-ness"—for understanding Wittgenstein, who, though he did not wish to become (as he put it in a letter to John Maynard Keynes) an "imitation Englishman,"[36] felt compelled to accept British citizenship in lieu of German following the *Anschluss*. Much less is known about the impact of Whitehead's decision—made, to be sure, under considerably less duress—to leave London for Massachusetts. The change of intellectual climate certainly seems to have inspired a freedom of expression and a blossoming of interests unpursued in the British context.

Although I have contrasted Whitehead's later literary style with the terse, and severely economic writing of Wittgenstein, still there are parallels. Whitehead's style of writing in his most technical work is difficult and weblike. He practices a kind of "recurrence method—continuously cycling back through topics already introduced and considered at some length, adding additional information or insights with each pass."[37] The later Wittgenstein was similarly non-systematic and recursive in his exposition. In the brief preface to the *Philosophical Investigations*, Wittgenstein describes his dilemma of being able only to provide "sketches of landscapes" which he is compelled to "criss-cross in every direction" yielding a book he characterizes as his "album" or as a kind of travelogue, compiled piecemeal "in the course of these long and involved journeyings."[37] Both writers, apparently, were attempting work of such complexity and intellectual demand, and were so "inside" their respective projects, that linear, systematic, topical exposition was apparently not possible. And in Whitehead's case, even though committed to providing an expository account of physical and metaphysical theories grounded, after the example of Mach, in experience, nevertheless he gravitated, as I argued earlier, increasingly toward the explicitly heuristic expression of the later Wittgenstein: in essence, we must "ignore what I'm saying; grasp what I'm trying to show."

Both received formal training principally in science and mathematics; of particular note, neither of these great philosophers received formal training in philosophy. Thus, in marked contrast to Moore, Russell, Collingwood, and many other contemporaries—neither Whitehead nor Wittgenstein was actually trained to pursue, nor did either apparently intend to pursue, the vocation for which they became most famous. Although it sounds shocking to say this, both were "amateur" philosophers. I do not mean, of course, that either was deficient in the practice of philosophy; rather, by "amateur" I mean they were largely self-taught and self-directed, and so informally educated as to what philosophy is and how it is done. This fact has the particular and important consequence that neither philosopher was ever forcibly indoctrinated through systematic study and apprenticeship into a community of discourse. Instead, each found his way into that community on his own. This led both to be perceived as mavericks; and, I think, permitted both to be path breakers rather than contributors to philosophy practiced simply as a "normal science" industry (in Thomas Kuhn's sense).

Wittgenstein is, of course, rather famous for this. It is well known that he deplored "professionalization."[39] Toulmin and Janik report[40] that Wittgenstein read comparatively little philosophy and saw himself as being none the worse for being a self-taught philosopher. Georg Henrik von Wright notes, in his famous biographical sketch of 1954, that Wittgenstein:

> had done no systematic reading in the classics of philosophy. He could read only what he could wholeheartedly assimilate.

Von Wright further notes that of the several philosophers Wittgenstein did read, and of the very few he could countenance, he (like Whitehead) apparently enjoyed Plato.[41]

Norman Malcolm, for his part, recalls that Wittgenstein once remarked to David Pinsent that he [Wittgenstein] was "extremely outraged," on finally reading some of the philosophers whose historical reputations he had heretofore somewhat naively presumed was warranted, at discovering the "stupid mistakes" they made.[42] Presumably among these stupid mistakes was Augustine's "theory of language acquisition" as an ostensive "naming game" that Wittgenstein found in the *Confessions*. What Wittgenstein scholars frequently describe as this "Augustinian theory" of language, with which Wittgenstein opens the *Philosophical Investigations*, serves as an important symbolic and rhetorical device—a kind of foil—for the later Wittgenstein, against which his own view of "language" as constituting an indefinite number of distinct and nonhierarchical "language games," loosely grouped according to family resemblance, is developed as an alternative.

But historians of philosophy would quickly object that it is clearly not Augustine, or anything central to Augustine's own philosophy, that Wittgenstein is attacking—rather, the "Augustinian theory" in fact names the view of language found in the British and in the *Wienerkreis*-positivists' "logical" reading of the *Tractatus*, and presupposed in the *Principia*'s efforts to ground mathematics in logic as the preeminent foundational language. What is rejected as unpromising and infeasible is likewise not Augustine's own philosophy, with which Wittgenstein was presumably not concerned, but the later efforts of contemporaries like Otto Neurath or A. J. Ayer, inspired by the logical interpretation of the *Tractatus*, to develop an incorrigible language in which philosophical perplexities would not arise.

In this sense, Wittgenstein's infrequent, selective, and sometimes idiosyncratic appropriation of the history of philosophy is somewhat comparable to Whitehead's, as in the example of John Locke cited earlier. Whitehead, however, was less impatient with his predecessors than was Wittgenstein, tending to be instructed from them by inspiration, and willing for the most part to overlook their "stupid mistakes." Whitehead's sharpest barbs are aimed at Kant and at the so-called epistemological turn in philosophy after the Enlightenment. Whitehead portrays his own later philosophy as an attempt to recur to "pre-Kantian" modes of thought, a revealing but nonetheless problematic assertion that has not aided in a sympathetic approach to his own thought, particularly in Europe.[43] Nonetheless, the later Whitehead found his way from ahistorical analysis back into the historical tradition of philosophy, within which constructive philosophical thought is conceived of as a dialogue with the positions of philosophers in the past. Wittgenstein apparently did not, in the end, find anything in that self-defined historical tradition worthy of detailed pursuit, and remained, as did his colleagues in both British analytic and European logical empiricism, largely outside of it.

Finally, as noted, both philosophers produced sharply divergent points of view in two distinct phases of a career. The degree of discontinuity between the earlier and later work of each philosopher is a much-disputed matter in the interpretation of both. There is, I believe, something quite remarkable about this Heideggerian *Verkehren*, this presumed radical conversion or transformation in the later orientation of both philosophers; and with this I turn at last to my concluding point. In his aforementioned biographical note on Wittgenstein, von Wright comments about this perceived *Verkehren* of Wittgenstein:

> The young Wittgenstein had learned from Frege and Russell. His problems were in part theirs. The later Wittgenstein, in my view, has no ancestors in the history of thought. His work signals a radical departure from previously existing paths of philosophy.[44]

In a note to the second edition of this sketch, von Wright goes on to observe:

> I have seen this statement, and the one preceding it, contested. But I think they are substantially correct and also important. The *Tractatus* belongs in a definite tradition in European philosophy, extending back beyond Frege and Russell at least to Leibniz. Wittgenstein's so-called 'later philosophy,' as I see it, is quite different. Its spirit is unlike anything I know in Western thought and in many ways opposed to aims and methods in traditional philosophy.[45]

I do not now propose to quarrel directly with Professor von Wright, who was attempting to refute any suggestion of indebtedness or influence, during this later period of Wittgenstein's, to the work of G. E. Moore. The sharp differences from Moore's specific philosophy, on which von Wright quite rightly insists, are clearly apparent in Wittgenstein's detailed commentary upon Moore in *Über Gewissheit*,[46] in which Wittgenstein transforms Moore's epistemological and ultimately metaphysical claims regarding what we can know indubitably into a dramatically different, attitudinal account of the *language* of certitude.

I want to call attention to something else entirely. Although I have labeled this a "critique of Enlightenment" according to prevailing philosophical fashion, in fact there is nothing so clear or precise in what I now present. There is, I will argue, a strain of irony emerging from the rarified philosophical air of Cambridge that, surprisingly, represents a rather severe distrust of, and even a reaction against, philosophy itself. While this reaction against the power of philosophical reason stops short of traditional skepticism, it does place a heavy emphasis on fallibility. It would not be unfair to label it "ironic" in the Socratic sense. Wittgenstein and the later Whitehead, I will argue, are representative of this tendency. Moore, in some respects at least, belongs to this reaction as well.

Russell and Frege, along with the Viennese positivists Schlick, Carnap, Reichenbach, Neurath—all sought to provide an "exact" scientific philosophy and logically precise language. Frege's work on sense and reference, followed by Whitehead and Russell's *Principia Mathematica* were considered pioneering efforts toward this goal. All of them apparently took it for granted that the early Wittgenstein of the *Tractatus* both honored this commitment to exactitude and promised its fulfillment.

The later Wittgenstein, by contrast, as we know, was extremely skeptical about the possibility of such "exact" philosophy, always in regard to ethical propositions, and increasingly concerning metamathematical and metatheoretical conceptualizations in his later years. Jaakko and Merrill Hintikka make this observation in the course of a brief discussion of Wittgenstein's "finitistic, constructivistic . . . anti-platonist" philosophy of mathematics. Wittgenstein's later beliefs in language as a universal medium, in the ineffability of semantics, and in the consequent view that "there cannot be any metatheoretical considerations about language" lead him consistently, they argue, to a "descriptivistic and apparently resigned attitude to ordinary language" *and* to a concomitant "highly critical attitude to mathematical, especially metamathematical, practice."[47]

To a surprising degree, Whitehead, the early philosopher of mathematics and coauthor of the *Principia*, developed, quite independently, a similar view of logic and of mathematical formalization. One of the later Whitehead's most widely quoted, scandalous passages states: "It is more important that a proposition be interesting than that it be true"; another is, "In philosophical discussion, the merest hint of dogmatic certainty as to finality of statement is an exhibition of folly" (PR x). Whitehead goes on to observe, "the chief error in philosophy is overstatement . . . [which] consists [in part] in a false estimate of logical procedure in respect to certainty, and in respect to premises" (PR 11). And the onetime coauthor of *Principia* Mathematica then suggests that "Philosophy has been misled by the example of mathematics" (PR 8).

The later Wittgenstein and the later Whitehead represent a growing movement toward the position finally formalized in Gödel's Incompleteness Theorem, that the sort of exactitude sought by the likes of Russell and Frege was a massive deception, and unattainable. Moore, as I read him in this context, at least to some extent shared in this ironic attitude toward philosophy itself. Let me explain.

Wittgenstein's original mentor, Russell, was intelligent, quick, sharp, and above all, clever; he disdained ordinary language and common sense in particular. Moore, by contrast, often portrayed himself as slow and somewhat dull-witted, and this made him cautious. He was trained in the Cambridge classics stream, rather than the science curriculum; he distrusted mathematics; he essentially abandoned attempts to employ formal logic in his analysis of common sense. Indeed, it seems that he apparently distrusted "clever" people. In contrast to Russell in particular, Moore had a high regard for the world as we find it, and for the abilities of ordinary people to get along in this world. He spent his efforts as a philosopher focusing on the meanings of everyday language and propositions, and like Hume, invested his efforts toward putting clever "false" philosophers and their fantastic theories about such language and ordinary knowledge to flight.

It seems to me that there is a rather stunning consensus on this ironic, antiphilosophical attitude, that helps to pinpoint the origins of a historical dynamic that only now, at the end of this century, are we in a position to appreciate fully. I would state it thus.

In what I referred to in my opening remarks as "the Cambridge Trinty" of Whitehead, Russell, and Moore, two radically different streams of the Western philosophical tradition are refracted. The first is thoroughly Enlightenment and modernist, stressing exactness and precision (that von Wright traces through Russell and the early Whitehead, back "at least as far as Leibniz"). The second stream emerging from Cambridge, however, has a history even older and more venerable than the first stream as traced by von Wright. This second, alternative perspective on what philosophy is and how it is best pursued stretches back through Hume at least to Gassendi and to other Renaissance scientists and humanists who relied on history, custom, and textual evidence as well as on experiment and mathematical modeling in the quest for scientific truth and philosophical wisdom.

With the exception of Hume, none of the earlier representatives of this alternative Western tradition completely disavowed the power of science, nor did they shrink from the quest for verifiable knowledge. They were not, by and large, outright skeptics; nor were they early harbingers of the contemporary postmodernist attack on reason, rationality, and objectivity. Rather, in this alternative, long-standing philosophical tradition we perceive a fear of the growing hegemony, for example, of Galileo's exclusive reliance on mathematical method in the sciences. To critics like Gassendi and later, Hume, such an approach offered a misleading promise of precision at the expense of engagement with the actual, just as the philosopher's Cartesian concomitant reliance on mathematical logic and logical method seemed to promise the possibility of a false precision in philosophy. Gassendi and his followers lost this quarrel, and have been largely forgotten to history in comparison with Galileo and Descartes. And thus it became this triumphant modernist-Enlightenment faith in progress and perfectibility, based on the power of human reason, that Hume was obliged to attack from the margins of the dominant culture.

Toulmin and Janik comment on the "neo-Humean (and so pre-Kantian) empiricism of Moore, Russell and their colleagues" (p. 22), but they do not follow up this cultural setting with anything like the attention they devote to the Viennese. For many historians (and I think this is a serious mistake) to be steeped in Hume, as Russell was, is to be steeped in the long-standing tradition of British Empiricism. But I would argue in contrast, to be steeped in Hume, the apostate from "false philosophy," the author of the histories of

England, and the advocate of tradition and a fuller understanding of British "common life," is to be steeped in another attitude altogether—one which results either in outright philosophical skepticism, or else in a tempering of the quest for exactness with an acute, ironic awareness of fallibility. Whitehead writes:

> Metaphysical categories are not dogmatic statement of the obvious, they are tentative formulations of the ultimate generalities . . . The useful function of philosophy is to promote the most general systematization of civilized thought. There is a constant reaction between specialization and common sense. It is the part of the special sciences to modify common sense. Philosophy is the welding of imagination and common sense into a restraint upon specialists, and also into an enlargement of their imaginations. By providing the generic notions philosophy should make it easier to conceive the infinite variety of specific instances which rest unrealized in the womb of nature. . . . Error [by which Whitehead means here, "logical imprecision, vagueness, ambiguity"] is the price we pay for progress. (PR 8, 17, 187)

The oft-noted feature of the early Wittgenstein is that his *Tractatus* came to embody the premier statement in this century of the tendency toward exactness and precision, and in a sense, could be portrayed as the culmination of the Enlightenment–positivist project. Wittgenstein, as we know, was extremely uncomfortable with this reading of the *Tractatus* by Russell, Schlick, and others, though his reasons for this discomfort were never adequately conveyed to his puzzled followers—and, indeed, were all but unintelligible to them. Wittgenstein subsequently proposed explicitly to abandon the central role of logic derived from the earlier *Principia Mathematica* of Russell and Whitehead, relegating logic to the status, at best, of one of many descriptive "languages" whose particular syntax and even semantics could be discerned only by entering into the varieties of human practices within which each originates. When this shift became evident, Russell commented bitterly:

> The later Wittgenstein . . . seems to have grown tired of serious thinking and to have invented a doctrine which would make such an activity unnecessary . . .We are now told that it is not the world that we are to try to understand, but only sentences, and it is assumed that all sentences can count as true except those uttered by philosophers.[48]

I am now suggesting that the later Wittgenstein, by rejecting his earlier work and this Enlightenment/modernist reading of it, developed an utterly unique variation of a second stream of tradition present all along, but never named, at Cambridge: namely, this deep-seated *distrust* of exact philosophy and of those Hume had labeled "false philosophers." Precisely the measure of Wittgenstein's uniqueness and his greatness is that, once again, the *Philosophical Investigations* (and also the *Bemerkungen, On Certainty*, and other work from this later period) represent premier documents in this ironic reaction against the preeminent status of logic and philosophical rationalism.

Joachim Schulte provides evidence for my interpretation in a discarded draft of Wittgenstein's foreword to the *Bemerkungen* of 1930. There Wittgenstein wrote (cited in Schulte, *Wittgenstein*, p. 20):

> This book is written for those who can appreciate its spirit. This is a spirit different from that of the main current of the European and American civilization of which we all are part . . . whose expression is the industry, architecture, music, fascism, and socialism of our time.

And what is this "main current" of European and American civilization against which Wittgenstein sets himself? Presumably it is that attitude, that orientation, represented by the "logical" rather than the "ethical" reading of the *Tractatus*, that positivism with which Wittgenstein consistently refused to be associated and assimilated, that belief against which virtually all his later writing is set: the quest for totality and closure, the belief that logical precision and clarity in all human affairs are in the end an attainable goal of philosophical reflection, that all else is nonsense—in sum, that confidence in the final power of reason above all else that is the social legacy of the Enlightenment. (Indeed, we find Wittgenstein here coming dangerously close, like Collingwood, to accusing his academic colleagues of facism.)

Like Moore and Whitehead, this later Wittgenstein is not an enemy of reason, and does not discard the desire to know the truth. But all three exhibit a strong sense of Socratic irony: they are clearly distrustful of the arrogance of reason, suspicious of the promise of easy attainment of clarity, and most of all, doubtful about the Enlightenment promise of progress toward perfectibility of human knowledge. Our Austrian engineer and logician, like Moore, and like the later Whitehead, came to criticize the chief artifacts of social engineering, and to see in these products the manifestation of a fundamental flaw in the dominant cultural worldview or what Wittgenstein, in this passage, calls "spirit," rather than a casual or unfortunate mistake in some specific detail or procedure. How else are we to understand the mature Wittgenstein's distrust of social engineering and of the overconfidence of social engineers like Russell,[49] his utter contempt for the high-flown moral theorizing of professional philosophers like Schlick (whose work he regarded as "twaddle"),[50] or his evident belief that the most important aspects of human existence, for example, ethics and morality, could be shown or seen, but could not be "said."

Galileo's project of "reforming" science, the Cartesian project of "reforming" philosophy, and the Enlightenment project of "reforming" humanity itself are all expressions of this modernist confidence that Reason constitutes a wholly self-sufficient resource, capable of defining the Good in terms of practical, desirable human aims and goals, and setting forth strategies for the eventual realization of these goals. Russell in philosophy, logic, and mathematics, and the members of the Bloomsbury circle in aesthetics and literature, are all typical representatives of these tendencies. It was beyond question to them, moreover, that the young Wittgenstein of the *Tractatus*, and the young Whitehead of the *Principia* and *The Principles of Natural Knowledge* were to be numbered among them.

There developed at Cambridge, I am arguing, another, rival view—one which perceived the Good as indefinable, as that in terms of which all else is defined, as that toward which all things tend as a limit. Reason is not an expression of freedom, nor an instrument for engineering a certain path to perfection. Reason is employed, not in the quest for certainty, but in the quest for the Good, and has the Good as its limit. That the Good is beyond definition, and that toward which all things tend, can be shown but cannot be said. This, of course, is precisely Moore's position in the *Principia Ethica*, and the famous "naturalistic fallacy" described there is only a fallacy if this larger orientation is adopted. Despite Wittgenstein's distaste for that work of Moore's, this fundamental orientation is also his in the closing of the *Tractatus*, and ever afterward. In a conversation in 1929 he is reported to have said:

> In ethics, people are forever trying to find a way of saying something which, in the nature of things, is not and can never be expressed. We know a priori: anything which one might give by way of a definition of the Good—it can never be anything but a misunderstanding.[51]

It is in this sense that we can speak of Wittgenstein's "influence" from Moore, and his commonality with Whitehead. All three reveal themselves in interesting ways as increasingly uncomfortable with the fundamental tenets and intellectual orientation of modernism. As a result, all three, each in his own way, developed a critique of the Enlightenment confidence in the power of Reason and its connection with freedom, progress, certainty, and perfectibility. That the later Wittgenstein ends up with Moore and with the later Whitehead arrayed *against* modernism is all the more remarkable when we recognize just how thoroughly both the younger Wittgenstein and the younger Whitehead began, or at least were taken without question by their contemporaries to be, on the side of the moderns. The rejection of the primacy of logic, the desire to recur to "pre-Kantian modes of thought" (PR xi), the distrust of certainty, the endorsement of common sense and the wisdom of common language and common life, the reconception of metaphysics as hypothetical, heuristic, and grounded in experience, and a belief in the ineffability of semantics and the indefinability of the Good, however, together link these three Cambridge philosophers in an ironic challenge to the worldview of their contemporaries, and place them thoroughly on the side of the ancients against the moderns, as critics of the false promise of Enlightenment.

Even more clearly and more important, in giving credence to this profound divide in twentieth-century British thought, and positioning Wittgenstein centrally within it, we make a permanent place for him after all in the great dialectical sweep of Western thought, of which he is now so clearly a preeminent part. Of the many divisions that constitute this profound, deeply troubled, Picassoian figure—the early and the later, the British and the Austrian, the Cambridge and the Viennese—this final divide between Wittgenstein the modern versus Wittgenstein the *critic* of modernism may well prove to be the most illuminating and important of all.

Notes

1. Justus Hartnack in the second edition of his seminal study, *Wittgenstein and Modern Philosophy*, prophesied in 1986: "The intense interest in the philosophy of Wittgenstein probably has reached its peak, to decline in coming years" (South Bend: University of Notre Dame Press, p. xii). But about such matters, Whitehead had earlier observed: "Philosophy *never* reverts to its old position after the shock of a great philosopher" (cf. PR 11, a point to which Hartnack goes on to assent [p. xiii]).

   In 1992, I was delighted to have the honor of publishing in my philosophy series at the State University of New York Press an English translation of Joachim Schulte's recent *Wittgenstein: An Introduction*. Like Hartnack, I, too, supposed that the tremendous interest in Wittgenstein must by now have peaked; and so I was unprepared for the tremendous interest this fine volume generated. It became, instantly, a book that outsold every other volume of philosophy published in that series, indicating that interest in Wittgenstein still remains extremely high in the United States, as it does throughout the world.
2. Alan Janik and Stephen Toulmin, *Wittgenstein's Vienna* (New York: Simon & Schuster, 1973), p. 22
3. New York: Random House, 1959.
4. Heller, *Artist's Journey*, p. 107.
5. Norman Malcolm reports on the "great distaste" that Wittgenstein had for English culture: cf. *Ludwig Wittgenstein: A Memoir* (Oxford: Oxford University Press, 1958/1984), p. 26.
6. Among these, I would number prominently George L. Kline, Donald W. Sherburne, and Lewis S. Ford, whose work I cite in this essay, and from whom I have been privileged to be instructed over the past twenty years.

7. Cf. Part I of Collingwood's *Essay on Metaphysics* (Oxford: Oxford University Press, 1939). See also the discussions of "tacit knowledge," in Michael Polanyi, *Personal Knowledge* (San Francisco: Harper & Row, 1958).
8. The main reference for these details is Victor Lowe, *Alfred North Whitehead: The Man and His Work*, 2 Vols. (Baltimore, MD: Johns Hopkins University Press, 1985/1990).
9. For a more detailed account, see *The Rehabilitation of Whitehead: An Analytic and Historical Assessment of Process Philosophy* (Albany, NY: State University of New York Press, 1989), chapter 10.
10. New York: Macmillan, 1925.
11. New York: Macmillan, 1929. The "Corrected Edition" was issued in 1978. All references in this essay are to that second edition.
12. Victor Lowe recounts the difficulties Whitehead encountered in delivering these lectures the year after Arthur Eddington, describing them as "a fiasco." Cf. Lowe, *Alfred North Whitehead*, vol. II, p. 250. See also his earlier, somewhat more detailed account: "Whitehead's Gifford Lectures," *Southern Journal of Philosophy* 7, no. 4 (Winter, 1969–1970), pp. 329–338.
13. Lowe describes Whitehead as "one of the most quoted philosophers of our century—and one of the least understood." (*Alfred North Whitehead*, vol. 1, p. 3.) I think this is fundamentally correct.
14. Cf. Lowe's chapter on "The Migration to Harvard," in *Alfred North Whitehead*, vol. II, esp. pp. 142ff.
15. Not much is actually known about Whitehead's participation in the Bloomsbury circle; Victor Lowe tends to discount this.
16. Such a transformation from analytic to "continental" figure is much discussed in the case of Richard Rorty; cf., for example, David Hall, *Richard Rorty: Prophet and Poet of the New Pragmatism* (Albany: State University of New York Press, 1994). Tracing a similar, more recent evolution of Hilary Putnam, Professor Edward Pols (in his 1987 Presidential Address for the Metaphysical Society of America) suggested that Putnam was on the road to becoming, by intention, "The Complete Continental Philosopher." "On Knowing Directly: The Actualization of First Philosophy," *Review of Metaphysics* 41 (1987), 229–230.
17. Cf. John Locke, *An Essay Concerning Human Understanding*, Book II, chapter XIV, section 1; cf. *Process and Reality* (New York: Macmillan, 1929), pp. 222–223.
18. Cf. Alfred North Whitehead, AI, Part III, chapter 11: "Objects and Subjects." This constitutes the main text of Whitehead's Presidential Address for the American Philosophical Association in 1931.
19. Cf. PR 157–167.

20. I have not bothered to honor the distinction, so dear to Whitehead scholars, between the monistic theory of events in *Science and the Modern World* and the later Leibnizian and reductionistic account in *Process and Reality*, which I regard as a blind alley subsequently abandoned by Whitehead. For more on this, see my *Rehabilitation of Whitehead*.
21. Cf. George L. Kline, "Form, Concrescence, and Concretum," in *Explorations in Whitehead's Philosophy*, eds. Lewis S. Ford and George L. Kline (New York: Fordham University Press, 1983), pp. 104–146. See also his "'Present,' 'Past,' and 'Future' as Categoreal Terms and the 'Fallacy of the Actual Future,'" *Review of Metaphysics* XL, no. 2 (December, 1986): 215–235.
22. *Tractatus Logico-Philosophicus*, for example, at 5.252 and 5.452.
23. *Tractatus* 1.1.
24. Cf. Hartnack, *Wittgenstein*, p. 39.
25. L. Wittgenstein, *Philosophical Investigations*, trans. G. E. M. Anscombe (New York: Macmillan, 1968), Part I, section 116.
26. Cf. Joachim Schulte, *Wittgenstein: An Introduction*, p. 43.
27. Although he speaks of death, God, and things beyond the world in the closing sections of the *Tractatus*, Wittgenstein denies that these can be elucidated meaningfully. In the *Investigations* he remarks (Section 119): "The results of philosophy are the uncovering of one or another piece of plain nonsense and of bumps that the understanding has got by running its head against the limits of language. These bumps make us see the value of the discovery." It is hard to resist the inference that much of what Whitehead wrote would be classified as "one or another piece of plain nonsense."
28. Cf. *The Rehabilitation of Whitehead*, pp. 87–91.
29. See Toulmin and Janik's excellent account of this in relation to the *Tractatus* in *Wittgenstein's Vienna*, chapter 6; esp. pp. 139–40; 179–185.
30. I note in passing that this connection is mine; Whitehead mentions Hertz (referred to as Herz) twice in passing in *Science and the Modern World*, and not at all subsequently.
31. Cf. the essay, "Intentional Systems" in *Brainstorms* (Montgomery, VT: Bradford Books, 1978); also "Intentional Systems in Cognitive Ethnology," *Behavioral and Brain Science* 6 (1983): 343–390.
32. In comparison with Kant, whose categories of understanding sought to explain how all *knowledge* was possible, Donald Sherburne aptly suggests that Whitehead's categorial scheme aimed to define those more general conditions or constraints that make experience (of whatever sort, in whatever possible world) possible. Cf. *A Key to Whitehead's Process and Reality* (New York: Macmillan, 1966; reprinted by the University of Chicago Press, 1986), p. 41.

33. Toulmin and Janik call attention to this problem in the later Wittgenstein regarding his (perhaps unjustified) continuation of his early beliefs that rational discourse on ethics is impossible.
34. I read much of Whitehead's later metaphysical work as of this sort: once the basic principles are grasped, the detailed accounts can be discarded. When I first gave such an account of his work over ten years ago, I was much influenced by Wittgenstein's account of conceptual modeling in the *Tractatus* at 6.341 and 6.342. I confess that this interpretation was not well understood or well received by those whose investment in literal metaphysics is greater than my own. Cf. *The Genesis of Modern Process Thought: A Historical Outline with Bibliography* (Metuchen, N. J.: Scarecrow Press, 1983), pp. 211–217.
35. I borrow this term from my colleague, William Desmond: see his *Desire, Dialectic, and Otherness* (New Haven: Yale University Press, 1987) and *Being and Between: Metaphysics and Transcendence*, forthcoming from SUNY Press.
36. March 18, 1938; quoted in Schulte, *Wittgenstein*, p. 11.
37. Lewis S. Ford, in his brilliant reconstruction of the phases of development of Whitehead's later metaphysical views, provides this account of his approach toward his written work: cf. *The Emergence of Whitehead's Metaphysics: 1925–1929* (Albany: State University of New York Press, 1984).
38. Preface, p. v. Cf. Hartnack, *Wittgenstein* pp. 100–101.
39. Cf. Malcom, *Memoir*, p. 28.
40. Toulmin and Janik, *Wittgenstein's Vienna*, p. 176.
41. Cf. Malcom, *Memoir*, pp. 18–19.
42. Here I cite Malcom's account of Wittgenstein in the *Encyclopedia of Philosophy*, vol. 8, ed. Paul Edwards (New York: The Free Press, 1967), p. 327.
43. I discussed Whitehead's treatment of Kant in explicit detail in my lecture for the Chair of Logic at Copernicus University in Torun, Poland: see "The Interpretation of Kant in Whitehead's Philosophy," *Ruch Filozoficzny Kwartalnik* 47, nos. 3/4 (1990): pp. 213–230.
44. Malcom, *Memoir*, p. 14.
45. Malcom, *Memoir*, p. 14, n. 17.
46. *On Certainty*, ed. G. E. M. Anscombe and G. H. von Wright; trans Denis Paul and G. E. M. Anscombe (London: Basil Blackwell, 1969); cf. *Investigations*, Part II, Sec. X on "Moore's Paradox," which Wittgenstein does take seriously and positively.
47. Merrill B. Hintikka and Jaakko Hintikka, *Investigating Wittgenstein* (Oxford: Basil Blackwell, 1986), pp. 25–27.
48. Cf. Bertrand Russell, *My Philosophical Development* (London: Allen & Unwin, p. 216f.

49. Schulte reports that "when Russell was on his way to give a speech at a congress dedicated to humanitarian goals and Wittgenstein showed his disapproval, Russell asked if he would prefer an organization for war and slavery. Whereupon Wittgenstein answered, 'By far, by far!'" (*Wittgenstein*, p. 23).
50. Cf. Toulmin and Janik, *Wittgenstein's Vienna*, p. 194.
51. Cited in Toulmin and Janik, *Wittgenstein's Vienna*, p. 195

Part II

Process Philosophy and Issues in Analytic Metaphysics

Chapter 4

Disanalogies Between Space and Time

RICHARD M. GALE

Editor's Comment: While Professor Gale can hardly be described as a "process philosopher" in the sense of one who adheres to many of the "core doctrines" of process thought in specifically the Whitehead-Hartshorne tradition (e.g., panexperientialism, theism, etc.), as this essay shows, he is nonetheless an ardent analytic proponent of some very basic and central tenets of process philosophy, namely, the semantical objectivity of the temporal modi, the resolute rejection of the tendency to "spatialize time," and the intrinsic connection between these tenets and moral agency. His essay thus represents one example of ways in which analytic philosophers can provide important philosophical resources for process thinkers. (Consequently, as submitted in chapter 1, the streams of influence ought to be perceived as running in both directions.) On combining Gale's arguments with Rescher's for the assets of process semantics, Goodwin's for the utility of the metaphysics of objective temporal modi in resolving disputes between Quine and Kripke on possible worlds semantics, and Shields/Viney's for the assets of a process doctrine of objective temporal modi in handling the vexing and clustered problems of future contingents, it is submitted that a strongly plausible cumulative case is built up in this volume for the theory of de re *temporal process—the theory that past, present, and future are "real," that is, among others items, the temporal modi are not mere "ways of referring" to events, are not merely reducible to tense neutral token-reflexive expressions, and as Gale insists, are not reducible to spatial concepts.*

Introduction

While space and time obviously are different, for space is space and time is time, it still might be the case that they are analogous in all philosophically important respects. It is not difficult to find some disanalogies between them. While *kiss me now* sounds a bit desperate, it has none of the lewd overtones of *kiss me here*. *Wish you were here* sounds more intimate than *wish you were now*. And *there is no time like the present* does not sound quite as chauvinistic as *there is no place like here*. Such disanalogies, however, are of more interest to a lover, vacationer, or travel agent than a philosopher.

For the philosopher bent on clarifying our concepts of space and time, only a modally based disanalogy will count as important. A modal disanalogy requires that the spatial or temporal analogue to a given sentence or proposition has a different modal status, in which a spatial or temporal analogue to a given sentence is formed by substituting for every temporal term in it a corresponding spatial one and vice versa. In forming analogues the temporal indexical term "now" and "this time" are to be replaced respectively by "here" and "this place" and a date expression by a proper name of a place. For the time being we will agree to substitute "in front of" for "later than." It will be seen that it does not matter if "to the rear (right, left) of" is substituted instead.[1]

It might be thought that the most obvious and important modal disanalogy concerns the fact that there is no spatial analogue to temporal becoming: while it is necessary for the reality of time that there be a now or present that inexorably shifts to ever later times it is not necessary for the reality of space that there be a here that shifts in some spatial direction. The following pair of analogues attempts to make this modal disanalogy explicit:

T1. Every event later than now will happen.
S1. Every event in front of here will happen.

Unlike T1, S1 is not a necessary truth, since some of the events that occur in front of here might have already happened.

This, unfortunately, is a bogus modal disanalogy, since there is a temporal component of T1, the future tensed "will happen," that fails to get replaced in S1 by a corresponding spatial expression. The proper analogy is:

T2. Every event later than now happens later than now.
S2. Every event in front of here happens in front of here.[2]

But both are necessary truths, and therefore there is no modal disanalogy. There appears to be a totally trivial sense in which here and now "shift" in analogous manners, namely, it is necessary that tokenings of "now" at different times denote different times just as it is necessary that tokenings of "here" at different places denote different places. It will be seen that appearances deceive here. To avoid against bogus disanalogies, such as T1-S1, we must be scrupulous in making fully explicit all of the temporal and spatial elements in our analogues, something that I failed to do in my *The Language of Time.* I caution the reader to watch me carefully, since I am not to be trusted.

There is no way to articulate the becoming-based modal disanalogy because this concept of becoming is absurd. A contradiction can be deduced from the claim that the present or now shift to ever later times. The first step in this deduction is to point out that "now," like "this time" and "the present," is a singular referring expression that is used to denote a moment of time, whatever a moment of time might turn out to be on analysis. This is borne out by the fact that sentences such as "Now is the time for all good men to come to the aid of their country" and "This time is noon of June 29, 1996" are used to assert an identity between times. These temporal demonstratives behave in the typical way that indexical words do in that they are rigid designators in Kripke's sense, meaning that the sentence "Now might not be now" expresses a necessarily false proposition whenever tokened. Ask yourself under what conceivable counter factual circumstances this very time—now—would not be this time. There are none.

Therefore, it is impossible for now (the present, this time) to shift to a later time; for then this time would cease to be identical with this time, that is, would cease to be identical with itself, certainly a manifest repugnancy.

That an impatient bridegroom says to his bride in the course of the wedding ceremony, "If only it were now eleven P.M. rather than one P.M., we would be making love," hardly constitutes a counterexample. He is no more envisioning a situation in which now is a different time than it is than I am envisioning being a different person when I say to you "if I were you, I would sell IBM stock." I am merely saying that anyone in your situation prudentially ought to sell IBM, and all our overeager bridegroom is saying is that it is now 1 P.M. and they are not making love and at a later and better time, 11 P.M., they will be making love.

Although the conception of temporal becoming dear to the hearts of A-Theorists is absurd, there still might be significant modal disanalogies between our temporal and spatial indexical perspectives. I will follow a three-stage format in my pursuit of these disanalogies. I begin with our untutored common sense beliefs, often expressed in metaphorical and pictorial terms, as to how time and space differ. Next, I refine these beliefs by translating them into more precise literal statements, being careful to make explicit all of their temporal and spatial commitments. Finally, I attempt to explain and justify these beliefs by unearthing the underlying modal disanalogies that serve as their cash backing. Sometimes these disanalogies will be formulated in the formal mode in which explicit mention is made of words and their rules of use. It will attempt to unearth them within our concepts of agency and objectivity.

Agency-Based Disanalogies

Whether an agent fills space and time in modally disanalogous ways will depend crucially on how we define an "agent." I will be making a somewhat technical or jargonistic use of "agent," the justification for which will come at the end of this section when I discuss the connection of my use of "agent" with certain forensic uses of "person." According to my use, it is required that an agent, in addition to being rational and self-conscious, has as its overriding goal to achieve self-realization. An agent will rationally deliberate about the best way to achieve this goal and will then intentionally carry out her/his decisions in a free morally responsible manner. Since an agent's *summum bonum* is to be an active and free cause of her own self-realization, an agent accepts a causal theory of value in which the goodness of an outcome, result, upshot, denouement, or culmination depends in part on its being brought about in the right way, the right way involving the agent as an active and free cause. Means and ends interpenetrate, each deriving its meaning and value from its functional relation to the other. As is the case with other causal theories, such as those for perception, memory, and reference, we are able to recognize in many cases when a given sequence is or is not of the right sort, but notoriously are not able to specify in general what is the right sort of causal sequence.

To summarize, an agent is a rational self-conscious being who deliberates about the best way to achieve self-realization and then intentionally carries out her decisions in a free, morally responsible manner. For the time being we will accept this as a merely stipulative definition for the sake of the ensuing discussion. It now is to be shown that this concept of agency entails striking modal disanalogies between the manner in which an agent exists in space and time consisting in there necessarily being a direction to time but not space, regardless of its dimensionality.

Some important and startling modal disanalogies concerning an agent's axiological commitments follow logically from my concept of an agent when it is conjoined with the following modal disanalogies concerning causation and the dependent notions of deliberation and choice:

T3. An action performed now can bring about something later but not earlier than now[3]

S3. An action performed here can bring about something in front of but not to the rear of here

in which the "can" is the weakest one of mere logical or conceptual possibility. No difference is made if "to the rear (right, left) of here" is substituted for "in front of here" in S3, as will be the case with all of the modal disanalogies to follow.

The T3-S3 modal disanalogy entails this modal disanalogy:

T4. An agent can now deliberate about and make choices and have intentions in respect to her conduct later but not earlier than now.

S4. An agent can here deliberate about and make choices and have intentions in respect to her conduct in front of but not to the rear of here.

There might be circumstances in which I have the capacity and opportunity to bring about things only to the front but not to the rear of here—I would literally have my back to the wall—but it is still *logically* possible that I bring about something to the rear of here and thus *logically* possible that I deliberate about doing so. And thus T4 and S4 differ modally, T4 alone being necessarily true. Similar considerations hold for T3 and S3, provided their use of "can" is interpreted as expressing logical possibility.

Given that an agent's *summum bonum* or primary project is to be the right sort of cause of her own self-realization and that causation cannot go temporally backwards though it logically can go in any spatial direction, it follows that an agent, in virtue of being rational, will have axiological commitments that are modally disanalogous between space and time. These disanalogies hold only for beings in different cultures and socio-economic groups who value the past, present, and future differently—some being more future oriented, while others give greater importance to the past or present. For this reason, the following would not express a modal disanalogy:

T5. Human beings care more about what befalls them later rather than earlier than now.
S5. Human beings care more about what befalls them in front of rather than to the rear of here.

1. Let us begin with the old saws, "All's well that ends well" and "Consider no man fortunate until after he is dead." That it sounds funny to say that all's well that spatially terminates well in front of here or that you should count no man fortunate except from a place in front of where he dies is some indication that we have modal disanalogies in these cases, but it is not easy to give an explicit formulation of them.

   Plainly, the following pair of analogues will not do, since they both seem to be *contingent* generalizations and false ones to boot:

   T6. A temporal succession of events is good if it temporally terminates later than now in a good state of affairs.
   S6. A spatial order of events is good if it spatially terminates in front of here in a good state of affairs.

   Lynne McFall has presented me with numerous counterexamples to T6 consisting in cases in which a deathbed conversion or final moment of beatific bliss does not render good or valuable a life that prior to that was one of long and unremitting immorality or suffering. The moral of these examples is that the length and intensity of evil that leads up to the favorable upshot or culmination must be taken into account.

   The McFall-type counterexamples might be met by requiring that the earlier succession of events is both the right sort of an agent-cause of the terminating state and is morally outweighed by it, resulting in:

T7. A temporal succession of events is good if it temporally terminates later than now in a state of affairs that morally outweighs it and for which it is the right sort of agent-cause.

S7. A spatial order of events is good if it spatially terminates in front of here in a state of affairs that morally outweighs it and for which it is the right sort of agent-cause.[4]

Whereas T7 seems a plausible candidate for being a necessary truth, S7 does not, since an agent does not necessarily give greater axiological value to any one particular spatial direction over the others.

There are other ways of reformulating T6 that might work as well as or even better than the T7 way, as for example:

T8. An agent holds that if it is better to be in state Y than state X, then it is better to be in state X now and state Y later rather than earlier than now, provided that she/he brings Y about out of X in the right sort of agency manner.

S8. An agent holds that if it is better to be in state Y than state X, then it is better to be in state X here and state Y in front of rather than to the rear of here, provided that she brings Y about out of X in the right sort of agency manner.

T8, for example, requires that an agent who believes that it is better to be a philosophy professor than a pickpocket believes that it is better to be a pickpocket now and a philosophy professor later than now rather than vice-versa, provided that she/he agency-causes the professorial state to evolve from the pickpocket one in the right way, as, for example, by using her/his ill-gotten gains to pay the way through graduate school. But without any additional information, our agent will be indifferent between being a pickpocket here and a philosophy professor in front of here rather than vice-versa. Given additional information, the agent might prefer the former, since here could be New York City, a good place for a pickpocket, and Pittsburgh could be in front of here, a good place for a philosophy professor but a bad place for a pickpocket due to its being economically depressed. But this hardly shows that S8 is a necessary truth, for this preference is based on extra nonspatial information of a contingent sort, whereas the preference in T8 is not based on any extra nontemporal information of a contingent sort, thereby showing that T8, unlike S8, is logically necessary.

It is interesting to note that the T8-S8 modal disanalogy underlies the prevalent soul-building theodicy, which holds that God is justified in permitting past evils if they serve as a necessary condition for an agent to grow freely in morally desirable ways. In determining the goodness of a world we do not just mechanically add up the goods and evils in it, but also consider the temporal plot into which they enter. Their spatial plot or concatenation is irrelevant. The greater value that T8 accords to the future does not mean that progress is inevitable or that future persons are to be given a privileged status when formulating social policies, a point that was forcefully made in discussion by George Kline.

Phil Quinn has presented me with a counterexample to T8's necessity that indicates the need to further qualify it. He imagines an agent of sixty who has been in poor health all his life reasoning as follows:

> It is better for me to be rich than to be poor, for wealth is bound to be helpful in the project of self-realization if wisely used. But clearly it is not better for me to be poor now and rich later, provided I earn my wealth, than for me to be poor now and rich earlier. Even if I can still earn a fortune at my age, by the time I have done so I will be too old and feeble to make much use of it in advancing my project of self-realization. But if I had a fortune when I was a mere youth, I would have spent it all on my project of self-realization and would have made a lot more progress in this project than I actually did, which in turn would have given me internal resources I do not now have to enable me to make the best of my present poverty.

One way to meet this ingenious counterexample is to require that we consider only the intrinsic value of the successive states X and Y in T8, thereby precluding consideration of their instrumental value in promoting other goods, such as that of self-realization, which is what Quinn's sixty-year-old man does. A technical device for assuring that only the intrinsic values of X and Y be considered is to require that they be described in "temporally pure" ways. A descriptive predicate "F" is temporally pure just in case the proposition expressed by "A is F at time" in which "A" is a non-descriptive denotator of an individual, is such that it (1) does not entail that there are any times other than t_7 and (2) is compatible with there being any number of instances of F at times other than t_7. Condition (1) rules out "drinking the fatal glass of beer," since it entails that the drinker dies at some future date as a result of the "drinking" and (2) does so for "drinking the first (last) glass of beer" since this entails that the drinker does not drink a glass of beer at any earlier (later) time.

2. Another agency-based axiological/asymmetry between past and future that has no modally equivalent spatial analogue concerns this difference between an agent's attitudes toward her past and future finitude:

T9. An agent regrets that his or her existence does not extend beyond some time later than now but does not regret in the same way that her or his existence does not extend beyond some time earlier than now.

S9. An agent regrets that his or her existence does not extend beyond someplace in front of here but does not regret in the same way that her or his existence does not extend beyond someplace to the rear of here.

The reason for the "in the same way" qualification will emerge from the ensuing discussion. S9 is not a necessary truth; for, an agent's regret that he or she does not exist at someplace in front of here is based on contingent considerations that are not necessary for her/his being agent; for example, Las Vegas could be in front of here and she/he loves to gamble in different casinos and thus would regret never existing in Vegas. But is T9 necessary?

To establish the necessity of T9 it must be shown to be a logical consequence of my definition of an agent. Since an agent has as its summum bonum her own self-realization and there is no upper limit on the possibility for the development of one's character, knowledge, ability, and talents, and so on, an agent ought to regret its future demise.[5] To be sure, it might take only a finite future time for an agent to realize all of her present first-order intentions, but because there is no upper boundary to an agent's potential for self-realization it is of the very essence of an agent always to be on the make, always to be incomplete. Thus, at every time an agent has a second-order intention always to have a new intention, always to have its projected horizon recede as it succeeds in satisfying former intentions; and, thus, death always represents a cutting off of its possibility for a fuller self-realization of its inherent potentialities.

Annette Baier has pointed out that there could be extratemporal contingent considerations that could lead an agent not to regret her death, such as now suffering from an incurable illness that prevents the agent from progressing now or in the future in her self-realization project. This problem could be met by stipulating that her agency is not impaired later than now.

T10. An agent regrets that her or his existence does not extend beyond some time later than now but does not regret in the same way that her or his existence does not extend beyond some time earlier than now, *provided nothing prevents her from functioning as an agent later than now.*

But, in contradistinction from T10, a necessary truth does not emerge when the analogous restriction is made in S9:

S10. An agent regrets that his or her existence does not extend beyond someplace in front of here but does not regret in the same way that her/his existence does not extend beyond someplace to the rear of here, *provided nothing prevents her from functioning as an agent in front of here.*

An agent might grow weary of being an agent for nonmedical reasons and thus no longer want an unlimited future. This, however, is just a case of an agent no longer being an agent, and thus not a counterexample to T10.

An agent might regret that her past existence is finite—he or she is a historian of ancient Greece and thus regrets having been born too late to have been an eyewitness to the going-ons in that era. But while the agent's past finitude limits his or her knowledge, it does not limit in any way her/his opportunity to realize him- or herself and, in particular, as a historian, her/his excellence as an historian not being diminished by his or her not having certain data that it is not possible for her/him to obtain. Since the agent's regret at having a finite future is not topic-specific, unlike the historian who regrets that his or her past is finite, T10's temporal asymmetry between past and future is unscathed by this example. This is the reason for the *does not regret in the same way* qualification in T10.

T10 ceases to be a necessary truth when applied to human beings in general. Mystical individuals seem to have no asymmetry in their attitudes to birth and death, since they take time to be unreal. Derek Parfit has argued that we would be happier if we lacked the T10-type of temporal bias. He imagines a passive, contemplative sort of chap, named "Timeless" who is not concerned with being an agent but only with finding a psychologically satisfying way of viewing the world around him. Timeless is someone:

> who takes life's pleasures as they come. And, to the extent that we are like this . . . we would be happier if we lacked the bias towards the future. We would be much less depressed by aging and the approach of death. If we were like Timeless, being at the end of our lives would be more like being at the beginning. At any point within our lives we could enjoy looking either backward or forward to our whole lives . . . I have claimed that, if we lacked the bias towards the future, this would be better for us . . . On any plausible moral view, it would be better if we were all happier.[6]

Timeless poses no threat to T10's necessity, since he or she is not an agent. Whether it is better to be an agent, and thereby have a T10-type bias, is an entirely different matter. No doubt Timeless has more peace of mind, is in a more mellow mood, than an agent. She/he is happier in the feeling-happy sense. But whether it is better to have the sort of psychological happiness of a Timeless than be in the mentally perturbed state of a striving, incomplete agent is irrelevant to the truth of T10. I happen not to share Parfit's "ethical" intuitions. I believe that those who have a capacity to become agents have an obligation to do so, even at the expense of their *ataraxia*.

3. It is an empirical fact that most human beings prefer that their painful experiences be in the past and their pleasurable ones in the future but do not have the analogous spatial preference, it mattering not at all whether their pains and pleasures occur in any particular direction from here. It does not seem to be necessary that *human beings* have these preferences, but is it necessary that *agents* do? Is the following a modal disanalogy?

T11. An agent prefers that his/her painful experiences occur earlier than now and her/his pleasurable experiences later than now.

S11. An agent prefers that her/his painful experiences occur to the rear of here and his/her pleasurable experiences in front of here.

While it is obvious that S11 is not necessary, that T11 is must be argued.

Before attempting this, the descriptions of the painful and pleasurable experiences in T11 must be restricted to temporally pure ones, so that no demands are made on what obtains or fails to obtain at times earlier or later than that at which the pleasure or pain occurs. Without such a restriction the following sort of counterexample can be produced. It is reasonable for an agent to prefer that a painful amputation of his or her leg occur in the future instead of the past, since this gives her more time in which she/he has use of the leg and thereby a leg up on her self-realization project. But the description of a pain as "the pain of having one's leg amputated" is temporally impure because it entails that one has this leg before the painful experience and lacks it afterward.

It is very difficult to show why T11 is necessary, assuming that it is. Plainly, we can not do so by saying that a past pain, since it already has become present, is of no moment whereas a future one, since it has yet to do so, is. For this is just to say that the past pain has already happened while the future one has not yet happened, leaving unexplained why this difference should be significant. And, for reasons already given, we cannot explain why T11 is necessary by invoking the notion of temporal becoming that involves a shift of the present moment to ever later times.

Given that it is better to be in a pleasurable than a painful state, it could be claimed that T11 is a special instance of

T8. An agent holds that if it is better to be in state Y than state X, then it is better to be in state X now and state Y later rather than earlier than now, provided that he/she brings Y about out of X in the right sort of agency manner.

The problem with this derivation is that an agent's T11 preference does not seem to require that she/he be a causal agent in respect to the painful and pleasurable experiences in question. Thus, there is a possible range of cases to which T11 applies but T8 does not, and therefore the necessity of T11 is yet to be explained.

Another possible way of grounding T11 in the concept of an agent is supplied by the following phenomenological insight of William James:

> The fact is that our consciousness at a given moment is never free from the ingredient of expectancy. Everyone knows

how when a painful thing has to be undergone in the near future, the vague feeling that it is impending penetrates all our thought with uneasiness and subtly vitiates our mood even when it does not control our attention; it keeps us from being at rest in the given present.[7]

It could be objected that James's phenomenological generalization is at best a contingent truth about human beings, and thus cannot establish the necessity of T11. But agents, unlike human beings, are not as a contingent matter of fact expectors and anticipators but are essentially so, and anticipation of an impending harm is not only upsetting but, more important, distracting, thereby undermining their efficiency as agents.

Furthermore, a future pain is harmful to their self-realization in a way in which a past pain is not. Thus, it is fitting and proper for an agent to have T11 type preferences. This defense requires that T11 be restricted to anticipated and remembered pleasures and pains.

It is not hard to tell a story in which a future pain is not deleterious to an agent's self-realization but even necessary for it. In such a case an agent does not prefer that the pain is in the past. Therefore, it seems necessary to add yet another restriction to T11, requiring that the pleasures and pains are respectively beneficial and deleterious for self-realization.[8] My defense of T11's necessity is starting to take on too many epicycles to be very convincing, but unfortunately, it is the best that I am able to do right now.

In concluding this section, I will consider Richard Bernstein's very trenchant objection to my general procedure for deriving agency-based modal disanalogies. My stipulatively defining "agent" in such a way that it entails the desired axiological modal disanalogies is nothing but a trivial exercise in gerry mandering. The plums that I gleefully pull out of my pie have been put there by me. My response is in two stages. Even if I am gerrymandering, my task hardly is trivial, since, as the preceding discussion attests, it is no easy matter to show that my concept of an agent entails these disanalogies. One of the major tasks for philosophy, going back to Plato's science of "dialectics," is to articulate the logical interconnections between different concepts. Furthermore, my concept of an agent is not all that gerrymandered. It is similar to a prevalent definition of what a person is in the normative or forensic sense, the sense that qualifies an individual to be a bearer of rights, such as to be treated always as an end and never as a mere means. Thus, my concept is not made up out of the blue solely for the purpose of establishing modal disanalogies but is modeled on an important tradition for understanding the normative concept of personhood. That my agency-based analysis of personhood is controversial is readily granted but that is not grounds for the charge of gerrymandering.

Objectivity-Based Disanalogies

The doctrine of temporal becoming as involving a shifting now was supposed to offer a theoretical explanation for our gut feeling that our past-present-future perspective is objective in a way in which our here-there one is not. Because this doctrine is contradictory and thus explains nothing, it does not follow that we must give up our gut beliefs that there is a sense in which we are prisoners of time but not space, are spatially but not temporally free and rangy, and the like. You can choose to leave Pittsburgh for a wild weekend in Ambridge or McKeesport but can not choose to leave the twenty-first century for a high old time in the seventeenth century. It is just such beliefs in the coercive power of time that caused some of our forefathers to prostrate themselves before a god of time but not one of space. Our fear of heights, or in the case of the comedian Steven Wright, widths, is an entirely different matter. I will now attempt to legitimize these beliefs by unearthing the objectivity-based modal disanalogies that underlie them.

Our concept of objectivity comprises two components: being nonselective or imposed independently of our will; and being common to or shared by different observers. It will be shown that for each component there are modal disanalogies between space and time.

Nonselectivity Disanalogies

There are three different sorts of nonselectivity disanalogies: (1) perceptual; (2) referential; and (3) locomotive.

(1) For the sake of simplicity the discussion will be confined to visual perception, but it admits of generalization to the other senses. Space is an order of coexistent objects and time an order of successive events. Visual experience presents us with coexistent objects but not successive events.[9] At any given time we can see only those events and objects that happen or exist at that time. This gives rise to the following modal disanalogy:

T12. I can now see only what is happening now.
S12. I can here see only what is happening here.

in which "can" again is that of mere logical possibility, thus rendering it irrelevant whether I have a stiff neck that prevents me from turning my head.

While it is clear that S12 is not necessary, there is cause to doubt that T12 is necessary, due to the fact that light signals have a finite velocity, resulting in what is seen being earlier than the seeing of it. One way to meet this difficulty is to revise T12-S12 as:

T13. I can now see only what happens now or earlier than now.
S13. I can here see only what happens here or to the rear of here.

Because perception is a causal process, this modal disanalogy rests on the T3-S3 one concerning the impossibility of backward causation.

Another way to circumvent the problem is to adopt the convention that "now" in T12 refers to the class of events that are directly perceivable by me, the observer, that is, all those events are causally connectable with my here-now by a rectilinear light ray. This convention for saving the necessity of T12 squares with the Special Theory of Relativity and is less cumbersome, and therefore will be adopted in what follows. Thus a tokening of "now" or "this time" refers to the simultaneity class of events that stand in this light-ray relation, the cone of the past, to the time and place of the tokening.

The T12-S12 modal disanalogy, in turn, gives rise to this modal disanalogy:

T14. I can here and now choose whether to see events that occur now or then (or later than now).
S14. I can now and here choose whether to see objects that exist here or there (or in front of here)

in which "choose" distributes over the disjunction: I can choose *p* or *q* is short for I can choose *p* and I can choose *q*. Again, stiff necks are irrelevant.

(2) Because visual perception is selective among places but not times, there will be a selectivity in the use of spatial indexical terms that is lacking for temporal indexical terms. We will confine ourselves to the "primary use" of an indexical term, that is, one in which it does not pick up its reference by falling within the scope of some other referring term. A primary use of "this place" is spatially selective whereas a primary use of "this time" is not.

T15. I can choose whether my primary use here and now of "this time" denotes now or then (or a time later than now).
S15. I can choose whether my primary use now and here of "this place" denotes here or there (or a place in front of here).

This modal disanalogy, cast in the formal mode, results from a difference in the rules of use for these indexical terms. The rules of use for "this place" specify that the denotatum of a tokening of it is the place ostended by the speaker. (Remember that I can point to the place I occupy.) No such act of ostending enters into determining the denotatum of a tokening of "this time."

To be sure, I can choose when to token "this time," but given that I token it at the time I do, I have no choice but to refer to that time. Herein I am requiring that the time at which a temporal indexical term is used be kept constant when we ask counter factual questions about its referent. This could be called be the principle of "contextual constancy."

It might come as a surprise, but exactly the same sort of disanalogy holds between the rules for the primary use of "here" and "now." *Pace* what was tentatively granted above, a token of "here" need not denote the place at which it is tokened, thereby giving rise to this modal disanalogy:

T16. A primary use of "now" must denote the time at which it is tokened.[10]

S16. A primary use of "here" must denote the place at which it is tokened.

A counterexample to S16 is my saying "Place the piano here," as I point to some place in front of me. It might be countered that S16 becomes necessary when restricted to a "naked" use of "here," that is, a use in which there is no accompanying ostensive act of pointing, gesturing, or staring. This must be granted; however, this restriction to a naked use gives rise to a different modal disanalogy.

T17. I can choose whether or not to use "now" nakedly.

S17. I can choose whether or not to use "here" nakedly.

Whereas, admitedly, S17 is necessary, T17 is not, since, as T15 has shown, a use of "now" or "this time" cannot involve an act of ostending.[11] Therefore, every primary use of "here," including the naked one, involves selection of some sort, unlike the primary use of "now."

(3) Not only is our past-present-future perspective, unlike our here-there one, nonselective in regard to perception and reference, it also is so in regard to our power of locomotion. We can move about in space at will but not time, thus the reason for it making sense to say "Come here" but not "Come now," assuming it is only the locomotive sense that is relevant. We can return to the same place but not the same time, which yields this modal disanalogy:

S18. I can exist here both now and at some time, t_2, later than now, and there at some time, t_1, temporally between now and t_2.

T18. I can exist now both here and at some place, P_2, in front of here, and then at some place, P_1 spatially between here and P_2.

This modal disanalogy is a consequence of the conceptual truth that a material object can occupy the same place at different times but not the same time at different places.

S19. I can exist here both now and then.
T19. I can exist now both here and there.

A philosopher of the likes of Richard Taylor would not accept these as genuine modal disanalogies. He would claim that a physical object is composed of both spatial and temporal parts. Thus, he would claim that both S18 and T18 are necessary truths; just as I can exist both here and there by having different spatial parts of myself occupy these two places, I can exist here both now and then by having different temporal parts of myself happen at these two times.

He is wrong, however, in his claim that physical objects, as contrasted with events, have temporal as well as spatial parts. When a man has his legs amputated, as did Ronald Reagan in an old movie, he can ask "Where's the rest of me?," for he is referring to some of his former spatial parts. But he cannot claim to be incomplete now because some of his "temporal parts," that is, events in his history, are not happening now. If my view of someone is obstructed so that I see only his back, I say that I see only a part of him, but I do not say this if I do not see some events in his past and future history. I would say that I see only part of his *history* rather than part of the *man.*

It might be replied that while we do not at present speak of a physical object's temporal parts, this might not be due to it being conceptually absurd to do so but simply because we have not yet had the proper contingent occasion to do so. It might be that the reason why we do not now speak of temporal parts is that an object's parts are connected with its sortal nature, and so far it has proven advantageous for the purpose of devising intellectually satisfying scientific systems of classification and successfully interacting with our environment to define the sortal or essential nature of objects solely in terms of how their spatial parts are concatenated. Think of the periodic table of elements in this connection. There are, however, conceivable circumstances in which it would no longer prove advantageous to define an object's essence exclusively in spatial terms; how it fills time, its history, would then be at least partially determinative of its nature. In fact, this is already the case in some areas of subatomic physics. It is part of the definition of certain kinds of mesons that they have a half-life of a certain duration. In such cases in which the definition of an object's essence makes demands on its history it might be appropriate to talk of an object's temporal as well as its spatial parts. Since our present spatially biased system of definitions of essences or sortal natures is revisable in this manner, it is doubtful that S18-T18 and S19-T19 are genuine modal disanalogies.

The reply to this is that this essay is a study in descriptive rather than revisionary metaphysics. The concern is with how we actually do conceive and talk about the world. No doubt, if we were radically to revise our empirical beliefs, this would occasion a conceptual revolution, such as is envisioned in the preceding response. How we play the language-games we do is a different question than why we do. A proper answer to the latter is not given by a description of linguistic rules but by an account of why the world rewards those who play them.

Fortunately, there are locomotive-based modal disanalogies that do not rest on an object's having only spatial parts. Because I can choose to move in any spatial direction but cannot backwardly cause something to happen, there is this modal disanalogy:

S20. I can choose here and now whether my use of "here" later than now denotes a place in front of or to the rear of here.
T20. I can choose now and here whether my use of "now" in front of here denotes a time later or earlier than now.

Other modal disanalogies that have the same conceptual underpinnings are:

S21. I can choose here and now whether to occupy here later than now.
T21. I can choose now and here whether to occupy now in front of here.

and

S22. I can choose here and now to occupy here at all times between now and five minutes later than now.
T22. I can choose now and here to occupy now at all places between here and five feet in front of here.

The reason for these two modal disanalogies is that I can now choose to bring something about neither in the past nor the present. Whether I now occupy both here and certain places in front of here, by having different spatial parts of me occupy them, can be caused only by past events such as an earlier decision of mine to overeat so that I would occupy these places now.

Shared-Perspectives Disanalogies

To complete my account of the objectivity-based modal disanalogies between our spatial and temporal indexical perspectives it remains to consider the other component of our concept of objectivity—that of being common to or shared by different observers. There is a sense in which both spatial and temporal indexical facts are objective. It is open to public verification both that someplace is here and that sometime is now, as well as that some event occurs here and that some event occurs now. The disanalogy I seek is implicated in the nature of the agreement in judgment or the unanimity test for verifying such facts. Because it is a necessary truth that

S23. Two observers who exist now at different places can both see what happens here now but false, and necessarily false, given my above convention for the use of "now," that

T23. Two observers who exist here at different times can both see what happens now here, follows that our here-there perspective is perceptually transcendable in a way in which our past-present-future one is not. Whereas only observers who exist now can directly verify or see what occurs now, observers who do not exist here can directly verify or see what occurs here. This is a variation on the T12- SI2 modal disananlogy. Thus, while it is necessarily true that

T24. Observers who can directly verify (see) what occurs now share the same temporal indexical perspective, that is, they both exist now,

it is not necessarily true that

S24. Observers who can directly verify (see) what occurs here share the same spatial indexical perspective, that is, they both exist here.

Often observers who do not occupy here can have a better view of what is here than do those who are here.

Thus, our agreement in judgment or unanimity test for objectivity, which, I might add, is only one of the relevant tests for objectivity, shows a modal disanalogy between now and here in regard to their being shared by or common to the *relevant* observers. The relevant observers for directly verifying or seeing what occurs now must share the same temporal indexical perspective but not the same spatial indexical perspective; they must all exist now but need not all exist here. This is why it seemed less chauvinistic to say that there is no time like the present rather than there is no place like here. Even if, *per impossible,* we could converse with Plato via some mysterious telephone connection, his testimony as to what he then perceives would be irrelevant for the purpose of determining what is happening now. Our unanimity test, therefore, presupposes a shared or be common now among the relevant observers but not a common here. And given that one mark of the objective is to be shared or common, it follows that our past-present-future perspective is objective in a way in which our here-there one is not. And when this modal disanalogy is conjoined with the nonselectivity modal disanalogy between these two kinds of indexical perspectives, there results a powerful conceptual case for now but not here being objective. These modal disanalogies are the cash that underlies our commonsense beliefs and feelings about being prisoners of time but not space, being spatially but not temporally free and rangy, and the like. There is no need, thank God, to appeal to the doctrine of temporal becoming that involves a shifting "now" to explain and justify them.

Conclusion

What connection, if any, is there between the agency-based axiological modal disanalogies and the various objectivity-based modal disanalogies? One would hope that there is a deep connection, and, fortunately, this hope is not disappointed. That our temporal but not our spatial indexical perspectives are objective gives an ontological grounding to an agent having axiological biases in favor of the future but not any spatial direction from here. If the past-present-future perspective were to be nonobjective, an agent's axiological biases in favor of the future would be merely subjective. There would be a serious and depressing bifurcation between agents and nature. The value-preferences of agents would be based on a mistaken view of reality in which how things are taken to be by agents is not how they really or objectively are. If I am right, this is not the case. The irreducibly tensed perspective of an agent as someone whose major concern is "What should I now do so as to create future value?" also is nature's own perspective.

Notes

1. I am fully aware that in making use of modal notions I am imposing on the goodwill of many readers. For those who are willing to countenance such notions, I give them license to fill in their own favorite account of modality in terms of linguistic rules, platonic forms, possible worlds, metaphysical necessities, and the like; while for those who view the modal distinction between necessity and contingency as an untenable dualism, I leave them free to reinterpret my talk about necessity in a Quinean way concerning how deeply embedded or central in our web of belief a given proposition is. For the latter my project is to show that there are truths about time whose spatial analogues are not as deeply imbedded or central in our web of belief.
2. Strictly speaking, "event" should be replaced by "object," since objects are composed of spatial parts and events of temporal parts. And since objects exist but do not happen, "happens" should be replaced by "exists." No harm is done here by not making such replacements, but we must be on our guard to see that no harm results in subsequent cases. Furthermore, none of the disanalogies that figure in this paper are

based on a difference in the dimensionality of space and time. They hold even if space were to be only one dimensional.

3. For a defense of this see chapter 5 of my *The Language of Time* (London: Routledge & Kegan Paul, 1968).
4. The agent-causation in S7 must be of the simultaneous sort, such as figures in the laws of classical physics, for otherwise some temporal component of T7 would fail to be translated in S7.
5. I am assuming that an agent cannot perform a so-called supertask, consisting in the performance of an infinite number of distinct acts in a finite time by performing each task in half of the time of its immediate predecessor.
6. *Reasons and Persons* (Oxford: Oxford University Press, 1984), pp. 176–177.
7. *The Will to Believe and Other Popular Essays in Philosophy* (Cambridge, Mass.: Harvard University Press, 1979), p. 67.
8. It is worth pointing out that what an agent prefers from a tensed perspective might differ from what she prefers from a tenseless one. If an agent existing now has a choice between suffering one unit of pain tomorrow or eight units of pain yesterday, he or she will prefer to have already suffered eight units of pain yesterday rather than one unit of pain tomorrow; but if this same agent adopts a tenseless Myth of Ur perspective on her/his life and is given the choice between suffering one unit of pain at t_9 or eight units of pain at t_7, she will prefer to suffer one unit of pain at t_9 rather than eight units of pain at t_7. Assume, as is possible, that tomorrow is t_9 and yesterday is t_8. In this case his or her tensed preferences conflict with her/his tenseless ones. This result should not surprise us, for we know that coreferring expressions that differ in sense are not intersubstitutable *salva veritate* within the scope of the verb "prefer," since it creates a nonextensional context. Thus, even though t_7 = yesterday and t_9 = tomorrow, these coreferring expressions, given that they differ in sense, are not intersubstitutable *salva veritate* within the scope of "prefer."
9. This might be challenged by appeal to the doctrine of the specious present according to which each pulse of perceptual experience has a sensory content comprised of successive events, thereby enabling us to perceive a succession of events in a single pulse of experience. This has the consequence that when I see an arm rise I really am seeing a Hindu-type god, and thus am seeing not a temporal succession but a concatenation of coexistent arms, and that when I hear the final note of a melody I am hearing a chord. (If Mozart had an auditory specious present of thirty minutes, being able to hear an entire symphony all at once, he must have had some horrible headaches.) For a fuller account see my

essay, "From the Specious to the Suspicious Present: the Jack Horner Phenomenology of William James," *Journal of Speculative Philosophy* 11, no. 3 (1997): 163–189.

10. Sean Gallagher has shown that there are some surface counterexamples to this, for example, "Now he has won" and "Now he will do it." But these are stylistic variants respectively for "He has just won" and "He will do it shortly."
11. It is interesting to note that there are some analogous ways in which we can choose the context for our use of spatial and temporal indexical terms. For example, for both types of indexes, one can adopt the rule of having their referent determined either *quoad* the place or time of the tokening, as is usual, or *quoad* the place or time of the perception of the tokening.

Chapter 5

Relational Particulars and Whitehead's Metaphysics

JOHN W. LANGO

Editor's Comment: Portions of an earlier draft of this essay were presented at the 1998 International Silver Anniversary A. N. Whitehead Conference at Claremont (where contributors Bradley, Lango, McHenry and the editor were able to meet personally for the first time) and at the 1994 Marvin Farber Conference on the Ontology and Epistemology of Relations held at SUNY Buffalo. Published here for the first time, Lango presents us with an excellent example of how Whiteheadean resources might be brought to bear relevantly on analytic discussions of the most basic and time-honored issue of the nature of particulars. Work by Professor Lango is a natural choice for inclusion in a volume on process and analytic philosophy as he has devoted a good deal of his professional career to discussion of Whitehead's philosophy in the context of issues in logic, philosophy of mathematics, and other topics of pointed interest to analytic metaphysicians.

In *Abstract Particulars*, contemporary analytic philosopher Keith Campbell argues that certain instances of properties, even though abstract, are particulars (AP 2).[1] But he also argues that there are no relational particulars—that is, that the category of abstract particulars does not include instances of relations. In contrast, in *Process and Reality*, Alfred North Whitehead holds that "'relatedness' is dominant over 'quality'" (PR xiii) and that prehensions are "Concrete Facts of Relatedness" (PR 22).[2] In other words, prehensions are both relations and particulars. Accordingly, the project of this paper is twofold. By means of some comparisons with Campbell's views, I interpret a basic part of Whitehead's metaphysics. And I use that interpretation to illustrate the thesis that there are relational particulars.[3]

Foundationism

A central question of metaphysics should be: What sorts of things are there? In trying to answer this question, a fundamental distinction could be made between universals and particulars. But then we would have to face the problem of universals, a multifaceted problem, which includes the questions of what they are, how they can be known, and even whether there are any. And we should also have to face a corresponding problem of particulars, equally multifaceted, a problem that includes the following question: Which sorts of things are particulars? In this paper, I want to address a part of this last question, namely, the question of whether there are *relations* whose instances are particulars.

Common sense holds, it would seem, that bodies and persons are particulars, and that they have properties and relations. For example, I look at the bricks in my fireplace. Each brick is red and rectangular and next to other bricks. With respect to the problem of universals, we may ask whether, in addition to these particulars (i.e., the bricks) there also are universals (e.g., redness, rectangularity, and nextness). There are comparable questions that may be asked with respect to the problem of particulars. When I look at a particular brick and see that it is red and rectangular, am I also seeing two additional particulars—namely, an instance of the property of being red and an instance of the property of being rectangular? And, when I look at two particular bricks and see that they are next to each other, am I also seeing an additional particular—namely, an instance of the relation *being next to*?

Campbell argues that certain "cases of kinds, or instances of properties" are particulars, albeit abstract ones (AP 2). Following Donald Cary Williams, he calls these abstract particulars *tropes* (AP 4). Moreover, his is a one-(basic-) category ontology, which means that there are *only* tropes, both simple and complex (AP 20). Thus there are no universals, and an ordinary physical body (e.g., a diamond) consists of tropes that are *compresent* with one another (AP 20). For example, when I look at my fireplace, and see a particular brick; that brick is, for Campbell, nothing but certain abstract particulars (or tropes)—namely, instances of the properties of redness, rectangularity, hardness, roughness, and so forth—that are present together in the right way (i.e., compresent). A concrete particular such as the brick is, then, "a total group of compresent tropes"; we need posit no matter or substance or substratum in addition to these property instances (AP 21).

But he also argues that there are no relational particulars, that is, that the category of tropes does not include relation instances.[4] For he advocates what he calls *foundationism*, the thesis that

> For all relational facts there are corresponding foundational facts, and in every case the relational facts call for no ontology beyond that involved in the foundational facts themselves. (AP 101)

And sufficient for the foundational facts is the ontology of property instances. For example, when I see that two bricks in my fireplace have the same color, what I see is that both are red. According to his foundationism, this means that the relationship between them of having the same color has as its foundation the fact(s) that they both are red (cf. AP 101). Thus there is no need to posit, in addition to these two instances of the property of redness, a third particular, an instance of the relation of color sameness.

In this essay, I take for granted Campbell's view that there are abstract particulars, although I do not claim that there is no other (basic) ontological category. But I argue that the category of abstract particulars could also include relation instances, and so I challenge his foundationism. More specifically, I consider at some length a type of relation instance that is obtained from Whitehead's metaphysical system. Hence my aim is twofold: both to offer a sketch of what should be a controversial interpretation of a basic part of Whitehead's metaphysics, and to use that interpretation to illustrate the thesis that there are relational particulars.

Prehensions and Particularity

In contrast to Campbell's one-category ontology, Whitehead presents, in *Process and Reality*, a many-categories ontology, his "eight Categories of Existence": actual entities, prehensions, nexus, subjective forms, eternal objects, propositions, multiplicities, and contrasts (PR 22). Eternal objects, which are similar to Plato's forms, are (in effect) universals (PR 44). Multiplicities are similar to classes or sets. The remaining categories are all categories of particulars.

It might be objected that Whitehead would not have accepted such a use of the term *particular*. For he held that the "terms, 'universals' and 'particulars,' both in the suggestiveness of the two words and in their current philosophical use, are somewhat misleading" (PR 48). Nevertheless, he himself used the term *particular*. Note, for example, his remark that "prehensions are real, individual, and particular" (PR 20). Accordingly, although the term *particular* can be somewhat misleading, he should have accepted its use in interpreting his metaphysics, when it is used with suitable caution.

I have contended that all of his categories other than those of eternal objects and multiplicities are categories of particulars. This contention should not prove very controversial concerning the category that is most fundamental: actual entities. For God is an actual entity, and all of the other actual entities—also called actual occasions (or, more briefly, occasions)—are (in effect) minimal events (PR 73). Interpreting Whitehead's conception of God raises difficult metaphysical issues that I want to avoid, and so I shall limit my discussion to actual occasions. Note that for Campbell "events are particulars"; nevertheless, they do not comprise a distinct (basic) ontological category, because they can be understood in terms of tropes (AP 22). Similarly, actual occasions are, as minimal events, particulars. Moreover, since nexus also are events (PR 73) (because a nexus is, very roughly, an assemblage of actual occasions), they too are particulars (cf. PR 229).[5]

Are the entities in the remaining four categories of existence particulars? Among these categories, that of prehensions is primary (PR 18). For one of the "factors" of a prehension is its subjective form (PR 23), a contrast is the datum of a specific type of prehension (PR 228), and a proposition is a kind of contrast (PR 24). Therefore, the most important question of particularity concerning Whitehead's ontology, one that could prove quite controversial, is: Are prehensions particulars?[6] Note that he asserts that "any characteristic of an actual entity is reproduced in a prehension" (PR 19). Therefore, it would seem that, if actual occasions are particulars, the answer to this question must be an affirmative one.

To address this question more adequately, let us look more closely at the notion of being a particular. Campbell summarizes his criterion of particularity as follows: "And our abstract particulars are *particulars* because they have a local habitation, even if no name. They exist as individuals at unique place-times" (AP 3). More exactly, he does not claim that the concept of existing at a unique place-time serves to individuate tropes, for he holds that "*individuation is basic and unanalysable*" (AP 69). Instead, he maintains that the concept serves us in identifying them; it is "*what we use* to distinguish" them (AP 70). For example, the reason why he thinks that events are to be identified as particulars is that "they occur at specific places at specific times" (AP 22). This could also be why actual occasions should be construed as particulars; for they are minimal events, they have locations in space-time; more precisely, they occupy basic regions in what Whitehead calls the extensive continuum (PR 283).

Could this particularity criterion of location in a place and at a time be used to determine whether prehensions are particulars? According to Whitehead, the subject of a prehension is "the actual entity *in* which that prehension is a concrete element" (PR 23, emphasis added). Moreover, in contrast to the traditional locution "an idea in the mind," where the word "in" is to be understood as a kind of metaphor; this notion of *being a concrete element in* should be taken in a (roughly) spatiotemporal sense. More specifically, just as its subject occupies a basic region in the extensive continuum, so a prehension occupies a "subregion" of that basic region (PR 283–285). My point is that a prehension has a space-time location in the location of its subject, and thus that, by Campbell's particularity criterion, prehensions should be counted as particulars.[7]

It might be objected that my use here of Campbell's criterion does not correctly represent how Whitehead understood particularity. For Whitehead might have had a different criterion, one that does not establish that prehensions are particulars. Is there, then, a more suitable Whiteheadian criterion of particularity? The entities that evidently are not particulars—that is, eternal objects—do not come into being but instead always exist. In contrast, each actual occasion comes into being through a kind of process; more exactly, it *is* its process of becoming (PR 23). In short, a fundamental distinction between actual occasions and eternal objects is that the former come into being whereas the latter do not.

Perhaps Whitehead could have formulated a criterion of particularity in terms of his conception of becoming. Note that, given such a criterion, prehensions would be counted as particulars. For "in the becoming of an actual entity, novel prehensions, nexus, subjective forms, propositions, multiplicities, and contrasts, also become" (PR 22). But why should the fact that an entity comes into being serve to allow us to count it as a particular? The conception of becoming is implicitly temporal: when an entity comes into being, other entities have already come into being, and others have yet to come into being. Therefore, I would suggest that, if a Whiteheadian particularity criterion involving the conception of becoming were adequately formulated, it might not be so different from one involving the conception of spatiotemporal location.

A Foundationist Objection

Nonetheless, the claim that prehensions are particulars is problematic. For, in Whitehead's metaphysics, "'relatedness' is dominant over 'quality'" (PR xiii). Moreover, prehensions are "Concrete Facts of Relatedness" (PR 22). Could he mean by this that prehensions, even though being particulars (i.e., concrete facts), are still to be construed as some sort of relatedness?

It might be thought that the answer to this question is quite obvious. For it might be thought that, in calling them concrete facts of relatedness, he just meant that they are relational particulars. Note that, in discussing the "antithetical terms 'universals' and 'particulars,'" he remarked, in a footnote, that, in addition to actual entities, "prehensions and subjective forms are also 'particulars'" (PR 48). If this interpretation is correct, then Campbell's foundationism represents a challenge. For it could be argued that, even though Whitehead meant that prehensions are relational particulars, they are not, because they can be given a foundation (in Campbell's sense) in nonrelational particulars (e.g., actual occasions). One aim of this paper is to answer this sort of challenge.

Prehending always involves some subject—an actual occasion—prehending some datum (PR 23). Hence a prehension might be thought to be a fact of relatedness between a particular subject and a single datum, a relatedness that might be symbolized straightforwardly as follows: *sRd*. Here *s* stands for a particular occasion, the subject of the prehension; *d* stands for the datum prehended by the subject; and *R* stands for a relation of prehension holding between the subject and the datum.

With respect to this way of symbolizing a relation of prehension, our question of particularity becomes this: is there, in addition to *s* and *d*, a further particular, namely, an *instance* of *R*? That is, when there is a subject and a datum and the former prehends the latter, is there also an additional particular, namely, an *instance* of the relation of prehending that holds between the subject and the datum? Or, could this fact of relatedness have a foundation (in Campbell's sense) in nonrelational facts about the subject and the datum?

To grasp this last question more clearly, we need to understand how foundationism is based on the concept of *supervenience* (AP 100). Recall the example of the two bricks in my fireplace that have between them the relationship of being the same color because each has the property of being red. The nonrelational fact that one is red and the nonrelational fact that the other is red together determine the relational fact that they are the same color. For they cannot cease to be the same color and yet both remain red; rather, they can only cease to be the same color if one of them ceases to be red. Moreover (and speaking counterfactually), if one of them were not red, they would not be the same color; on the other hand, it cannot be the case that, had they not been the same color, they would still both be red. In this way, their being the same color is *supervenient* on their being red. In general, and very roughly speaking, a relation between two things is supervenient on certain properties of them if and only if when they have the properties there has to be the relation between them (that is, they cannot have the properties and fail to be in the relation).

Accordingly, there is the following objection, stemming from Campbell's foundationism, to the claim that prehensions are particulars: the relation of prehension is in this way supervenient; and, therefore, just as there is no need to posit an instance of the relation of color sameness as a particular, so there is no need to posit an instance of the prehension relation as a particular.

But what facts are there about subject and datum that could make prehension supervenient? There are many types of prehensions—for example, conceptual feelings, physical purposes, propositional feelings, and intellectual feelings—and so a full discussion of this question could be quite involved. However, in order to answer the objection, it is enough to show that it fails concerning just one type of prehension. Let us examine, then, those prehensions that are (genetically) fundamental: simple physical feelings.

Simple Physical Feelings and Supervenience

An actual occasion comes into being through a process of concrescence involving a succession of phases of prehensions, and the *initial* phase of this concrescence is that of simple physical feelings. Moreover, each such feeling is "an act of causation," an antecedent actual occasion being the "cause," and the feeling itself being the "effect" (PR 236). Also, the occasion that is the subject of the feeling is called the "effect" (PR 236).

The two actual entities that are respectively cause and effect are particulars. "In a simple [physical] feeling there is a double particularity in reference to the actual world, the particular cause and the particular effect" (PR 237). Does this passage mean that the simple physical feeling is itself a particular? Or, is its "double particularity" supervenient on the particularity of the two actual entities that are cause and effect? That the passage is thus ambiguous indicates that it is not after all obvious what Whitehead meant when he stated that prehensions are concrete facts of relatedness. For it is conceivable that a simple physical feeling is a *concrete* fact of relatedness because, even though it is not itself a particular, there is in it reference to two particulars.

The relation of simple physical feeling is at the same time a sort of relation of causation. Accordingly, if simple physical feelings are supervenient, then so (it would seem) should be the causal relation. After criticizing Hume's analysis of causation, Campbell argues, utilizing a "doctrine of *Causal Powers*" (AP 117), that the causal relation is a supervenient one (AP 121). For example, I put another log on a fire in my fireplace, and it catches fire and burns. According to Campbell, the fire causes the log to burn because it has in itself the power to burn the log, an active power that "can only act in the right circumstances" (AP 120). One such circumstance is that the log is dry; hence the log must be capable of being burnt, that is, it must have in it the right passive power. Such causal powers are natural and not occult, for they have a "basis" in the physics and chemistry of fire and wood (AP 121); and the "simplest" powers are "the fundamental forces acting in Nature" (AP 119). In this way, the relation of causation "has a foundation in both cause and effect" (AP 120); for the active power in the cause and the passive power in the effect together determine the causal relation between them.

Whitehead incorporates in his metaphysics something like this conception of power. In discussing John Locke's "doctrine of 'power,'" he asserts the following concerning simple physical feelings: "In Locke's phraseology the objectified [i.e., prehended] actual entity is then exerting 'power'" (PR 58). Hence, in support of the foundationist objection about prehension, it might be claimed that this power makes the simple physical feeling supervenient. More accurately, it might be claimed that this active power (exerted by the prehended occasion) and some passive power (in the subject occasion) together determine the relation of simple physical feeling.

How does an actual occasion exert such power? Whitehead's answer to this question presupposes his conceptions of objective datum and subjective form. When an antecedent occasion A is the cause of a simple physical feeling in a subsequent occasion B, B objectifies A by means of one of A's own prehensions. Hence A is the "initial datum" and A's prehension is the "objective datum" of B's simple physical feeling (PR 236). Furthermore, B can have more than one simple physical feeling of A, for B can objectify A by means of more than one of A's prehensions.

Additionally, a prehension has as an essential factor its subjective form—namely, *how* (i.e., the manner in which) its subject feels its datum (PR 23). Although his metaphysics makes relatedness dominant over quality, the concept of "quality inhering in particular substance" is exemplified by the concept of "subjective form inhering in feeling" (PR 232). Hence, in contrast to prehensions, subjective forms are nonrelational. Furthermore, if the subjective form is abstracted (in thought) from the feeling, "we are left with an eternal object" (i.e., a universal) (PR 232). This means that subjective forms are (in effect) instances of properties—that is, abstract nonrelational particulars.

Its subjective form is a property instance that holds of a feeling. Moreover, a simple physical feeling is merely the effect of its initial datum, and so its subjective form is merely the (partial) reproduction or "reenaction" of the subjective form of the prehension that is its objective datum (PR 237). Consider, accordingly, the following hypothesis: the *power* exerted by the objectified occasion stems from a nonrelational fact about it—namely, the *subjective form* of one of its prehensions (i.e., the objective datum). Note that each subjective form has "its qualitative pattern and its pattern of intensive quantity" (PR 233), and thus that this power could derive, at least in part, from something that has intensity, something that is quantitative.

Therefore, using this hypothesis in support of the foundationist objection about prehension, it could be claimed that two nonrelational facts—that subjective form in the cause and its reenaction in the effect—together determine the relation of simple physical feeling between cause and effect. Just as the relation of color similarity is supervenient upon color qualities, so the relation of simple physical feeling might be supervenient on qualitative subjective forms.

Counterexample

Having sketched what I think to be the best defense of the claim that simple physical feelings are supervenient, I want now to challenge that defense by means of a counterexample.

Campbell holds that metaphysics should concern itself with "the actual" (AP 1), and so his trope ontology is influenced by various scientific theories, especially the conception of physical fields (e.g., electromagnetic fields). Similarly, Whitehead thought that his metaphysics of actual occasions should interpret the order that science finds in nature. Basic to his interpretation of this order is the notion of *society*, a notion that covers such diverse items as electrons, rocks, and human bodies (PR 98). Briefly (and incompletely), a society is a nexus of occasions which are ordered by means of a "defining characteristic" (i.e., an eternal object); moreover, a necessary condition for this "social order" is that each occasion in the society has a (conceptual) feeling of that defining characteristic (PR 34).

My counterexample utilizes this notion of society, and is rooted in this passage (PR 56, emphasis added):

> The reason why the doctrine of power is peculiarly relevant to the enduring things [e.g., material bodies] . . . is that any *likeness* between the successive occasions of a historic route [i.e., a society] procures a corresponding *identity* between their contributions to the datum of any subsequent actual entity . . .

Drawing on this way in which likeness procures identity, I shall now state the counterexample.

A and B are actual occasions that are contemporaneous members of a society, and there is the following *likeness* between them: their feelings of the society's defining characteristic are exactly the same. Therefore, just as two instances of a color can be exactly the same, the subjective forms of those feelings are exactly the same. In other words, when one of the subjective forms is abstracted from its feeling, we are left with identically the same eternal object that we are left with when the other subjective form is abstracted from its feeling.

It might be objected that, because a subjective form gives to a feeling its "essential novelty" (PR 232), the two subjective forms cannot be exactly the same. However, although every actual occasion is a "novel entity" (PR 21), this does not mean that each of its feelings must be qualitatively unique, different in character from all other feelings. Indeed, "the origination of conceptual novelty" is essential for living organisms (PR 102); but, on the other hand, material bodies are deficient in novelty (PR 101–102). Thus the society in the counterexample could be a material body whose successive occasions are very much alike.

Let us continue with the counterexample. C is a third occasion in the society, and is subsequent to A and B, and thus has simple physical feelings of them. In particular, C's feelings of them have as objective data their feelings of the defining characteristic. Furthermore, the subjective forms of C's feelings reenact the subjective forms of their feelings. Now we reach a crucial step. The above *likeness* between A and B procures the following *identity* between their contributions to the datum of C: because A's subjective form is exactly the same as B's subjective form, C's subjective forms are exactly the same.[8]

D is a fourth occasion in the society, subsequent to C, and thus also to A and B, and with simple physical feelings of them. In particular, D has the following simple physical feeling of C: D feels C's feeling of *A*'s feeling of the defining characteristic. The subjective form of D's feeling is the reenaction of the subjective form of C's feeling (of *A*'s feeling).

Now recall that it is possible for D to have more than one simple physical feeling of C, for D can objectify C by means of more than one of C's prehensions. Nevertheless, crucial to the counterexample is this feature of it: D does *not* feel C's feeling of B's feeling of the defining characteristic.

Is D's simple physical feeling of C supervenient upon its subjective form and the subjective form of C's feeling (of A's feeling)? A subjective form is a property instance, and so our question should be, more accurately: Is D's simple physical feeling of C supervenient on the property instantiated in those two subjective forms? Recall that a relation between two things is supervenient on certain properties of them if and only if when they have the properties there has to be the relation between them. Hence D's simple physical feeling of C is supervenient on (the property instantiated in) the subjective forms only if the following is the case: Suppose that D and C were not to have those subjective forms, but instead were to have (numerically) different subjective forms that nonetheless are (qualitatively) exactly the same (i.e., identically the same property is instantiated both in the former and in the latter). Then D would still have to have that simple physical feeling of C.

I shall now show why D's simple physical feeling of C is *not* thus supervenient. D might have had a different simple physical feeling of C, but with exactly the same subjective forms. For, instead of feeling C's feeling of *A*'s feeling of the defining characteristic, D might have felt C's feeling of *B*'s feeling of it. But we have seen above that the subjective form of B's feeling is exactly the same as the subjective form of A's feeling, and thus that the subjective forms of C's two feelings are (by reenaction) exactly the same. Now, if D were to have felt C's feeling of *B*'s feeling of the defining characteristic, there would also have been the reenaction of exactly the same subjective form. Therefore, the subjective form of this simple physical feeling that D *might* have had is exactly the same as the subjective form of the simple physical feeling that D *does* have. Once again likeness procures identity (but this time counterfactually).

In conclusion, the simple physical feeling that D does have and the simple physical feeling that D might have had are different, because they have different objective data (i.e., C's feeling of A and C's feeling of B). And yet their subjective forms are exactly the same, and the subjective forms of their objective data are exactly the same. Therefore, the above foundationist objection is false; the relation of simple physical feeling does not have a foundation in a subjective form in the cause and its reenaction in the effect.

Since it is not thus supervenient (and assuming that there are not other properties in the cause and in the effect in which it has a foundation), a simple physical feeling is, we may conclude, a relational particular. Moreover, because physical feelings of the other types are derivative from simple physical feelings, they are (we should suspect) themselves relational particulars. Also, an actual occasion in the final phase of its concrescence is "one complex, fully determinate feeling" (of its actual world) (PR 26), and hence is itself a relational particular, or so I shall eventually argue.

Some Objections

I have challenged what I take to be the best defense of the foundationist claim about simple physical feelings with a counterexample. However, it might be objected that this defense is not the best one. For it might be held that the active power in the objectified occasion stems, not from the subjective form of one of its prehensions, but rather from that prehension itself (i.e., the objective datum). But then, rather than being supervenient on subjective forms, a simple physical feeling would be supervenient on its objective datum (together with some passive power in the subject). However, this objection fails. For, since the objective datum is a prehension (i.e., a type of relation), the objection does not show that simple physical feelings are supervenient on terms that are nonrelational.

There is another objection that derives from the category of eternal objects. Even though a simple physical feeling is not supervenient on its relata, it is not a relational particular. For, since Whitehead is a (Platonic) realist about universals, the relation of simple physical feeling is a universal (i.e., a relational eternal object). And thus the instantiation of that relation is to be understood, not as a relational particular, but merely as the inherence of a universal (i.e., the ingression of an eternal object).

To answer this objection adequately, I would have to discuss both the problem of universals and his attempt to solve it with his category of eternal objects. Why does he include that category in his ontology? Could eternal objects have a foundation (in Campbell's sense) in the other ontological categories? However, I cannot hope to answer such difficult questions here. Nevertheless, it should be evident that, if this objection were correct, his categories of existence would be considerably altered. For example, the category of prehensions would be conflated with that of eternal objects. Also, since an actual occasion is itself (in its final phase) one complex feeling, the fundamental category of actual entities would itself appear to be conflated with that of eternal objects. In short, the objection would seem to presuppose that there is only one basic ontological category in his metaphysics: universals.

Whitehead held that a metaphysics has to be coherent, that its basic concepts "presuppose each other so that in isolation they are meaningless" (PR 3). Nevertheless, in constructing the above counterexample, I have focused on a part of his metaphysics, largely in abstraction from the remainder. How, then, can I be sure that the foundationist challenge has been defeated? In drawing the conclusion that simple physical feelings are relational particulars, I assumed that there are not other properties in the cause and in the effect in which a simple physical feeling has a foundation. As my brief discussions of the above two objections should indicate, a full defense of this assumption would be a very complicated enterprise, one that I cannot engage in here. For example, it might be thought that the power exerted by an actual occasion on which a simple physical feeling of it is supervenient is its subjective aim; but this would entangle the foundationist challenge with the problem of final causation. Since my view is that the assumption could eventually be defended, I would claim, albeit without conclusive proof, that the above counterexample is definitive.

I have said that my aim in this paper is to sketch an interpretation of a part of Whitehead's metaphysics, and to use that interpretation to illustrate the thesis that there are relational particulars. I have focused on a part of it that involves the problem of (efficient) causation, and have (largely) abstracted from those parts of it that involve other problems, for example, the problem of universals and the problem of final causation. Although it could be claimed that Whitehead rejected such an analytical approach in metaphysics (cf. PR xii), I would not concur with such a rejection. If his metaphysics is to be of value for those who are not enthusiasts, we have to be able to learn from parts of it, to the exclusion of others.

Causation

The foundationist objection made use of an hypothesis that can be restated as follows: when occasion B has a simple physical feeling of occasion A, that feeling is caused by a power exerted by A, a power that stems from a *nonrelational* fact about A (i.e., a subjective form in A). In light of the counterexample, I would contend instead that the power exerted by A stems from a *relational* fact about A—namely, one of A's own prehensions (i.e., the objective datum of the simple physical feeling). And this contention suggests the following conjecture: that the active power in *any* cause derives, not from properties, but rather (at least in part) from relationships.

But Campbell holds that the active power in a cause is based on something that is nonrelational. Let me summarize some of his pertinent views. The active power in a cause is not a "bare power" (AP 119); for example, my fire does not have the power to burn the log simply because it has the (bare) power of being combustive. Rather, the power in a cause has an "inner complexity" (AP 119) that has a "basis" in scientific "features" of the cause (AP 120–121); thus the power in the fire has a basis (roughly) in the rapid motion of molecules. Finally, the power in a cause has "a monadic qualitative base" (AP 122)—that is, its basis in the cause consists in abstract particulars, namely, property instances.

Let us look at one of his examples. "When you drop it, it is the weight of this particular brick, not bricks or weights in general, which breaks the bone in your particular left big toe" (AP 113). Moreover: "Not the brick in its entirety, but rather the mass and solidity which in part constitute the brick, are the proper terms of this causal relation" (AP 114). Thus the active power in the (falling of the) brick is not the bare power to break things. Rather, this power has an inner complexity based in scientific features of the brick: its mass and solidity. Finally, mass and solidity are properties, and thus the power stems from instances of those properties being constituents of the brick.

In opposition to Campbell, I would claim that his example supports instead the conjecture that the active power in a cause derives (in part) from relationships. In the quoted passages, the words "weight" and "mass" appear to be used interchangeably. However, if an astronaut in a spacecraft orbiting the earth were to drop a brick on her toe, she would probably not suffer a fracture, since the brick would be weightless. Therefore, it is not merely the mass of the brick (which is virtually the same in the spacecraft as on the surface of the earth) but the brick's weight that gives it (part of its) causal power to break the toe. But, in contrast to its mass, which might seem to be a nonrelational fact about it; its weight stems both from its mass and from the mass of the earth. Thus its weight is a relational fact about it and the earth. My point, then, is that the active power in the brick to break a toe derives (in part) from something that is relational: its weight.

It could be objected that this relational fact is supervenient on certain properties: the masses of the brick and the earth. Nevertheless, in light of the general theory of relativity, the concept of mass might itself submit to a relational analysis (cf. Mach). Since there is no space to reply further to this objection, I must halt this brief discussion of the conjecture inconclusively. However, it is worth mentioning that, because Whitehead's account of causation rests on his conception of simple physical feeling, his metaphysics presents a way of understanding how the active power in any cause derives (ultimately) from relational particulars.

Spatial Relations

It might be thought that my way of constructing a counterexample is too roundabout, and that instead counterexamples lie ready at hand, in spatial relationships. Consider, for example, how a counterexample might be obtained using the relation *being next to.* I see two red bricks in my fireplace that are next to each other. When the fireplace was constructed, they might have been placed in it differently, so that they were not next to each other. Had they been thus placed apart, they would still have had exactly the same properties. Hence, even though their redness determines that the relation of color sameness holds between them, the relation *being next to* is not supervenient on their properties. This suggests that, in addition to the two bricks, there is a third particular: an instance of that spatial relationship.

A brick is a concrete particular that, according to Campbell, consists of tropes that are compresent with one another. An analogous counterexample could (arguably) be constructed for trope theory. Using spatial location as a criterion of particularity, it could be argued that the spatial parts of certain property instances—for example, instances of colors—are themselves property instances (cf. AP 136–138). For example, there is one instance of red located in the left half of a brick in my fireplace, and a different instance of red located in the right half. However, even though these two instances of red determine a relation of color sameness, they do not determine a relation of nextness. This suggests that the relation of nextness is not here a supervenient one, and thus that there is, in addition to the two instances of red, an instance of that spatial relationship between them.

In order to show that spatial (and also temporal) relations have a nonrelational foundation, Campbell develops a "field version of the trope theory" (AP 155). Note that earlier in his book (i.e., prior to about AP 124) he seemed to be following Williams in taking "manifest tropes" (e.g., color instances) to be fundamental (AP 138). However, this field version of trope theory is a holistic theory (cf. AP 129–133, 144). Most important for the present discussion, "Space-Time" is a single trope "containing no real, detachable parts" (AP 132; cf. AP 144–145). Instead, the manifest parts of space-time are to be understood merely as pseudo-parts, and such pseudoparts of a single holistic trope are only quasitropes (AP 66, 91, 130, 148, 152). In general, then, Williams's manifest tropes are in Campbell's field theory only quasitropes (AP 151–155). Hence the book can be interpreted as presenting two quite different theories of tropes.

In summary, much of Campbell's book is devoted to the very difficult project of showing that spatial relations and temporal relations are supervenient on nonrelational quasitropes. My view is that this project is incomplete, especially because the notion of quasitrope is obscure, and needs to be developed more fully. However, my purpose here is not to critically examine his project, but rather simply to make this point: counterexamples to foundationism that involve spatial (or temporal) relationships do not lie ready at hand, but instead have to be defended by elaborate argumentation.

Could such a counterexample be obtained from Whitehead's metaphysics? Unfortunately, his views on space and time are quite complex. What follows is a brief (and partial) summary: underlying space-time is "one extensive continuum" (PR 66), which is divisible into regions that are interrelated by a relation of "extensive connection" (PR 294). Even a summary of this brevity allows us to discern problems. Are regions of the extensive continuum particulars? Are relations of extensive connection between regions relational particulars? We see, then, that constructing a Whiteheadian counterexample to foundationism that involves a spatial (or spatiotemporal) relationship would require an intricate dialectic, which is not feasible here. Since Whitehead advances what is in effect a causal theory of spatiotemporal ordering, a counterexample involving the relation of causation is more readily constructed than one that involves a spatiotemporal relationship.

Events

Why should Campbell be so concerned to provide nonrelational foundations for relational facts? His commitment to foundationism must be quite deep, for it leads him to abandon D. C. Williams's intuitively graspable manifest trope theory, in favor of a highly counterintuitive Spinozistic holism (AP 154). To venture a partial answer to this question, let me suggest that (among other motives) he might be trying to avoid what could be called the problem of dangling relational particulars (cf. AP 97–99).

In order to make this problem concrete, let us have an example. One billiard ball strikes another. Each ball is, on the (manifest) trope analysis, nothing but a complex of compresent tropes (e.g., an instance of the property of sphericity). Now suppose that there are relational particulars, and that, when one ball strikes the other, there occurs an instance of the causal relation of striking, that is, a causality trope. It might be thought that this causality trope is one of the compresent tropes that comprise each ball. This would mean that the two balls share a trope, whereas they would appear to be distinct objects. There would also be a problem of identity through time, for the balls before the collision did not include this causality trope, and yet they would not appear to be themselves (internally) changed because of the collision. The conclusion is that the causality trope is not part of the balls.

But then this relational particular is left dangling. For it is not part of either ball, but nonetheless it (somehow) exists between them, linking them together.[9] In order to try to solve this problem of dangling relational particulars, it might be claimed that the causality trope is itself related to the balls by two additional relations, relations that are themselves supervenient. Alternatively, it might be claimed that a relational particular by its very nature links together its relata; and, moreover, that this relational nature is ontologically fundamental, and cannot be grounded on something more fundamental. Since each of these claims requires a subtle defense open to various objections, it should not be surprising that Campbell prefers foundationism.

In raising this problem, I have allowed the causal relation of striking to hold between the billiard balls. It might be objected that causal relations hold between events, and thus that the striking relation holds between events involving the balls. Nonetheless, assuming that events are complexes of nonrelational tropes (cf. AP 22), the problem still remains. One event causes another event. Now suppose that there are relational particulars, and that there occurs between the two events an instance of the causal relation. This causality trope cannot be one of the compresent tropes that constitute each event, because each event is a complex of nonrelational tropes. Therefore, the relational particular is left dangling, existing (somehow) between the events, linking them together.

But why should we assume that events are complexes of nonrelational tropes? The substance metaphysics would appear to be entrenched in our ordinary ways of thinking (cf. Strawson). Moreover, events are commonly pictured as four-dimensional analogues of substances. Now substances are traditionally understood to be essentially nonrelational (i.e., their relationships are mere accidents). Therefore, in accordance with the substance picture of events, it could seem that events too should be construed as essentially nonrelational.

This substantializing of events has been reinforced by the authority of science. For relativity theory, understood as uniting space and time into a four-dimensional space-time, has suggested an ontology of point events (i.e., events occurring at space-time points). In accordance with the substance picture of events, it could seem that a point event should be construed as a substancelike entity. Now each such point event is causally influenced by earlier point events (in its light cone). Hence, if the relation of causal influence between two point events were itself a relational particular, it would (somehow) exist between them, linking them together. We can, of course, depict this relationship on a blackboard by joining two dots with an arrow. But, in this relativistic point-event ontology, a space-time line connecting two point events is just the locus of a series of point events. And thus such a line cannot be (literally) the location of a relational particular, an instance of the relation of causal influence (cf. AP 60). Our blackboard depiction is just a kind of metaphor.

However, there is a radically different way of understanding events. Rather than picture them as four-dimensional analogues of substances, we could understand them to be intrinsically relational. Accordingly, the relativistic point-event ontology could be reinterpreted as follows: each point event is constituted by the causal influences of earlier point events; that is, it is nothing but the causal relationships that it has with them.[10] If events are analyzed as complexes of tropes, then a point event becomes a complex of compresent causal-influence tropes. And so our problem is solved, for these causality tropes no longer dangle between the point events, but instead constitute them.

Similarly, Whitehead's actual occasions are minimal events. Moreover, they are not substancelike entities. Instead, they are acts of becoming. And they are, I have claimed, relational particulars. For an actual occasion comes into being through a process of concrescence involving a succession of phases of prehensions. Each incomplete phase is nothing but a multiplicity of prehensions, whereas the final phase is "one complex, fully determinate feeling" (PR 25–26). In other words, during each incomplete phase, there is a multiplicity of prehensions, but that multiplicity is not yet a single relational particular (for the subject occasion is what emerges from the completion of the process of concresence). In the final phase (i.e., when the process of concrescence is complete), the multiplicity of prehensions becomes a single relational particular (i.e., the emergent subject occasion). The point is that, just as its prehensions are relational particulars, so is the actual occasion itself a relational particular. We see, then, that the category of entities that is fundamental in Whitehead's ontology—actual occasions—is a category of relational particulars.

I have said that my interpretation of Whitehead should be controversial, and what I have especially in mind is this last claim. For interpreters of Whitehead, despite his disclaimers, have tended to construe actual occasions as (in some sense) substancelike. But my main point is that Whitehead's metaphysics furnishes one very interesting way in which events could be understood as relational particulars.

It might be objected that it is a basic principle of (philosophical) logic (or ontology) that there cannot be relations without there also (ultimately) being terms that are not relational—in short, no nonrelational terms, no relations (AP 98). For otherwise (it could be argued) there would be a vicious infinite regress. (Cf. Leibniz's famous dictum that, because there are complexes, there must be simples.) However, there can be a mereology without atoms; that is, the part-whole relation can be defined on a class of individuals none of which is without parts. In light of such mereological tolerance, my view is that it would be a serious philosophical error to ban ontologies of relational particulars by logical (or ontological) fiat.

Notes

1. References of this form (AP) are to Keith Campbell, *Abstract Particulars* (Oxford: Basil Blackwell, 1990). For recent discussions of the topic of property and relation instances, see also John Bacon, *Universals and*

Property Instances: The Alphabet of Being, Aristotelian Society Series, vol. 15 (Oxford: Basil Blackwell, 1995); and D. W. Mertz, *Moderate Realism and Its Logic* (New Haven and London: Yale University Press, 1996). For the sake of simplicity, I focus here on Campbell's book.

2. Note that Campbell refers briefly to Whitehead's process philosophy (AP 8) and to process philosophy in general (AP 76).
3. For a different kind of illustration, see my "Relation Instances and Musical Sounds," *Australian Journal of Philosophy* 78 (2000): pp. 176–169.
4. In contrast, John Bacon's *Universals* supports a conception of "particularized relations," and Mertz advocates a conception of "relation instances." For some criticisms of Campbell's foundationism, see Mertz, *Moderate Realism*, pp. 156–169.
5. For a defense of this claim, see my "Whitehead's Category of Nexus of Actual Entities," *Process Studies* 29 (2000): 16–42.
6. For example, in attempting to formalize the relation of prehension using predicate logic, Granville C. Henry assumes that prehensions are not particulars. See his *Forms of Concrescence* (Lewisburg: Bucknell University Press, 1993), esp. p. 39.
7. In light of Whitehead's fallacy of simple location (PR 137), it might be objected that he could not have accepted Campbell's criterion of particularity. However, to say that something cannot be (in the sense of that fallacy) simply located is not the same as to say that it has no location at all. Moreover, Whitehead's assertion that an actual occasion has a basic region implies that he held that there is a conception of location that avoids the fallacy.
8. It might be objected that this reenaction is only partial, and thus that the subjective forms are not exactly the same. For Whitehead asserts that "the re-enaction is not perfect" (PR 237). My view is that he should have said that the reenaction need not be perfect; but this would mean that reenaction includes the limiting case where the subjective forms are exactly the same. However, suppose that reenaction cannot be perfect, and thus that one of C's subjective forms is only partially the same as A's subjective form, and the other one of C's subjective forms is only partially the same as B's subjective form. Nevertheless, C's two subjective forms can still be exactly the same as the other. Similar remarks hold of what is said in the next three paragraphs about D's subjective forms. The point is that, if reenaction has to be partial, a slightly more complex counterexample than the one given in the text can still be constructed.
9. Campbell notes that this sort of problem was raised by McTaggart (AP 98).
10. This suggestion is influenced by Donald Davidson's causal criterion of event-identity. See his "The Individuation of Events" in his *Essays on Actions and Events* (Oxford: Oxford University Press, 1980), p. 179.

11. See, for example, William Christian, *An Interpretation of Whitehead's Metaphysics* (New Haven: Yale University Press, 1959), pp. 115–118; and Ivor Leclerc, *Whitehead's Metaphysics* (London: George Allen and Unwin, 1958), esp. pp. 17–28.

Chapter 6

Whitehead and the Analysis of the Propositional Function

JAMES BRADLEY

Editor's Comment: An earlier version of this paper was presented at the 1998 International Silver Anniversary A. N. Whitehead Conference held at the Center for Process Studies in Claremont, California. This highly original essay, revised and published here for the first time, argues for a profound connection between Whitehead, Wittgenstein, Dummett, and some others in the analytic tradition insofar as all these thinkers have constructivist and finitist leanings in the philosophy of mathematics. Arguing that Whitehead generalizes Frege's propositional function to its limits, Bradley contends that Whitehead's way of philosophically situating this generalization satisfies the speculative thrust toward the self-explanatory and at once harmonizes constructivism and realism. This essay is perhaps best read as a complement to George Lucas's piece (chapter 3) as both authors are arguing for divergent and even conflicting relationships between Whitehead and Wittgenstein, especially where they concern the import of constructivism and finitism for the question of "semantical ineffability."

Speculative metaphysics is primarily distinguished from analytical metaphysics, and from various kinds of naturalism and pragmatism, by the fact that it maintains a strong as opposed to a weak theory of existence. It is my contention that the difference between strong and weak theories of existence is central to Whitehead's speculative thought.

The Weak Theory of Existence

Weak theorists characteristically follow Hume and Kant in regarding existence as a notion about which little can or should be said except as a corrective to strong theories. As the Hume-Kant view of existence is nowadays usually stated in the form Frege gave it, a form which plays a crucial role in Whitehead's thought, a brief summary of Frege's position is relevant here.

Frege's fundamental idea is to generalize the mathematical function beyond mathematics and to use it as a model or analogue for the analysis of the logical structure of propositions. In this context, Frege maintains that statements of the form "*x* exists" are not, as one might ordinarily suppose, statements about *x* in the sense that they predicate existence of *x*. Existence is not a predicate of *x*, for *x* is not an individual object but a first-order class or kind. Indeed, existence-statements do not ascribe any predicate or property to individual objects at all. Instead, statements of the form "*x* exists" are second-order statements about the *term x*, the first-order class or kind *x*. That is, such statements of the form "*x* exists" are thus to be interpreted as quantificational statements about the term *x*, to the effect that the term *x* refers to a class that is not empty but has instances or examples.

On this view, existence is exhaustively definable as the satisfaction or instantiation of the existentially quantified variable of the propositional function. To exist is to answer a description. Whether one is talking about prime numbers or about concrete objects such as stones and people, statements of existence are defined in the same way: as saying that something (or everything) satisfies a description. In this respect, propositional-functional analysis can be regarded as putting a premium on rationality; for the existent is now through and through describable in terms of its predicates, with no mysterious residues. Indeed, on a Fregean analysis, it is evident that the weak theory of existence is not properly a *theory* of existence at all. Existence is simply removed from the realm of reflection and replaced by an account of the logical structure of language.

The Strong Question of Existence

Such claims would not, however, impress strong theorists of existence, the speculative metaphysicians. For speculative metaphysics holds that existence is much more than the silent, featureless pendant of the propositional function, at least as it is usually understood, and thus it refuses to assimilate the "is" of existence to the "is" of instantiation.

The basic difference between speculative and other kinds of metaphysics can be stated like this. All metaphysics of whatever kind is concerned with the nature of the real understood as that which is incapable of further demonstration, that which is not further derivable, that which is ultimate in the order of analysis, over against which anything else can be shown to be derivable, partial, abstract or whatever. However, speculative metaphysics maintains that the so-called ultimates of other kinds of philosophy are in fact open to further inquiry and derivation. For speculative metaphysics pushes philosophy's commitment to intellectual inquiry to its limits by asking whether or not whatever is claimed to be the ultimately real can be understood to be *self-explanatory*. The self-explanatory real, if there be such, is whatever may turn out to satisfy intellectual inquiry in that is description shows that its nature is nor further demonstrable or derivable, for it carries all the reasons for itself in its own nature. In this context, Whitehead's speculative metaphysics is to be conceived as putting to quantificational analysis the strong question of existence: Why is there sometimes that which answers a description?, Why is there sometimes that which satisfies the propositional function?[1]

This question is a contemporary expression of the traditional speculative attempt to establish a strong theory of existence as something more than merely a matter of quantification. Its purpose is to point out, no matter how successful in mathematics and logic, the generalization of the function as the propositional function has its limits in that it does not offer a complete theory of existence. That is, to take the simplest and least contentious examples, it does not explain in the case of concrete objects such as stones and people why there is sometimes that which satisfies the function. To that extent, the propositional function is not self-explanatory. The strong question thus opens up for fresh investigation the various strategies employed by weak theorists to secure the propositional function as the basis of philosophical reflection.

The Activity Debate

However, none of the points made so far on behalf of the strong question need disturb the weak theorist.

The fact is, speculative metaphysics since Plato had maintained *activity* to be an essential element in the analysis of existence. For the speculative claim is that the search for the self-explanatory ultimate is only satisfied by analyzing existence primarily in terms of some principle of "actualization," of "active" or "actual" existence (where "actual" is the adjectival form of "act"), which alone can explain why there is sometimes that which answers to a description. That is, a strong theory of existence is necessarily a theory of the activity of actualization. This is the crucial difference between analytical and speculative metaphysics.

It is the appeal to a theory of active existence implied by the strong question which for weak theorists vitiates the speculative enterprise *tout court.* In support of this view they offer a number of arguments, among which the primary argument is that relations are self-explanatory and so require no reference to any principle of activity to account for their connectivity. On this view, to put the strong question to the propositional function is tacitly to revive old conundrums, beloved of speculative philosophers, such as How do relations relate? Yet to ask how relations relate is mistakenly to view relations as abstract objects or third terms over and above their elements, rather than, with Frege, as structurally incomplete, partial objects that cannot occur without relata to complete them. Once relations are regarded as incomplete objects that are as such intrinsically connective, there is clearly no need to invoke any kind of activity as a third term or glue holding the relations and relata together.

This powerful account of the self-explanatory or intrinsic connectivity of relations lies behind a second powerful argument of weak theorists against any speculative appeal to activity. The claim here is that it is the very being of a function to have values. In this context, it is generally held that intrinsic connectivity of function and value means that their relation is to be understood in terms of rule-following, the practice or procedure that Wittgenstein terms a *process*. Rule-following is not conceived as a matter of any activity of decision or synthesis on the part of a directing, totalizing subject, cognitive or metaphysical. Rather, the process involved is a purely mechanical, "automatic calculation," an algorithm, which constitutes a differentiating series of which human subjects are, among other things, the effect.[2]

Now it is indeed the case that it is the very being of a function to have values, and functions are in that sense self-explanatory. Furthermore, there can be no doubt that theories of rule-following provide striking, even if disputable, accounts of the generation of mathematical objects, and other special kinds of entities such as language and social practices. Yet there is nothing in this weak theory of process which answers the strong question of existence. That is, there is nothing about the intrinsic connectivity of function and value, or about rule-following procedures, which explains why (to take the simplest examples again) there is sometimes that which satisfies the propositional function in the case of concrete objects such as stones and people. The mathematical model of calculation breaks down precisely here.

It is at this point that the weak theorists deploy a third argument against speculative theories of activity. The argument is that any questions about concrete instantiations—any questions about what Frege calls *Wirklichkeit*—are to be referred to natural science. Any other procedure would be guilty of stepping outside the limits of experience.

The power of an appeal to natural science cannot be underestimated. The problem is that natural science, at least in its current state, makes no claim to be either self-explanatory or exhaustive of the nature of experience. That philosophers in the empiricist and positivist traditions have often claimed it to be so is irrelevant here, for that is precisely what is at issue between strong and weak theories. Indeed, in the context of propositional-functional analysis, such claims have an inevitable circularity about them, for they are usually based on the view that *Wirklichheit* is to be understood in terms of a weak theory of process as mechanical or algorithmic (the simplest example is the regularity theory of efficient causation). However, no modern proponent of the algorithmic character of the natural order would ever pretend it to be self-explanatory, or anything other than an ultimate that has simply to be taken as given. The difference between strong and weak theorists at this point is that strong theorists view such a position as constituting premature abandonment of the experiment of intellectual inquiry.

Yet weak theorists have good reason to reject such a view of their position here, on the basis of a fourth argument, which, although negative, is as telling as the first argument. This fourth argument may, for brevity, be termed the objection from nonrelationality. It is based on the fact that strong theorists have traditionally regarded relations as requiring a further principle of connection. As a result, strong theorists have defended a form of regress argument in respect of relations: if there is a reason for connectivity of relations, it must apparently be more than any relation, for, were it not, it would require some further reason for its connectivity, and so ad infinitum. To formulate the same point in propositional-functional terms: if there is a reason beyond the relation of instantiation that is the reason for that relation, such a reason must apparently be more than a relation, for relation of instantiation includes the instantiation of any relational expression. Thus, if there is a reason for the relation of instantiation beyond the fact of instantiation, that reason must apparently be nonrelational or suprarelational in nature. The upshot of the strong question thus seems to be that whatever may be the reason for the connectivity of relations, it cannot itself be a relation and so must be nonrelational or suprarelational

This is why Hume, Kant, and Frege object to any attempt to answer the strong question even though they grant that the question is intelligible.[3] For reason or reflection operates in terms of relations, so that which is more than relational is beyond the grasp of reason or reflection. It would therefore seem that any attempt to answer the strong question inevitably ends up in the realm of the ineffable.

The ineffable is whatever at some point turns out to be describable only as that which cannot be rationally and intelligibly described. It is not rationally describable, for it cannot be brought under a relational order or a rule. It follows that it is not through and through intelligible, for, even if it is usually claimed to be in some sense irreducibly given in experience, its nature is such that it cannot be understood. In consequence, while the strong question may indeed indicate that there is a feature of experience that cannot be explained by the propositional function, to overstep the limits of reflection as defined by the propositional function is to take reflection into realms where, apparently, it has no business to be—a conclusion that seems to be borne out by the mystery or ineffability usually associated in the speculative tradition with principles of actualization, whether Plato's Good, Aristotle's Unmoved Mover, Plotinus' One, the transcendent Creator God, Spinoza's divine substance, the Kantian subject, the Idealist's Absolute, Bergson's *duree*, Peirce's boundless and primordial spontaneity, or Heidegger's *Ereignis*. In this context, justifiably, weak theorists over the last hundred years either have looked for the self-explanatory elsewhere than in theories of active existence, or have in various degrees given up on the search for the self-explanatory (Rorty would be the most extreme and perhaps most consistent example).

It is here, however, that the significance of Whitehead's speculative thought clearly emerges. For he regards the propositional-functional analysis, and the twentieth-century critique of speculative metaphysics in general, as guilty of the fallacy of irreformability. This is the fallacy of assuming that a particular line of thought such as speculative theory is intrinsically tied to whatever shortcomings and limitations of method may have characterized it in the past; for example, the treatment of the principle of sufficient reason as an axiom, the assumption that relations are not intrinsically connective, and the orientation of speculative philosophy toward the ineffable. It is then concluded that speculative philosophy is irreformable and so irredeemable (AI 223). Whitehead's extraordinary counterclaim is that the logic of the function provides resources for answering the strong question in such a way that it makes possible a renaissance and transformation of speculative philosophy. Thus he is ready provisionally to suspend the view that the propositional-functional analysis of Frege and his followers is ultimate, and to reexamine in what sense or senses functional analysis can claim to be so. In other words, he is prepared to embark on the experiment of answering the strong question.

However odd such an enterprise may at first sight appear to be, it should not be forgotten that in Frege, Russell, and their followers propositional-functional analysis has always carried with it considerable ontological baggage, even if, for many weak theorists, it is so much taken for granted as to be almost invisible. Most notably, there is the view that the real is in some sense complete, eternally present, and awaiting discovery, even though it may be essentially unpredictable or even random in nature. This usually goes hand-in-hand with the claim that, insofar as time is real, it is tenseless, that is, the qualitative differences between past, present, and future are at best subjective modes of temporal apprehension and that objective time is analyzable in terms of "dates" or quantitative before-after relations. The tenseless view of time allows the existentially quantified function to be said to have an absolute and invariable truth-value (true or false), so that the truth-value of a proposition is held to be timeless in that it is not dependent on the tensed context of its utterance. This gives rise to the program of analyzing all discourse in terms of "eternal sentences," that eliminate all references to tensed time.

Whitehead sums up the ontology of propositional-functional analysis by pointing out that it completely takes for granted the "invariableness" or "self-identity" both of the connectives and of the variables of the function. That is, it is assumed in propositional-functional analysis that "each symbol indicates one and the same individual thing in its repetitions throughout the complex pattern." Further, "it is assumed that the inevitable variation of meaning is infused into these basic symbols of interconnection by the diversity of the variable is not such as to affect the meaning which the pattern contains for the observers in question." In other words, propositional-functional analysis is closely tied to the view that the connectives and variables of a function in its different instantiations are merely numerically different. This means that there has been no consideration of what may be involved in the possibility of "the suffusion of the connective by the things connected" opened up by Russell's view of the function as meaningless apart from its instances.[4] In his response to the strong question, Whitehead will pursue the implications of Russell's view in order to reconsider the ontological implications associated with functional analysis.

Whitehead's Generalized Mathematics

It is no accident that Whitehead calls his speculative philosophy a "generalized mathematics" (ESP 109). For in *Process and Reality* (1929), as the revision and culmination of his work in *Principia Mathematica* (1910–1912), he builds on the brilliant success of the Frege-Russell generalization of the mathematical function as the propositional function. In this respect, his work is close to other Cambridge figures such as Ramsey and Wittgenstein. Moreover, like Ramsey in his last writings and Wittgenstein after 1929, the position Whitehead develops from the early 1920s onward is predominantly constructivist and finitist in character.[5] The difference is that Whitehead pushes the generalization of the function as far as possible: he develops it into a theory of existence, so as to render functional or rule-defining structure capable of answering the strong question and thus self-explanatory.

In embarking on the experiment of seeing how far the generalization of the function can be taken, and what its implications are, Whitehead endorses the Frege-Russell position that relational analysis is the principle of intelligibility—that reason operates in terms of relations—and that relations are structurally incomplete, partial objects that cannot occur without relata to complete them. He further argues with Frege and Russell that relational structure has ultimate status, at least to the extent that its nature is such that it renders questions about the relatedness or connectivity or relations otiose. Thus, the principle of experimental reason is in his hands an attempt to discover just how far relational analysis can be taken in the search for the ultimate: the self-explanatory is to be experimentally treated as intrinsically a matter of relational structure in some sense, whatever else it may be.

At this point, we encounter another area in which Whitehead is at one with Frege and Russell: namely, he accepts the function at least as a model or tool for the analysis of relations. That is, he accepts as ultimate Frege's definition of a relation as a function with two arguments.[6] It follows that if the self-explanatory has a relational structure, its structure is at least to be defined as a function with two arguments. The question now is: In terms of what function with two arguments is the structure of the self-explanatory to be defined?

The Theory of Serial Recursion

Although it has gone wholly unrecognized, Whitehead's speculative metaphysics is a generalization of the modern mathematical definition of natural numbers, as elaborated, for example, by Frege.[7] On this account, no number is a collection. The statement that 3 = 2 + 1, which is the definition of three, does not mean that 3 is "a 2 and a 1," but that 3 is a term of the integer series that comes "next after" 2. There is, in other words, no principle that is the series of numbers, or, as Plato put it, there is no form of number as such.[8] Rather, each number is a form, or more precisely, each number is a serial relation or connective in series with functional structure $n + 1$, known as the "successor operator," and its relata are themselves relations or connectives in series with that structure. Generalized by Whitehead as the binary structure of existence or "process" (even God's), the successor operator constitutes "the category of the ultimate," which he terms "Creativity"; it defines the nature and relation of "occasions," which are the basic units of existence, and of their complex internal phases of development or "prehensions."[9]

The particular interpretation of the successor operator which Whitehead generalizes is a form of free-variable finitism.[10] The following points will indicate what this means.

First, Whitehead's account of the serial connective is modeled on a nonclassical version of mathematical induction, which does not posit the existence of infinite sets or classes and defines natural numbers in terms of predecessor-successor relations. In the same way, Whitehead's account of existence as having the intrinsic structure $n + 1$ is a way of establishing a description of existence in terms of predecessor-successor relations.

Second, that description is established by Whitehead in terms of a form of primitive recursion: the serial structure $n + 1$ takes for its basis the result of its own operations (cf. PR 21). Part of the significance of Whitehead's recursive definition of seriality is that he can thereby avoid Russell's Paradox, the paradox of the class of all those classes that are not members of themselves.[11] For, defined recursively, no connective includes itself; it includes only its predecessors and is included only by its successors. (Formally stated: functions of stage $n + 1$ accept in their arguments only the results of the functions of stage n.) In other words, the serial connective is a matter of intrinsically finite iteration, so there is in serial analysis no completely realized real to generate reflexive paradoxes.

Third, and more precisely, the serial connective $n + 1$ is for Whitehead a matter of recursive succession. That is, every element of the serial structure requires an "initial value" or predecessor (there is no boundless, primordial spontaneity in Whitehead); and every element of the serial structure "contains" its predecessor (which Whitehead analyzes in terms of a complex theory of immediacy or "feeling"). In other words, seriality for Whitehead is cumulative (PR 237) in precisely the sense in which mathematics uses that term, in contrast to a mere additive concatenation (which is why any elements of the real are properly series and not mere sequences). It follows that serial connectives constitute a unidirectional, irreversible, series of differences that stand to one another asymmetrically, transitively, irreflexively, and consecutively.[12] Every connective is therefore next after its predecessor and it is the condition or potential of its successor. There is in the nature of the case no such thing as a single serial connective: the completion of one serial connective is the beginning of the next, and each is intrinsically situated in its position in the series.

Fourth, defined as a matter of recursive function, the variable of the function (+ *1*) is a free variable. That is, the values of any given serial connective are not knowable in advance but are defined by context. The operations of the function are thus said to be unique in that on this analysis the function $n + 1$ constructs its own domain (cf. PR 210).

It is at this point that the full implications of Whitehead's ontological generalization of the recursive function as a theory of existence begin to emerge. His purpose is twofold: to show that, when fully generalized, functional theory cannot dispense with the speculative notion[13] of activity, and to show that, when redefined in terms of the finite, recursive function, the speculative notion of activity becomes for the first time in the history of speculative metaphysics rationally and intelligibly describable without qualification.

Activity, Synthesis, Freedom: The Recursive Subject and the Nonconceptual Real

The key here is this. When, in response to the strong question, the recursive function or serial connective is generalized as a theory of existence, Whitehead's claim is that the functional order must necessarily be understood as a matter of constructive or synthetic activity. However, recursive succession is not for Whitehead as it is for mathematical intuitionists a matter of synthetic activity understood as the mental activity of a directing mathematical subject.[14] His argument is quite different, and runs as follows: if the recursive structure $n + 1$ is generalized as the mind-independent structure of existence, *it must necessarily be a synthetic activity in that it (and nothing else) constructs its own nature out of its predecessors.*

Here we reach the heart of Whitehead's position: the complete generalization of the function discloses the indispensability of the speculative notion of activity. More precisely stated, his claim is that the serial nature of existence means that there is no such thing as direct, simultaneous relations between contemporary occasions or prehensions in different series, for in the nature of the case there is nothing to respond to until an occasion is completed. In serial theory all direct relations are relations to completed, immediately antecedent occasions or prehensions. Thus, the way in which and the extent to which any new term added to the series derives from the determinacy of the antecedent terms always involves some element of situated, free construction, which is what Whitehead means by "spontaneity" (AI 255, 258). That is, the recursive connection is the principle of its own synthetic activity; in Whitehead's words, his recursive acts or occasions are minimally free as "self-actualizing" (PR 47; AI 198). On this analysis, therefore, existence is primarily to be understood on the basis of a universal (transcendental[15]) theory of freedom: existence is a matter of activity in the particular sense that it is a recursive synthetic activity of self-actualization.

It follows that, in each of its instances, the serial act or occasion defines itself as intrinsically topic-relative or topic-saturated and so as always different, always unique (hence Whitehead terms the connectives "occasions"). Moreover, like numbers, serial acts or occasions can play a multiplicity of roles in any subsequent successor series; they become "factors," as Whitehead likes to put it. In serial analysis, the values of the variables of the recursive connective are themselves variables with infinite polyvalency in respect of their successors. A serial act or occasion is thus completely determinate in itself and ontologically value or indeterminate in respect of its relation to its successors (PR 215). By thus developing the Russellian view of the function as having meaning only in virtue of its values in terms of an ontologically generalized, free variable account of the successor operator, Whitehead is able to define his recursive connective as actual only in virtue of its instances (PR 7) and to secure the radically immanent finite character of the real.[16]

While the implications of Whitehead's analysis of the dynamical serial connective are too numerous to be drawn out here, four points are particularly relevant in terms of his relation to analytical metaphysics and to the speculative tradition.

In the first place, it is evident that Whitehead's dynamical serial connectives are synthetic subjects, or the "prehensive" components of synthetic subjects. In his terminology, they are acts or occasions of actualization, or the prehensive components of acts or occasions, which have the status of *cognitive* subject-occasions or prehensions only in certain instances. Thus, speculative serial analysis rejects the idea that there is an overarching, substantial unity that is the ground of synthesis, or that in cognition there is an ego that accompanies all our representations. The recursive, finite subject-occasion is not a transparently reflexive, transcendental unity of apperception that is completely present to itself as such, nor any kind of completely realized Absolute Subject. In this respect, Whitehead is close to Wittgenstein and to pragmatism in abandoning the traditional concepts of "mind" or cognition as a model for the principle of order. However, Whitehead's serial subject-occasion is not a mere effect of the differential structures of an algorithmic process, as in analytical metaphysics. Indeed, Whitehead's claim is that the rule-following proccsses that can be said to generate certain types of entities always require a reference to the agency of subject-occasions.[17] Serial process is not a relational activity without an actor, but is realized only through the activities of the situated subject-occasions of which it is the condition—as will be more fully explained in what follows.

In the second place, it is evident that the concrete act or occasion is offered by Whitehead as a self-explanatory ultimate that is not further derivable or explicable in terms of higher concepts. And the crucial point here is that it is not an ultimate that is nonrational or inconceivable. For Whitehead bypasses the usual opposition of the conceptual and ineffable by defining the ultimate as the nonconceptual; more specifically, as the nonconceptually given, irreducible unity of recursive structure and activity. That is to say, the concrete act or occasion, because it is the unity of rule-defining structure *with activity*, can be reduced neither to its component parts, nor to concepts, not even to the concept of functional rule (PR 20–22). And as an always situated or intrinsically unique differentiating activity, the concrete act or occasion can only be described by the same concept or concepts (PR 55). Nevertheless, on the model of Kant's account of the nonconceptually given or intuited nature of time (cf. PR 113), the nature of the concrete act or occasion is rationally and intelligibly describable through and through, and requires no further principle to unify it: there is no general serial connective of which particular serial connectives are instances, just as there is no general time of which particular times are instances.

More explicitly put, third: the concepts of "relational structure" and "activity"—the poles of the debate between analytical and speculative theories of process—are to be understood, not as fundamental opposites, or in terms of some order of priority or suprarational real, but as twin predicates of the concrete nonconceptual unity of the individual act or occasion. Their binary, equiprimordial relation is in Whitehead defined in terms of "convertibility": structure and activity are distinctions that are indissociable from and "convertible" or correlative with, one another, in that anything that has one character necessarily has the other character, and both are coextensive in the sense that they express a character which necessarily belongs to every element of the analysis. Another way of stating this is to say that, for Whitehead, in line with the speculative tradition, the unity of structure and activity is to be found in the intrinsically relational concept of power (PR 57–58, 213).

However, power is now defined, not in terms of a completely realized real, but as finite serial act. Moreover, in contrast to the analytical and speculative traditions alike, Whitehead subsumes both structure and activity to the finite serial act so that neither are endowed with any kind of priority or fundamental status, nor do they need to be suprarelationally transcended. Rather, both together express the ultimate, primordial complexity of the nature of the serial act.[18]

For Whitehead, what this means on the side of intrinsically relational or rule-defining structure is that, in contrast to analytical claims, it cannot be rendered fully intelligible or self-explanatory without reference to activity, understood as the self-actualizing activity of recursive subjects. What it means on the side of activity is that, in contrast to the traditional speculative position, relational or rule-defining structure is no longer a feature or predicate of some ineffable, non- or suprarelational activity of spontaneity; rather, activity or spontaneity is now a feature or predicate of the relational or rule-defining structure of serial order. Whitehead thus installs complex relational structure as intrinsic to the nature of spontaneous activity by defining it in terms of the functional rule of finite supersession. He removes the mystery of ineffability from spontaneous activity, but not the wonder of its nonconceptual ultimacy, by making it an intrinsic element of serially recursive process. In consequence, the nonconceptually given or intuited unity—the "togetherness" of predicates—that is the concrete serial act or occasion (PR 21–22) does not for Whitehead constitute any kind of problematic intuition of an ineffable that renders relations intrinsically connective, nor is it the "semantically confused" notion of Coffa's analytical history of philosophy.[19] Rather, the nonconceptually given or intuited unity of recursive structure and activity that is the concrete, serial act or occasion is rationally and intelligibly describable through and through precisely because it is an ultimate and irreducible given that is intrinsically rule-governed.

Thus, finally, the significance of Whitehead's concrete, serial act or occasion resides in this: there is no need here either to claim that the rational *is* the real, or to abandon speculative reflection for some rule-based operationalism or naturalism. Everything can be articulated in terms of recursive acts, without in any way compromising the serially constituted, irreducible gap between thought and existence. One day, perhaps, analytical and speculative philosophers will be ready to take the measure of Whitehead's claims, which amount to a massive attempt to fuse together two otherwise mutually indifferent, even mutually dismissive, traditions.

Notes

1. The strong question as formulated here, and its analysis throughout this essay, are offered as extended interpretations of what Whitehead

says about the explanatory purpose of philosophy at PR 20. I should add that an epistemic version of the strong question could be formulated as: Why do the rules of the function apply? For Whitehead, however, as will become evident, this epistemic question can only be answered ontologically, by making the functional structure of cognition an instance of structures larger than itself. The reason why, for Whitehead, the limits of reflection are not defined by the propositional function (or any cognate theory of language, meaning, or human action) will emerge in his response to the strong question about instantiation.

2. For Wittgenstein's influential view of "process," see his *Remarks on the Foundations of Mathematics*, ed. G. H. von Wright, R. Rhees, and G. E. M. Anscombe (Cambridge, Mass.: MIT Press, 1983), esp. pp. 68, 69, 95, and 246. For an excellent discussion, see Mathieu Marion, *Wittgenstein, Finitism, and the Foundations of Mathematics* (Oxford: Oxford University Press, 1998). The theory of calculative process has its origins in the *Tractatus* theory of recursive "operations" and issues in the later theory of "language games." The extraordinary convergences of the thought of Wittgenstein and Whitehead will become evident below, as also will the crucial differences.
3. See David Hume, *A Treatise of Human Nature*, ed. L. A. Selby-Bigge (Oxford: The Clarendon Press, 1968), Book I, Part III, Section V. On Kant, see G. Buchdahl, *Metaphysics and the Philosophy of Science* (Oxford: Basil Blackwell, 1969), chapter 8. On Frege, see Peter Geach, *God and the Soul* (London: Routledge and Kegan Paul, 1969), chapter 5, and Leila Haaparanta, "On Frege's Concept of Being," in *The Logic of Being*, eds. S. Knuuttila and J. Hintikka (Dordrecht: D. Reidl, 1986), pp. 269–289.
4. ESP 127–128; cf. MT 107. See Bertrand Russell, "On Denoting," in *Logic and Knowledge*, ed. Robert C. Marsh (London: Routledge and Kegan Paul, 1956), pp. 39–56. For an example of the numerical difference of the function, see Ludwig Wittgenstein, *Wittgenstein's Lectures on the Foundations of Mathematics, Cambridge 1939*, from the notes of R. Bosanquet, N. Malcolm, R. Rhees, and Y. Smythie (Ithaca: Cornell University Press, 1976), p. 237, which is discussed by Marion, *Wittgenstein, Finitism, and the Foundations of Mathematics*, pp. 158–159.
5. See F. P. Ramsey, *Notes on Philosophy, Probability, and Mathematics*, ed. M.-C. Galvotti (Naples: Bibliopolis, 1990). On Wittgenstein, see note 4 above.
6. See G. Frege, "Function and Concept (1891)," in *The Frege Reader*, ed. M. Beaney (Oxford: Basil Blackwell, 1997), p. 146.
7. See G. Frege, *The Foundations of Arithmetic*, trans. J. L. Austin (Evanston: Northwestern University Press, 1980).

8. For a Fregean interpretation of the later Plato's unwritten lecture on "Mathematics and the Good," see A. E. Taylor, *Plato: The Man and His Work* (London: Methuen and Co., 1926), chapter 19. Whitehead refers to this standard work in PR and uses Plato's title for an important late lecture of his own delivered in 1941 (see ESP 97–114).
9. Whitehead's theory of universals or "eternal objects" is too complex and problematic to be dealt with here. There can be no doubt, though, that it is an attempt to shift the theory of universals from its traditional basis in language into the framework of mathematical logic. To the present writer, it seems an increasingly redundant realist hangover as Whitehead's constructivist theory of occasions develops.
10. The form of free variable finitism which, I am suggesting, is Whitehead's speculative model is akin to that developed by the mathematician Thoralf Skolem in 1923. See T. Skolem, "The Foundations of Elementary Arithmetic established by means of the Recursive Mode of Thought Without Use of Apparent Variables ranging over Infinite Domains," in *From Frege to Goedel: A Sourcebook in Mathematical Logic, 1879–1931*, ed. J. van Heijenoort (Cambridge, Mass.: Harvard University Press, 1967). Whether or not Skolem's famous work, which was written in response to *Principia Mathematica*, provides the actual model for the theory of occasions developed in *Process and Reality* (1929) is irrelevant here, though it is highly unlikely that Whitehead did not know it. My point is this: a form of free variable finitism like Skolem's provides a powerful and illuminating model for Whitehead's theory of the nature of existence.
11. The paradox of the class of all those classes that do not contain themselves can be formulated thus: If such a class contained itself, it would not contain itself; for it contains *only* those classes that do not contain themselves. But, if it did not contain itself, it would contain itself; for it contains *all* those classes that do not contain themselves. Thus, contradictorily, any such class would contain itself if and only if it did not contain itself. See *Principia Mathematica*, chapter 2; for Whitehead's comments, see ESP 127–128. On the role of reflexive paradoxes in modern philosophers besides Whitehead, see Hilary Lawson, *Reflexivity* (La Salle, Ill.: Open Court, 1985).
12. A relation is asymmetrical when, for example, if x is earlier than y, y is not earlier than x. Asymmetry is the property of being incompatible with the converse (for an explication of this in terms of modern truth-functions see G. W. Shields, chapter 1 in this volume, section entitled "Analytic Themes in the Philosophy of Hartshorne"). A relation is transitive if and when it holds between A and B and also between B and C; it therefore holds between A and C; so that, for example, if x precedes y

and *y* precedes *z*, then *x* must precede *z*. A relation is irreflexive when no component of a series has those relations to itself that it has to other components of the series. Finally, because actualization is nothing else than the activity of serial acts or connectives, serial acts or connectives are necessarily consecutive in that the relation between any two terms in the series has no intermediate term or terms. On the series in mathematics, see B. Russell, *The Principles of Mathematics* (London: Routledge and Kegan Paul, 1992), chapter 24; *Introduction to Mathematical Philosophy* (London: Routledge and Kegan Paul, 1993), chapters 3-4; *Our Knowledge of the External World* (London: Allen and Unwin, 1914), Lecture II.

13. I follow Whitehead in employing the useful term *notion* here. Anything of which we have a notion (as opposed to a concept) is nonconceptual in nature, in a sense that will be defined below.

14. On Whitehead's relation to intuitionism, see my "Act, Event, Series Metaphysics, Mathematics and Whitehead," *The Journal of Speculative Philosophy* 10, no. 4 (1996): 233–248. Wolfe Mays has noted Whitehead's convergences with mathematical intuitionism in his *Whitehead's Philosophy of Science and Metaphysics* (The Hague: Martinus Nijhoff, 1977), chapter 3. Although I would regard MT as the most explicitly intuitionist or constructivist of Whitehead's works (see especially MT 91–93, 97), his constructivism is as clear as daylight once he announces in PR that the continuum is potential and not actual, as he had previously thought (PR 35, 61, 283; cf. PNK 202). As will become evident, however, his ontology of the recursive function places constructivism on a philosophical basis quite different from Kant, Husserl, Wittgenstein, Brouwer, or Dummett. See esp. note 18 below.

15. Contrary to the more or less universal, quasi-naturalist interpretation of Whitehead as maintaining that acts or occasions are extensive, tiny little contents of the world, I have argued elsewhere that the various categories of Whitehead's theory of process constitute a *new* kind of transcendental analysis: they are transcendental conditions of actualization. (As such, serial acts or occasions are not themselves extensive but are the conditions of extension.) See my "Transcendentalism and Speculative Realism in Whitehead," *Process Studies* 23, no. 3 (1994): 155–190. It is by means of this transcendentalism that Whitehead would resolve the debate between his colleagues McTaggart and Russell on the priority of dates (before/after) and tenses (past/present/future). See J. M. E. McTaggart, "The Unreality of Time," in his *Philosophical Studies* (London: Edward Arnold, 1934), pp. 110–131; B. Russell, "On the Experience of Time," *The Monist* 25 (1925): 212–223; C. D. Broad, *Scientific Thought* (London: Kegan Paul, 1923), chapter 2; D. H. Mellor, *Real*

Time (Cambridge: Cambridge University Press, 1981). Whitehead's transcendentalism allows him to hold that both dates and tenses are real, mind-independent features of time and that changes do not need to change in order to introduce real movement into the world. Moreover, he can sidestep the debate between empiricists and Kantians on the relative priority of time and causation, for both find their condition in the transcendental recursive series (PR 237, AI 202). For comments on my transcendental reading of Whitehead, see *L'effet Whitehead*, ed. I. Stengers et al. (Paris: Vrin, 1984), pp. 132–133; and Lewis S. Ford, "Structural Affinities Between Kant and Whitehead," *International Philosophical Quarterly* 38 (1998): 233–244.

16. In this context it is important to note that Whitehead's speculative categories are self-referentially inclusive in that they are fallible and revisable, in line with his constructivist leanings. For the constructivist, universally quantified propositions are not statements or assertions, but are "rules for judging" (Weyl) or "variable hypotheticals" (Ramsey) to the effect that, as Ramsey puts it, "If I meet a *phi*, I shall regard it as a *psi*." In Dummett's words: "Even if we operate with the classical conception of a large class of utterances that constitutes assertions with determinate truth conditions, we shall still need to acknowledge that not all informative utterances belong to that class. Other informative utterances may be classified, not as assertions of statements, but as expressions of claims; statements are to be assessed as true or false, but claims are justified or unjustified" (as cited in M. Marion, "Wittgenstein and Finitism," *Synthese* 105 (1995): 141–176; all the quotes given above are from this excellent article). Because they are not assertions but "schemes" (his word), Whitehead's categorial rules or claims are not determinately true or false; that is, the principle of bivalence does not apply to them (PR 8). And although bivalence is a semantic principle that makes no mention of negation, the nature of a claim can also be formulated in terms of the logical laws of the object-language to the effect that the law of excluded middle (either *p* or *not-p*) does not apply to the claims for they are not assertions. A consequence of this is that a given set of rules or claims is not exclusive of alternative rules or claims (PR 7–8) Further, the proof or construction of a claim is an example. That is, a proof or construction is a method for obtaining categorial "applications," as Whitehead calls them (PR 8; cf. AI 221–223, FR 43). There could be no clearer indications than these that Whitehead defines the status of his speculative categories on the model of constructivist mathematical definitions of the status of general arithmetical propositions about natural numbers.

17. Thus, for Whitehead, "existence" in the primary sense of the term refers to subject-occasions. However, in the widest sense it refers to whatever is a factor in, or "makes a difference to," the activities of subject-occasions, such as mathematical objects, languages, social practices, even fictional entities. He sometimes uses the term *real* to distinguish these secondary, derivative types of existents from the acts or occasions that construct them (AI 197, 294; cf. 119–120), but such reals are all possible subjects of quantification. Like Russell, but unlike Quine, quantification is not for Whitehead a criterion of the nature of ontological commitment (see the discussions of McHenry and Quine, chapters 7 and 8 in this volume).
18. It may be asked here if functional form and activity are to be understood as real, virtual or formal distinctions, and as principles that are in some sense prior to the concrete, serial act, and consequently derive their unity from some still higher term. In serial analysis, however, distinctions are not distinctions *in* independent substances, as on the medieval model, but distinctions among the modes of the complex of relations of the serial connective. The traditional metaphysical debate between types of distinctions is here a matter of indifference, for relations of situation or perspective are part of the serial order of the ultimate, which is nothing else than the connectivity of acts or occasions. In Whitehead, to put it broadly, there is no opposition between metaphysical realism and constructivism, for the real is itself an activity of construction. Hence the traditional types of distinction, while they can be usefully employed in certain contexts, in serial analysis no longer have final metaphysical significance.
19. See Alberto Coffa, *The Semantic Tradition from Kant to Carnap: To the Vienna Station* (Cambridge: Cambridge University Press, 1991), chapter 1.

Chapter 7

Quine and Whitehead

Ontology and Methodology

LEEMON McHENRY

Editor's Comment: McHenry's interesting comparison between Quine and Whitehead elicited Quine's own response in the proceeding chapter. Originally composed while serving as a visiting research scholar in the Department of Philosophy at UCLA (where McHenry was enabled to receive input from such Quine scholars as Roger Gibson), this essay represents a pointed example of contributions to the "seamless sensibility" of some contemporary historiographers mentioned in the introductory essay as one aim of this book. Aside from the important comparative aspects of this chapter, I find it extremely helpful as a quite lucid overview of Quine's general philosophical project. Unlike numerous discussions of Quine that concentrate on a few specific positions (e.g., the indeterminacy of translation thesis), McHenry calls attention to the importance for Quine of his view of philosophy as systematic revisionary metaphysics of nature guided by advances in the empirical sciences. In the light of this interpretation, Quine thus appears to be clearly and fundamentally connected to that wing of the analytic tradition which is preoccupied with the empirical scientific worldview—namely, the tradition of Russell, Broad, Carnap, and the Whitehead of the "panphysics" period—as opposed to the descriptive metaphysicians of P. F. Strawson's and Donald Davidson's ilk.

Introduction

The very idea of a basis for comparing the philosophies of W. V. Quine and A. N. Whitehead may be surprising to most philosophers, including Quine himself. Both produced systems of thought that have taken philosophy in two completely different directions. Quine's thought has remained at the forefront of contemporary analytic philosophy for the better part of the twentieth century, while Whitehead's influence has been reserved for a relatively small number of devotees who have cut their own path. With regard to the latter, Anthony Quinton has remarked: "Outside the sequestered province of the cult, Whitehead is regarded with a measure of baffled reverence, mingled with suspicion."[1] While Whitehead was clearly made of "the right stuff," says Quinton, his philosophical writings have been utterly incomprehensible to the general philosophical community.

In this paper, I make a case for a number of common themes between Quine and Whitehead in their approach to ontology, especially when Quine's views are compared with the work of Whitehead's middle period on the foundations of physics. Allegiance to one or the other of the warring factions within philosophy, that is, the analytic versus the speculative, has prevented notice of these common themes. I hope to show that the boundary that separates the two thinkers is not as precisely drawn as most have supposed.[2] Moreover, as new "-isms" have emerged on the philosophical scene as of late (e.g., deconstructionism, postmodern relativism), the gulf that separates Whitehead and analytical philosophy is not as great as it used to be.[3]

Before I begin to explore the affinities, as well as some contrasts, between Quine and Whitehead, a word of caution is in order. It is well known that Quine wrote his doctoral dissertation, "The Logic of Sequences: A Generalization of *Principia Mathematica*," under Whitehead's direction.[4] Quine also took two of Whitehead's seminars at Harvard, "Science and the Modern World" and "Cosmologies Ancient and Modern," but he says that he "responded little to these courses" and "took refuge in his relatively mathematical material on 'extensive abstraction.'" Despite Quine's statement that he "retained a vivid sense of being in the presence of the great," he does not acknowledge any philosophical influence from Whitehead. Rather, Carnap and Russell are cited as the inspirations of Quine's early development.[5]

When Quine overlapped with Whitehead at Harvard, Whitehead was deeply involved in working out the details of his metaphysics of process—a philosophic vision that ran against the spirit of the times. Just prior to Whitehead's "metaphysical period," however, he had devoted his attention to a general ontology of physics and a theory of natural knowledge. This is where Whitehead and Quine connect.

General Common Themes

Although most interpreters of Quine's philosophy focus their attention on disparate doctrines (e.g., inscrutability of reference, indeterminacy of translation) in isolation from the broader framework, Quine is clearly a systematic philosopher. That is, unlike a philosopher such as Wittgenstein whose thought promoted reflection on bite-size analytical problems of an antimetaphysical nature, Quine's thought forms a systematic whole in which the apparently disparate doctrines have their place. Quine is a linguistic philosopher, but not one who takes a piecemeal approach to philosophical problems. As Roger Gibson persuasively argues, "Quine's philosophy is a systematic attempt to answer, from a uniquely empirical point of view, what he takes to be the central question of epistemology, namely, 'How do we acquire our theory of the world?'"[6] The answer that follows is a system in which logic, mathematics, linguistics, ontology, and natural science form a whole. The key elements to this system are: naturalism, physicalism, and empiricism.[7]

Quine is also credited, along with Strawson, with resurrecting metaphysics from the hands of the logical positivists. As Quine came to recognize the failure of such projects as Carnap's attempt to reduce all theoretical language of science to experiential terms, he became increasingly committed to a holism in which the theoretical and experiential terms of a scientific theory hang together when confronting experience. The positivists who sought to separate these two had thrown the baby out with the bathwater because much of a scientific theory is unverifiable in principle. Metaphysics, for Quine, is the general and abstract end of a continuum with the natural sciences. It is not the transcendent or speculative metaphysics of the rationalists, but rather a naturalized metaphysics that originates in the natural sciences and forms an essential part of our theory of the world.

Quine's naturalism contends that our attempt to discover what there is cannot rise above our scientific theories and, in particular, our theories of physics (TT 67–68; LPV 44). This view commits him to the revisionary over the descriptive approach to metaphysics. Strawson's espousal of the descriptive approach has privileged the role of ordinary language in our attempt to make meaningful sense of the world (IDM 9–12). Grammar is the guide to ontology. For Quine, however, the descriptive metaphysician does not begin to do justice to the role of science in shaping our worldview. In fact, it appears to sidestep science completely in the attempt to discover another way to truth by restricting philosophy to mere conceptual analysis. This is not to say that the turn to language was wrong, but that the linguistically oriented philosopher must conduct his or her inquiry within the framework of the scientific enterprise. Philosophy, in this manner, works with the cutting-edge discoveries of science in the pursuit of truth. If physics posits an ontology that is contrary to common sense (and ordinary language), so much the worse for common sense. The revision of the categories is always a genuine option for philosophy and science. In this way, particles such as quarks and leptons or the space-time regions of field theory may turn out to be ontologically basic rather than the macrobodies of perception.

The last general theme concerns the relation between logic and metaphysics. The logical positivists regarded logic as a neutral instrument that could be used with great effect because it did not commit one to any ontology at all. Quine, however, has always been interested in the metaphysical implications of logic. Specifically, he has focused on the problem of how our statements commit us to what there is (LPV 1–19; OR 95–96). Quine argues that we commit ourselves to the existence of entities by the use of the bound variable in quantification logic. To be is to be the value of the bound variable (LPV 12). This criterion does not tell us what there is, but rather what we are committed to saying there is. As mentioned above, the attempt to determine our ontology is another matter of fixing our overall conceptual scheme that best accommodates science.

In his foreword to Quine's *A System of Logistic*, Whitehead seems to have anticipated the general point of Quine's theory when he wrote that: "logic prescribes the shape of metaphysical thought."[8] For example, in *Principia Mathematica*, Whitehead and Russell put Φ and Ψ in quantifiers—for example, '(∃Φ)(x)Φx' such that attributes become variables in their own right. As Quine says, "The effect of letting 'Φ,' 'Ψ,' etc. occur in quantifiers, now, is that these letters cease to be fragments merely of dummy matrices 'Φ,' 'Ψ,' etc., and come to share the genuinely referential power of 'x,' 'y,' etc."[9] Throughout Whitehead's philosophy, he proposes an ontology that is dualistic in the sense of recognizing both individuals and properties. In Quine's logic, however, individuals and classes are properly quantified over—for example, '(∃x)(Φx)'—but not attributes (LPV 102–103, OR 91–92). This has an important consequence for "the shape" of Quine's ontology in that he does not recognize properties or attributes in addition to objects or individuals. As he puts the point: "Properties were vaguely assumed in *Principia* as further denizens of the universe, but they serve no good purpose that is not better served by classes, and moreover they lack a clear criterion of identity."[10]

With regard to these general themes—the importance of systematic philosophy, naturalism, revisionary metaphysics, and the metaphysical implications of logical theory—there is little with which Whitehead would disagree. As a systematic philosopher, Whitehead's early concern was to demonstrate the unity of the natural sciences by producing a general science of nature. He called this endeavor "pan-physics" because the central motivation behind his project was the crisis in physics at the turn of the century—the second "awakening from dogmatic slumber" (R 4). The revolutionary theories of gravitation and electricity have "made urgent the question, What are the ultimate data of science?" (PNK v). Once the foundations of physics are recast in an ontology that accommodates the advances, the other natural sciences, such as astronomy, geology, and biology, should follow suit. Whitehead's system, then, involved the latest mathematical, scientific and philosophical thought converging to produce a novel metaphysics and epistemology.

It should be obvious that this system is naturalistic in one important sense of Quine's meaning. Naturalism, Quine says, "sees natural science as an inquiry into reality, fallible and corrigible but not answerable to any supra-scientific tribunal, and not in need of any justification beyond observation and the hypothetico-deductive method" (TT 722). At this point in Whitehead's philosophical development, he claimed not to be engaged in "metaphysics" because his inquiry excluded consideration of the nature of the observing mind (CN 2–4). His panphysics, however, is metaphysical in the sense of being at the general end of a theory that originates in natural science. This contrasts sharply with the traditional conception of metaphysics as a pure, *a priori* discipline with some special grasp of truth apart from scientific investigation. As Quine puts the point, naturalism abandons the goal of a "first philosophy."

In holding that it is cutting-edge science, not armchair speculation or an *a priori* investigation of the categories, that determines our general ontology, Whitehead and Quine are in general agreement about the legitimacy of revisionary conceptual schemes. This of course does not imply that anything goes, but rather that a system of thought that revises our ordinary thought has to be firmly grounded in the advancing natural sciences. The gods of Homer or astrology will not compete as "best theories" in this sense.

Whitehead long held that ordinary language of the standard subject-predicate form distorts our conception of reality. The descriptive projects of Strawson and his intellectual predecessors, such as Aristotle, have taken as basic a historical accident of the structure of Greek and other Indo-European languages, such as English. The result is a conception of substance as the ultimate substratum. But this has been a disaster as an epistemological foundation for the empirical sciences (CN 16–20). As Berkeley discovered, the concept of matter has thereby become disconnected from the complex of immediate fact and survives as a mere abstraction of thought.

When Whitehead repudiated substance philosophy and posited an ontology of events in its place, many such as Strawson would claim that he ceased to make sense (IDM 46–47, 59–86). If Whitehead is right, however, Einstein, Bohr, and Heisenberg, not ordinary language philosophers, are at the forefront of making sense.

The advances in logicomathematical schemes at the outset of the twentieth century provided the impetus for Whitehead's first major contributions, *Universal Algebra* and (with Russell) *Principia Mathematica.* On the one hand, these advances led to the reformulation of the definition of mathematics, from "the science of discrete and continuous magnitude" to the more general concept of "the science concerned with the logical deduction of consequences from the general premises of all reasoning."[11] on the other hand, specific technical devices developed in Whitehead's early works provided the tools for the organization of thought in other endeavors such as cosmology and metaphysics. One such device with enormous metaphysical implications for Whitehead was the logic of relations, initially pioneered by Peirce and DeMorgan.

Paraphrasing Russell, the logic of relations gave thought wings whereas the categorical logic of Aristotle caused it to flutter.[12] Instead of thinking of relations as attributes of substances—as reducible to the subject-predicate pattern—polyadic relations of modern symbolic logic allow us to treat each term in the relation as an individual in its own right. So "*x* is larger than *y*," symbolized *xLy*, preserves the two individuals in the relation rather than absorbing *y* into the predicate. The immediate consequence was crucial for the foundation of mathematics in *Principia Mathematica* because it allowed all sorts of distinctions of order and sense for quantitative differences, for example, transitive and asymmetrical relations.[13]

For Whitehead, the logic of relations provided a basis for metaphysical pluralism against the antirelational arguments of monists such as Bradley. This new logic was put to work in his Royal Society paper of 1906, "On Mathematical Concepts of the Material World," and was applied further to the structure of events in *The Principles of Natural Knowledge.* The primary relation of "extending over" is his fundamental idea from which all else, such as points, lines and planes, are derived (PNK 101). Later, in *Process and Reality,* the asymmetric relation of the temporal process becomes fundamental and his theory of extension is modified so that extension is derived from process.

The Ontology of Events

Moving now from the general to the specific, the main point of contact between Quine and Whitehead is their view of the physical world: an ontology of events consistent with the four-dimensional structure of space-time.

In *Word and Object*, Quine advances his project of regimentation of ordinary language in order to create an extensional language for science.[14] In accordance with the Einstein-Minkowski concept of space-time, for example, he translates tensed sentences into a canonical notation that interprets a specific time as a "slice of the four-dimensional material world, exhaustive spatially and perpendicular to the time axis" (WO 172). Physical objects in this world, he says, "are not to be distinguished from events or, in the concrete sense of the term, processes" (cf. WO 171, ER 167). "A body is thus visualized eternally as a four-dimensional whole, extending up and down, north and south, east and west, hence and ago. A shrinking body is seen as tapered toward the hence; a growing body is tapered toward the ago" (PL 30). These are the "worms" of space-time, or the "world-lines" of Minkowski's theory.

Quine's generalized notion of a physical object or event is intentionally broad so as to accommodate whatever objects are posited by science, such as particles, waves, electromagnetic fields, and organisms. It also allows us to think of mass substances, such as all the world's sugar, sand, dirt, or water, as discontinuous physical objects (TT 10). All of the above constitute the values of the variables of quantification.

Because ordinary bodies fail to provide clear criteria for identity and individuation, Quine says that his liberal notion of a physical object, as any portion of space-time, spares us this pointless task (WPO 497). Furthermore, as physics continues to probe the subatomic realm, the same problem increasingly applies to particles. It was only by rough analogy that the comparison between bodies and particles was useful anyway. With the convertability of matter and energy, "field theory is the order of the day" (WPO 499). It is in relation to field theory that the notion of an event is especially promising as an ontological foundation for physics; the various states are ascribed to regions of the electromagnetic field and bodies seem to fade altogether from the picture. Once again, whether we call this an ontology of "physical objects," "events," or "portions of space-time," it is all the same for Quine.

As discussed above, when Whitehead asked the question about the ultimate data of science, which had been made urgent by advancing physics, he was in search of a unifying concept. Substances and physical bodies in the Aristotelian sense no longer answered the question. With the fusions of time and space, and matter and energy, in Einstein's theory of relativity, a new ontology was required. Whitehead saw this requirement as an opportunity to set physics back on solid empirical foundations by proposing that the basic particulars are events. As he says: "What we discern is the specific character of a place through a period of time. This is what I mean by an 'event'" (CN 52).

Physical objects in Whitehead's theory are conceived in roughly the same way as they are in Quine's view. All aspects of endurance and stability in nature must be explained in terms of events of varying durations. His example is *Cleopatra's Needle* on the Embankment in London. The enormous and seemingly permanent structure may not appear to be an event by comparison with the short duration of the traffic accident below. Whitehead argues, however, that the abiding structure is simply a relatively stable situation in the stream of events constituting this permanence of character, and the difference between it and the traffic accident is merely one of time-span (CN 165–67). *Cleopatra's Needle* just happens to be a rather monotonous, long-lasting event.

Within the duration of one's specious present, we discern subordinate events by, whole-part relations, from which we can eventually construct the elements of geometry via the method of extensive abstraction. Working outward from the specious present, the larger space-time structure is known only as *relata* in relation to the entities in the discerned Field. This is what Whitehead calls the "discernible." For example, the orbits of planets in distant galaxies are not at present discerned but are, in principle, discernible. The discerned is always part of the broader field of the discernible. This notion, that events are interrelated to form the space-time structure of nature, is the basis for Whitehead's doctrine of significance. Space-time is, in fact, an abstraction from the concrete order of events.

Given the interrelatedness of events, how are events identified and individuated? Sense-awareness does not apprehend definite spatiotemporal limits in events. Whether events are longer or shorter, extended over or extending over, depends on our descriptions of them. The properties ingredient in events, however, provide certain natural boundaries for our attempts at demarcation (CN 144).

Quine's very definition of a physical object or event, as "the material content of any portion of space-time, however irregular and discontinuous and heterogeneous," recognizes the fact that there are no precise lines to draw (TT 10; WO 171). Space-time is 'gerrymandered' to suit our purposes. Language creates a "vaguely varied and very untidy ontology," that Quine's regimentation seeks to tame (TT 9). "There is room for choice," he says, "and one chooses with a view to simplicity in one's overall system of the world" (TT 10). His generalized ontology allows us such theoretical latitude in that it does not tie our hands to any specific way that events or physical objects must be conceived. It is, after all, the business of science, not ontology, to tell us specifically what there is.

As to whether there are functionally relevant groupings in nature in the Whiteheadian sense, Quine's theory is less clear. Quine's discussion of natural kinds seems to point in this direction, given his view that there are both intuitive and taxonomic kinds that are useful for language learning and more general theoretical pursuits, but he refuses to admit properties to his ontology in favor of classes (OR 1 14–38).

Physical objects or events are identical, Quine argues, if and only if they are spatiotemporally coextensive. In other words, two events *e* and e' are identical when they occupy the same place at the same time. But how do we individuate the identical regions of space-time in the general sense? Quine says that formal logic does the job with the notion of an *extension family*—a family of vaguely delimited classes, each class being comprised of nested [events]" (ER 168). Each event consists in the activities of some region so that a spatially small event is contained in a Chinese box of larger ones extending outward to the vast event of the whole universe. This certainly sounds like the Whitehead of *Principles of Natural Knowledge*, but again, how does Quine make sense of the boundaries of the space-time regions without recognizing the existence of properties?

Whitehead's ontology is dualistic, containing events and properties (which he called "objects"). Quine's ontology is also dualistic, containing events (which he calls "physical objects") and classes. Do the two fundamental and irreducible types do the same work in the end? Whereas Whitehead's "events" are nonrepeatable particulars, his "objects" are the "recognizable permanencies in nature of various grades of subtlety" (PNK 82). His objects, on the other hand, are the recognizable and repeatable entities in nature. Examples include: sense objects, such as colors and sounds; perceptual objects, such as ordinary macroscopic bodies; and scientific objects, such as electrons and molecules. Without them, science would be impossible; laws of nature are discoveries of patterns of objects in the passage of events (PNK 87).

In Quine's well-swept ontology, classes were only begrudgedly admitted for services rendered. As he puts the point:

> Physical objects in this generous sense constitute a fairly lavish universe, but more is wanted—notably numbers. Measurement is useful in cookery and commerce, and in the fullness of time it rises to a nobler purpose: the formulation of quantitative laws. These are the mainstay of scientific theory, and they call upon the full resources of the real numbers. (TT 13–14)

Since numbers are ultimately reducible to classes, the latter are the abstract entities that Quine finally recognizes. Like Whitehead, he sees that science would be impossible without them (WPO 500-01).

Some Important Differences

Although classes and properties may do some of the same ontological work for science, they are not the same entities. For Quine, however, the legitimate needs that apparently called for properties can be dealt with by classes. In his view, the scientific demand for exactitude requires that we reject properties as bona fide members of our ontology. His stringent requirement for admission is summarized by his criterion, "No entity without identity" (TT 102). For any entity considered as a real object, there should exist some general criterion of identity for all things of the general kind to which the entity belongs. Classes are identical when their members are identical. But there is, Quine argues, no such clear principle for properties. As he says, if he must comes to terms with Platonism, the least he can do is keep it extensional (TT I 00).

Whereas Quine identifies physical objects with events in the broadest sense, for Whitehead they are not identical: physical objects are conceived as relatively stable patterns in events. Events are primary; objects are secondary. Whitehead's reason for this distinction is based on his claim that events are the entities we directly perceive. Nothing is known in an instant. The primary objects of knowledge are events known only within the specious present of an observer.

This difference in the way Whitehead and Quine understand events is rooted in their different approaches to empiricism. For Whitehead's theory of natural knowledge, all that there is for knowledge is contained within nature itself. On one front, he argues against the pure phenomenalism of Berkeley by attempting to secure the independence of nature from the knowing mind. On the other front, he argues against the "bifurcation of nature" into two systems: a world of phenomenal appearances in the mind and a world of objects that are the inferred causes of the appearances. Descartes, Locke, and Kant were, in different ways, guilty of bifurcation. As an alternative to classical British empiricism, he affirms the "radical empiricism" proposed by William James. Whitehead's notion of an event closely parallels the duration of the specious present. Perception, he says, is an awareness of events or happenings (PNK 68). "Experience" means more than just sense experience; it is phenomenologically dense and includes the perception of time as an essential component. In this way, he contends, the immediate perception of events is our most important source of evidence for the pure ontology of events.

The place of the concept of the "specious present" in Whitehead's theory makes his version of empiricism significantly different from Quine's. They both hold that whatever evidence there is for science is sensory evidence, but "sensory evidence" for Quine is construed within the context of behavioristic psychology.

Defending science from within, for Quine, means that we start with empirical psychology in order to demonstrate how we account for the link between observation and theory—"between the meager input and the torrential output" (OR 83). Quine thus takes one step further back than Whitehead in his analysis of sensory evidence, because he starts not with perception but with *reception* construed as nerve endings receiving stimulation.

Conclusion

There is a tendency among analytic philosophers to consider Whitehead (if indeed they consider him at all) as having made major contributions to logic and philosophy up through *The Principles of Natural Knowledge* and *The Concept of Nature*. In this paper, I have limited my focus to these works simply for the sake of making the comparison with Quine's ontology, with no negative assessment of Whitehead's later work implied. In the later work, in which process became the fundamental idea, Whitehead developed a comprehensive metaphysics characterized by event-atomism, panpsychism, and a nontraditional theism. Quine's views, on the other hand, have been refined by a shift in emphases over the years. But the big picture, with its physicalism, naturalism, and quasi-Platonism remains the same.

After the dust settles from the twentieth century, it is up to the historians of philosophy to determine whether Quine's philosophy shares enough with Whitehead's to justify their membership in a common movement or trend. I have made my case mainly on the basis that both Quine and Whitehead are in serious pursuit of the way things are in contrast to the more limited view of philosophy as a kind of conceptual self-understanding.[16]

Notes

Works cited have been identified by the following abbreviation:

ER W. V. Quine. "Events and Reification," in *Actions and Events: Perspectives on the Philosophy of Donald Davidson.* Ed. by Ernest LePore and Brian McLaughlin. Oxford: Blackwell, 1985.

LPV W. V. Quine. *From a Logical Point of View.* New York: Harper and Row, 1963.

OR W. V. Quine. *Ontological Relativity and Other Essays.* New York: Columbia University Press, 1969.

PL W. V. Quine. *Philosophy of Logic.* Cambridge, Mass.: Harvard University Press, 1970.

TT W. V. Quine. *Theories and Things.* Cambridge, Mass.: Harvard University Press, 1981.

WO W. V. Quine. *Word and Object.* Cambridge, Mass.: The MIT Press. 1960.

WPO W. V. Quine. "Whither Physical Objects?," in *Boston Studies in the Philosophy of Science.* Ed. by R. S. Cohen et al. Dordrecht: D. Reidel, 1976.

IDM P. F. Strawson. *Individuals: An Essay in Descriptive Metaphysics.* London: Methuen, 1959.

1. Anthony Quinton, "The Right Stuff," *The New York Review of Books* 32, no. 19 (1985), p. 52 (review article on Victor Lowe's *Alfred North Whitehead: The Man and His Work*, vol. I: 1861–1910).
2. As analytical philosophy has recently become preoccupied with its own history there has been a certain amount of dispute over what constitutes the origin of the analytic tradition. On the one hand, Michael Dummett (*Origins of Analytical Philosophy* [Cambridge, Mass.: Harvard University Press, 1994]) has claimed that post-Fregian analytic philosophy is distinguished by the foundational role of the philosophy of language, particularly by the search for a viable theory of meaning. This has the odd consequence of denying Russell membership to the tradition, given his complaint that philosophy so conceived does not attempt to understand the world but only sentences. On the other hand, P. M. S. Hacker (*Wittgenstein's Place in Twentieth Century Analytic Philosophy* [Oxford: Blackwell, 1996]) sees a schism over the relationship between philosophy and science. Those who see a sharp distinction between the two

regard philosophy as a quest for human understanding via conceptual clarity. Wittgenstein, Ryle, Austin, and Strawson, then, are the quintessential analytical philosophers because they eschew the orientation of the scientific investigator as a guideline for philosophical work, that is, scientism. By contrast, those who see both philosophy and science as engaged in a collaborative effort for truth about the world have abandoned the true analytic ambition. But now if Russell, Carnap, and Quine are so charged, then there is even more reason to see the kinship between Whitehead and Quine.

3. In this connection, see chapter 1 of this volume and the Special Focus of *Process Studies* 25 (1996): "On the Interface of Analytic and Process Philosophy," ed. by George Shields. Also see George Lucas, *The Rehabilitation of Whitehead* (Albany: State University of New York Press, 1990), chapter 8.
4. Quine's dissertation was subsequently revised and published under the title, *A System of Logistic* (Cambridge: Harvard University Press, 1934).
5. "Autobiography of' W. V. Quine," in *The Philosophy of W. V. Quine*, The Library of Living Philosophers, Vol. XVIII. ed. Lewis Hahn and Paul Schilpp (La Salle, Ill.: Open Court, 1986), pp. 9–10.
6. Roger Gibson, in *The Philosophy of W. V. Quine: An Expository Essay* (Tampa, Fla.: University of South Florida Press, 1988), quotes Stuart Hampshire's comment that Quine is "the most distinguished living systematic philosopher" and notes how surprising this remark is for most analytic philosophers (p. xvii).
7. Roger Gibson, "The Key to Interpreting Quine," *The Southern Journal of Philosophy* 30, no. 4 (1992): 17–30. Also see, "Introduction" and Quine's "Three Indeterminacies," in *Perspectives on Quine,* ed. Robert Barrett and Roger Gibson (Cambridge, Mass.: Basil Blackwell, 1990), pp. xiii–xxiii and 1–16.
8. *A System of Logistic*, p. x.
9. See Quine's "Whitehead and the Rise of Modern Logic," in *The Philosophy of Alfred North Whitehead*, The Library of Living Philosophers, Vol. III, ed. Paul A. Schilpp (New York: Tudor Publishing Company, 1941), p. 145.
10. Quine, *The Time of My Life: An Autobiography* (Cambridge, Mass.: The MIT Press), p. 85.
11. A. N. Whitehead, "Mathematics," in *Encyclopedia Britannica,* 11th ed.; reprinted in *Science and Philosophy* (New York: Philosophical Library, 1974), pp. 282, 291.
12. Bertrand Russell, *Our Knowledge of the External World* (New York: Mentor,1956), p. 53.

13. See Bertrand Russell, "Principia Mathematica: Mathematical Aspects," in *My Philosophical Development* (London: George Allen and Unwin, 1959), pp. 86–101.
14. That is, given the anomalies of ordinary language (vagueness, ambiguity, and various failures of reference), Quine seeks a regimentation of scientific and ontological language by the purely extensional device of mathematical logic.
15. This question leaves aside for the moment Quine's fantasy of hyper-Pythagoreanism in which physical objects give way to classes constructed on the empty class (cf: TT 17–18; WPO 502–503).

I wish to thank David Griffin for the invitation to write this paper for first Forum of *Process Studies*. I am indebted to the UCLA philosophy department for a visiting scholarship and various forms of support during the time in which I wrote this paper. W. V. Quine, Roger Gibson, Kit Fine, David Kaplin, and David Griffin provided criticism and suggested improvements to an earlier draft.

Chapter 8

Response to Leemon McHenry

WILLARD VAN ORMAN QUINE

Editor's Comment: This chapter is one of W. V. O. Quine's last published writings prior to his death in 2000. It is particularly important and appropriate that he be directly represented in a book dealing with Whitehead and contemporary analytic philosophy, especially given that Quine went to Harvard University expressly to study with the great coauthor of the celebrated Principia. *It is also not to be forgotten that it was Quine alone who was entrusted with the task of treating Whitehead's contributions to the development of symbolic logic and modern extensions of algebra in the celebrated Open Court Library of Living Philosophers Series volume on* The Philosophy of Alfred North Whitehead. *Some of the issues concerning quantification discussed by Quine and McHenry are broached by James Bradley in chapter 6 (see especially note 17). Also observe the* prima facie *conflicting claims about Quine and the possibility of metaphysics in the essays by McHenry and Goodwin: for McHenry, Quine advocates a metaphysics much akin to that of the "middle period" Whitehead (a claim receiving an affirmation—with a qualification about properties—from Quine himself); on the other hand, for Goodwin, a truly adequate response to Quine's critique of quantified modal logic requires a commitment to the very "possibility of metaphysics." The different claims are perhaps to be explained semantically. Goodwin is using the term* metaphysics *in a sense signifying "specifications of transcendental conditions for coherent talk about possible worlds, individual identity, and essential properties," whereas McHenry is using* metaphysics *to signify Quine's project of "presenting a view of the whole as provided by the materials of the empirical natural sciences and as shaped by an extensionalist quantificational logic" (my language here). It is my suggestion that Quine can be seen as affirming metaphysics in the latter sense, but denying it in the first sense.*

McHenry ascribes to Whitehead a dualistic ontology of individuals and properties, and to me a monistic ontology of individuals, including classes. I protest that my ontology is as dualistic as Whitehead's and indeed the same as his except that classes have a clean-cut principle of individuation, namely coextensiveness, whereas properties have none. The nearest I can come to a principle of individuation for properties is that they are identical when they are necessarily coextensive. This I reject because of not understanding "necessarily." Hence my renunciation of properties in favor of classes; for there is no entity without identity.

I cannot recall seeing anything explained in terms of properties that could not be explained equally to my satisfaction in terms of classes. No wonder, since the only difference between classes and properties is the enigma of diversity of coextensive properties. Let us not confuse the mere use of an adjective phrase with the appeal to a property. Appeal to a property, or to any thing, involves reckoning it as the object of an essential pronoun, hence as the value of a variable. Perhaps this point bears on McHenry's puzzling puzzlement over how we can "make sense of the boundaries of the space-time regions without recognizing the existence of properties." Perhaps he is making sense of such boundaries by means of phrases, intelligible as such, which he takes to be names of properties.

It is over properties that my clear disagreement with Whitehead lies, and the only one I think of. It dates back sixty-eight years to my senior year as a mathematics student at Oberlin College, when I immersed myself in Whitehead and Russell's *Principia Mathematica*. The authors were chary of classes, but receptive to what they called propositional functions, which were properties and relations "in intension."

Whitehead and Russell were heedless of the individuation of propositional functions, but punctilious about justifying the extensionality of classes by contextual definition of classes in terms of propositional functions. Once these beclouded preliminaries were out of the way in favor of classes, the ensuing chapters of the three monumental volumes commanded my unbounded admiration.

I recall Sir Karl Popper's figure of a bottomless bog into which we have vertically sunk many long piles to support the structure which is our theory of the world. The swampy ground is our sensory input, instinct, and untutored common sense, and it affords a firm foundation thanks only to the depth and multitude of the piles. Could this have been Whitehead and Russell's intuition in starting with the unindividuated properties that reflect the vagaries of our undisciplined adjective phrases?

If this accounts for their procedure, it still does not justify it. For they had to quantify over properties, that is, propositional functions, in their contextual definition of classes. In so doing, they reified properties, incurring the responsibility, never discharged, of individuating them. They might better have assumed the classes outright. What was missing was a clear standard of ontic commitment. Hence my stress on essential pronouns and values of variables. But the properties stayed on in Whitehead's later philosophy as ill-individuated structural elements of science.

I agree with Whitehead in drawing no basic distinction between events and bodies. He draws the commonsense distinction, a matter of degree, with which I have no quarrel. I think that all of us who envision nature in terms of modern logic must share this attitude, for logic makes no distinctive structural provision for time and the tenses of verbs. We are already shunted into four-dimensional thinking quite independently of relativity physics.

McHenry asks how we individuate spatiotemporal objects. Perhaps he misses the answer because it is too close to his eyes: the objects are identical if they coincide; if they are coextensive. In individuation, for me, there is no requirement of observability. It is only a matter of an identity standard couched in terms as clear as the rest of one's science.

Nor is failure of individuation to be confused with mere vagueness. The so-called surface of what I call my desk is vague at the molecular level, and all of the myriad almost identical masses that are enveloped by that cushion of vagueness qualify equally as my desk. But I intend "my desk" to designate one and only one of those masses. The vagueness is in my words and not in their ineluctable physical designatum. Meanwhile the individuation is quite in order: spatiotemporal coincidence.

Chapter 9

De Re Modality and the Ontological Argument

GEORGE L. GOODWIN

Editor's Comment: This formidable essay puts forward, in a compressed way and with new discussions of relevant literature, a central argument of Professor Goodwin's impressive University of Chicago Ph.D. thesis on Hartshorne's ontological argument. Published in the American Academy of Religion Distinguished Dissertation Series in 1978, it consequently received attention from Hartshorne scholars, theologians, and philosophers of religion, but not from the community of analytic philosophers at large, despite its relevant subject matter and despite the fact that its main argument contra Quine was appreciated by Leonard Linsky, editor of the Oxford Readings on "Reference and Modality" and a dissertation committee member. Thus, one motivation for including this essay, published here for the first time in a non-European venue, is to help Goodwin's argument reach the wider analytic audience it merits. Moreover, this chapter is connected to the remaining ones in important ways: its argument for the intelligibility of de re *modality provides a significant background justification for the efforts of Billy Joe Lucas in his epistemic argument of chapter 10 (the first modal version that carries existential import), while in turn Lucas's argument helps buttress the crucial philosophical assumption of the ontological argument that the concept of God is coherent and logically possible. Likewise the intelligibility of* de re *modality is an assumption made in the course of presenting Hartshorne's solution to logicofatalism in the concluding essay authored by me and Don Viney, a presentation that provides further articulation of the metaphysics of temporal possibility discussed by Goodwin. On a more personal note, I observe that Goodwin's dissertation was the genesis of my own dissertation project on "The Semantics of Perfection" as I atttempted to flesh out in a systematic way all that would be necessary for justification of the crucial notion that "God is logically possible," thus buttressing Goodwin's case in what I argued is the required comprehensive manner.*

Preliminary Considerations

A sound ontological argument will be a modal argument. By this I mean that the argument will operate on what I shall call the modal principle, that is, the principle not that real existence is a predicate of a perfect being, but that modality of existence—the way a thing exists, the relation a thing has to existence—is a property of every being and every concept.

Every being exists either contingently or—if deity exists—necessarily. Obviously, no existent exists impossibly. Similarly, any mental concept is related to reality in one of three ways: either the concept must be instantiated in reality (2 + 2 = 4) or it might or might not be instantiated (my future son) or it necessarily could not be instantiated (round square). Necessity, contingency, impossibility: one of these three modalities of existence is a property of every being and every concept.

What a sound ontological argument proves, strictly speaking, is not that God exists, but that, of the three possible existential modalities, one is incompatible with the idea of a perfect being. God, or perfect being,[1] could not exist or fail to exist merely contingently; "contingently existing perfect being" is as contradictory as "round square."[2] Consequently, the existence of a perfect being is either necessary or impossible. In this sense, the ontological argument is an argument about the logic of theistic arguments.

It follows that we cannot coherently say that the existence of God is just "possible," at least not in the way we talk about the possibility of ordinary things. I may say that it is possible that it will rain next week or that there will be a permanent human colony established on the moon. These statements make sense because "rain next week" or "permanent human colony on the moon" describe contingent states of affairs, states of affairs that might or might not come to pass.

But I cannot talk about the existence of a perfect being in the same way. Just because the modality of contingent existence is ruled out in the case of divinity, leaving only necessity or impossibility of existence as viable options, any possibility of divine existence is already evidence of necessary existence. "Possible" means "not impossible," and where necessity and impossibility are the only alternatives, ruling out impossibility means ruling in necessity. This is Aristotle's insight that "with eternal things, to be possible and to be are the same" (*Physica* III, 4203b, 30).

This, then, is the structure of a modal ontological argument:

P1 Modality of existence is a predicate. (Assumption.)
P2 The existence of God is either necessary or impossible. (Definition of "God" or "perfect being.")
P3 The existence of God is possible. (Conclusion from other theistic arguments.)[3]
P4 The existence of God is necessary. (From P2 and the definition of "possible.")

C Therefore, God exists. (What necessarily is, is.)

The central premise in this argument is the assumption that the existence of God is possible, and this in two senses: (1) The argument assumes the logical possibility—the conceivability—of the divine existence; it is thus a *theory of divinity*. (2) The argument also assumes a *theory of modality*, that is, it assumes that the *logical* possibility of divinity guarantees the *ontological* possibility, and so the *ontological* necessity, of the divine existence. In this sense, the argument does move "from thought to reality."

Consequently, there are two chief ways to challenge the ontological argument: The *positivistic objection* challenges the meaningfulness of the idea of divinity. J. N. Findlay, for example, has argued that the ontological "proof" is a proof of the necessary nonexistence of deity.[4] The *modal objection* challenges the assumption that there is a correspondence between logical or linguistic modalities and real or ontological modalities. There are two versions of this modal challenge.

According to one version, logical modalities make sense and ontological modalities make sense, but they do not in fact correspond to one another. This is the objection to the ontological argument that Kant urged when he wrote in the *Critique of Pure Reason*: "This is a warning against arguing directly from the logical possibility of concepts to the real possibility of things."[5] David L. Paulsen expresses the same point when he writes:[6]

> If and when God's existence is shown to be *logically* possible, the probative value of ontological arguments will remain in doubt. For there will still remain the task of showing that God's real existence is ontologically possible . . . For whether or not some state of affairs, e.g., the existence of God, is ontologically possible is a function not (merely) of the coherence of our concepts, but of the ultimate nature of reality . . . Critics have long claimed that one cannot build bridges from concepts to non-conceptual realities by means of *a priori* reasoning.

Or, as John Hick has put it succinctly: "Logical necessity is not a case of ontological necessity, nor vice versa."[7] This is one of the strongest intuitive objections to the ontological argument: namely, that one cannot move from a logical argument to any conclusion about the nature of ontological reality.

A more radical version of the modal challenge is that there *could be* no correspondence between logical and ontological modalities, because the ontological modality of necessity is nonsensical. In other words, necessity is purely linguistic and the concept cannot make sense when it is construed ontologically. The most vocal proponent of this position is the American philosopher, W. V. O. Quine.

These, then, are the three major challenges to a modal ontological argument: the positivistic challenge that the idea of God is nonsense, the Kantian challenge that the logical and ontological modalities are not coextensive, and the Quinean objection that they could not be coextensive because ontological necessity is nonsensical. Any of the objections, if sustained, will ruin the argument.

My intent in this essay is to examine and answer Quine's challenge to the meaningfulness of ontological necessity. In doing so I will draw on principles that I am convinced—although I cannot demonstrate this here—also provide the resources required to answer the positivistic and the Kantian challenges as well. The principles I refer to are those of the neoclassical metaphysics of Charles Hartshorne, whose work on the ontological argument I take to be most significant in this century.[8] The key to Hartshorne's defense of the modal ontological argument is his metaphysics of temporal possibility, according to which the necessary is defined in terms of the possible and the possible is defined in terms of the future.

The Challenge to *De Re* Modality

We have seen that the success of the ontological argument depends on a cogent theory of the correspondence between logical and ontological modalities. The argument is committed to both the logical necessity and the ontological necessity of the divine existence.

The technical terms for logical and ontological modalities are modality *de dicto* and modality *de re*. By *de dicto* modality we mean the predication of a modal property (necessity or contingency) of another dictum or proposition, for example, "Necessarily, God exists," which means that "God exists" is a logically necessary truth. By *de re* modality we mean the predication of a necessary or accidental property of some object or individual, for example, "God exists necessarily," which says that God has the ontologically essential property of necessary existence. *De dicto* modalities thus express logical or linguistic properties, whereas *de re* modalities thus express ontological or real properties. (In terms of modal logic, the distinction between the two modalities is that in cases of *de dicto* modality, the modal operator—necessity or possibility—falls outside the scope of the universal or existential quantifier, whereas in the cases of *de re* modality, the modal operator falls within the scope of the quantifier.)

The ontological argument, then, is committed to both of the following propositions and to their mutual implication:

"N" for "necessarily"
"Ex" for the existential quantifier ("there is one x")
"Px" for "God" or "Perfect Being"

N(Ex) Px "God (or 'Perfect Being') exists" is logically necessary
and
(Ex) N (Px) God has the essential property of necessary existence.

W. V. O. Quine has argued that *de re* necessity is unintelligible.[9] He represents well the contemporary dogma that necessity can refer only to propositions and not to matters of fact. I will now review his argument and show that, finally, it is not just a logical or semantical—but a metaphysical—challenge and that, therefore, it can finally be assessed and answered only on metaphysical grounds.

Logic

Quine's attack on *de re* necessity begins in the realm of logic, and it depends on the two principles of *the indiscernibility of identicals* and *existential generalization.*

According to Leibnitz's principle of the indiscernibility of identicals, given a true statement of identity, one of its two terms may be substituted for the other in any true statement and the result will be true. Substitutivity is thus analytic of the idea of singular reference. For example, from the true statement that

the Vatican is in Rome
and the identity statement,
Rome = the capital city of Italy,
we can arrive at the true statement that
the Vatican is in the capital city of Italy.
But now consider another case. From the true statement that
Mary believes that Rome is in Germany
and the identity,
Rome = the capital city of Italy,
we arrive at a statement that is false,
Mary believes that the capital of Italy is in Germany.

What is the difference between these two cases? Why is it that in one case a true statement and an identity statement yield another true statement, while in the other case a true statement and an identity statement yield a false statement? Why does substitutivity work in one case but not in the other?

According to Quine, the difference has to do with the denotation of "Rome" in the two cases. In the first case, "Rome" refers precisely to "the capital city of Italy." But in the second case, "Mary believes that Rome is in Germany," "Rome" is clearly not referring to "the capital city of Italy." In

Quine's language, "Rome" in the second case has a referentially opaque (as opposed to transparent) occurrence, and this opacity is induced by the context of "believes that."

Here is another example of referential opacity:
"Bush" has four letters.
Bush is President of the United States.
The President of the United States has four letters.

Here the problem is clear: the "Bush" in "Bush has four letters" is referring to the *name* Bush; whereas the "Bush" in "Bush is President of the United States" is referring to the *person* Bush. Because of the ambiguity of denotation or reference, we cannot apply the principle of substitutivity. In short, *failure of substitutivity betrays referential opacity* (perhaps "referential ambiguity" would be better).

Quine next argues that referentially opaque contexts prevent existential generalization. (The existential generalization of a sentence says that something has the property which that sentence predicates of the denotation of its singular term.) For example:

The *Mona Lisa* is hanging in the Louvre.

This is equivalent to saying (by existential generalization),

There is something such that it is the Mona Lisa and it is hanging in the Louvre.

But from the statement,

There is no such thing as my twin brother,

I cannot move by existential generalization to the statement,

There is something such that it is my twin brother and it is not.

What is the difference between the statement about the Mona Lisa and the statement about my twin brother that allows me to perform existential generalization on the former, but not upon the latter? The problem, once again, is referential opacity: the "Mona Lisa" names or denotes an object, whereas "my twin brother" does not. Therefore, *referential opacity prevents existential generalization*.

These, then, are Quine's two principles: failure of substitutivity betrays referential opacity, and referential opacity prevents existential generalization. According to Quine—and this is the point of our investigation—*modal contexts* also cause referential opacity.

Thus, says Quine, from the *de dicto* proposition,
necessarily, 9 is greater than 7, that is, N(9 > 7)

and the true identity,

> the number of planets = 9,

we cannot conclude that

> necessarily, the number of planets is greater than 7.

Obviously, the number of planets could have been 5, and so it is not a necessary truth that the number of the planets is greater that 7. Substitutivity has broken down, and therefore the underlying problem is referential opacity: "9" is not referring clearly. Therefore, existential generalization also breaks down. We cannot move by existential generalization from the true *de dicto* statement that

> necessarily, 9 is greater than 7, i.e., N (9 > 7)

to the *de re* statement that

> there is a number which is necessarily greater than 7, that is, (Ex) N (x > 7)

Why not? Because, according to Quine, (Ex) N (x > 7) is nonsensical or at least lacks clear sense. What is the "x" that is said to have the property of necessary-greaterness-than-7? According to one interpretation, it is 9 that has this property, but that which is identical with 9, namely, the number of planets, does not have the property. On the same interpretation of "x" denotes (Ex) N (x > 7) is true and on another interpretation it is false. And this is precisely Quine's point: modal contexts are referentially opaque because terms in those contexts are not referring clearly or unambiguously. Apparently, necessary-greaterness-than-7 is not a property of *what* we are referring to, but is rather a matter of *how* we are referring: necessity is linguistic rather than ontological. "To be necessarily greater than 7 is not a trait of a number, but depends on the manner of referring to the number."[10] Or, more generally, "being necessarily or possibly thus and so is in general not a trait of the object concerned, but depends on the manner of referring to the object."[11]

Thus, to use another of Quine's favorite examples: Suppose that John is both a mathematician and a cyclist. *As a mathematician*, John is necessarily rational but not necessarily two-legged; *as a cyclist*, he is necessarily two-legged but not necessarily rational. Quine concludes that necessity attaches only to ways of referring to things, not to the things themselves.

In short, Quine represents the doctrine that all necessity is logical or analytic and has to do with relations of concepts and not with properties of objects. If this claim is true, then the statement that real necessary existence is a predicate of perfection is indeed meaningless.

One direct answer to Quine has been given by Arthur Smullyan[12] who has pointed out that all of Quine's examples of failure of substitutivity in modal contexts depend on interchanging definite descriptions for proper names (for example, "the number of planets" for "9"), and that definite descriptions induce "scope ambiguities." So, for example,

> Necessarily, the number of planets is > 7

is ambiguous. It may mean the true *de re* statement that

> The number that in fact numbers the planets is necessarily greater than 7

or it may mean the false *de dicto* statement that

> It is a necessary truth that the number that numbers the planets is greater than 7.

According to Smullyan, then, the problem is not with modal contexts as such, but with Quine's overlooking the difference between proper names and definite descriptions. He writes, "the modal paradoxes arise not out of any intrinsic absurdity in the use of the modal operators but rather out of the assumption that descriptive phrases are names."[13] Smullyan's proposal is that only singular terms in which scope ambiguities do not arise (i.e., proper names) will serve as valid substitution instances in modal contexts. So "the number of planets" will not serve as an unambiguously valid substitution instance for "9" in "N (9 > 7)"—not because of any paradox intrinsic to the modal context, but because "the number of planets" is not a proper name.

In his response to Smullyan, Quine does not *deny* that we can distinguish names and descriptions; rather, he argues that we have to pay too high a price to maintain the distinction. Drawing the distinction between names and descriptions involves "adopting an invidious attitude toward certain ways of uniquely specifying x, . . . and favoring other ways . . . as somehow better revealing the 'essence' of the object."[14] His final decision is that a "reversion to Aristotelian essentialism is required if quantification into modal contexts is to be insisted on."[15]

"Aristotelian essentialism" is understood as the doctrine that "an object, of itself and by whatever name or none, must be seen as having some of its traits necessarily and others contingently."[16]

In short, the issue between Quine and Smullyan is not so much logical as semantical; how are we to *interpret* quantified modal logic? Quine's problem with quantified modal logic, it turns out, is not that there are logical puzzles which attend it (for Smullyan has shown clearly how we may resolve those puzzles), but that resolving these puzzles in a certain way commits us to an interpretation of the meaning of necessity which Quine does not understand. Says Quine, "The general idea of strict modalities is based on the putative notion of analyticity as follows: a statement of the form 'Necessarily . . .' is true if and only if the component statement which 'necessarily' governs is analytic."[17] So, for Quine, it is built into the very meaning of "analytic" that "necessity" refers to a certain way of specifying an object, not to the object itself. Predicating necessity of objects is thus at odds with the only interpretation of necessity which Quine claims to understand. What does a statement of *de re* necessity *mean*? This is Quine's question.[18]

Semantics

Saul Kripke has provided a semantical framework that responds well to Quine's challenge.[19] Kripke develops a possible-world semantics according to which we may talk about individuals existing in the actual world and in some of the possible worlds that are accessible from the actual world. A definite description (e.g., "the tallest man in London") picks out different individuals in different possible worlds; a rigid designator (e.g., the proper name "George Walker Bush") names the same individual in every possible world in which it names at all; and a strongly rigid designator (e.g., God) names the same individual in every possible world. A property is *essential* to an individual if a rigid or strongly rigid designator picks it out every time it picks out the individual; otherwise the property is *accidental.*

We may use this semantics to interpret the proposition (Ex) N (x > 7): it means that there is some object, x , in this world, which has the property, greaterness-than-seven, in this world and in every world in which x exists. And (Ex) N (Px) means that there is a being in this world which has the essential property of necessary existence; therefore, "God" is a strongly rigid designator that picks out the same (existing) being in every possible world. (Of course, this does not prove that there is such a being; it simply gives a semantical account of what the claim about ontological necessity means.)

From Semantics to Metaphysics

Does the applied semantics answer Quine's challenge? Unfortunately not, because Quine (and others) have argued that there are serious conceptual problems involved in identifying the same individual from world to world. The difficulties have come to be known as the problem of transworld identity.

What, exactly, is the alleged problem of transworld identity? According to possible-world semantics, we speak about the *same* individual existing in several *different* possible worlds. For example, it is the same Mary who is sick in the actual world, but well in a possible world. In order to make sense of this talk, then, we need to resolve a logical puzzle: How can that which is the same yet be different? This is one aspect of the transworld identity problem, and I will return to it below. A second aspect of the problem is the getting clear about just which properties serve to identify an individual as precisely the same individual from world to world. If we use the term, "essence," to mean that collection of properties that are necessary to an individual and that, taken together, distinguish that individual from all others, then it would seem that we need to be able to say what those essential features are for a particular individual (other than the trivial property of being self-identical), so we can identify the individual from world to world. An example will illustrate the point. George W. Bush is now president of the United States. But obviously there are and have been possible worlds in which Bush is not President, so being president is not essential to the identity of George W. Bush. Is being Republican, or even a politician, essential to his identity? Could the same George W. Bush who is now a Republican President of the United States have been or one day be a professor of music and a Democrat? Could George W. Bush have been a soldier in the American Civil War or a medieval theologian? In short, what are George W. Bush's essential features?

Here we must be cautious. The question of precisely which features are essential to George W. Bush or to anything is an interesting and important question, but perhaps it is not exactly the question about transworld identity. As Peter van Inwagen has observed, "It does not follow from the fact that there are real philosophical problems that can be stated—that can *best* be stated, for that matter—in terms of transworld identity that there are real philosophical problems *about* transworld identity."[20] The issue here is not whether in any particular case we can state correctly which attributes are essential to someone, but whether we can clearly state a criterion for distinguishing essential features from accidental ones. Analogously, we may be clear about what the biological criteria of life are, and yet unclear in a particular borderline case about how to apply the criteria.

The problem of transworld identity, then, requires (1) a clear resolution of the logical paradox about identity and difference and (2) a clear formulation of the criterion used to distinguish essential from accidental properties.

Quine, of course, supposes that the problem of transworld identity cannot be resolved, because proponents of Aristotelian essentialism cannot provide a clear criterion for identifying essential properties (see the section on "Individual Identity" below for further discussion of this point). And, in general, he assumes that Aristotelian essentialism is fraught with problems because metaphysics itself is fraught with problems. If metaphysics does not make sense, then obviously metaphysical necessity does not make sense either. Thus we are left with the modern doctrine that necessity applies only to propositions and not to matters of fact. "The rejection of the Aristotelian scheme of essences eliminates absolutely necessary truths about the world . . . The theory of essences is thus replaced by a theory about concepts."[21]

Thus, Quine writes that, because he "can make little sense of identification of particulars across possible worlds" he "can make little sense of quantifying into necessity contexts when the values of the variables are particulars."[22] "So much the worse for quantified modal logic" is Quine's final judgment.[23] Such a judgment is not uncommon among contemporary philosophers and logicians: "Modalities *de re* are more recalcitrant than modalities *de dicto* (and Quine was right in laying his finger on that) and the opinion most widely received is that essentialism at least so far as it involves necessities *de re*, simply cannot bear scrutiny; in particular, although some, possibly justifiable, interpretations are available for *de dicto* modalities none is forthcoming, or likely, for modalities *de re*."[24]

What began as a logical puzzle has become, at the hands of semantical analysis, a specifically metaphysical issue, requiring a metaphysical solution. Just as previously we faced the challenge of providing an intelligible semantical account for quantified modal logic, so now we face the challenge of providing an intelligible explanation of our semantics. To ask for an interpretation and a criterion for essential properties is to ask a metaphysical question. I consider this an extremely instructive point: the *de re* issue should be viewed, finally, precisely as a metaphysical issue, not according to any extrinsic invasion of metaphysics into logic, but according to the intrinsic dynamics of contemporary philosophical logic itself. Quine's attack on quantified modal logic is really an attack on the intelligibility of metaphysics.

The Neoclassical Alternative

In what follows I will argue that, although Quine is exactly right that quantified modal logic commits us to essentialism, he is wrong to assume that it must commit us to *Aristotelian* essentialism. Aristotelian essentialism is—I will argue—just as metaphysically problematic as Quine takes it to be. But there is available to us another sort of essentialism that both satisfies the demands of quantified modal logic and avoids the problems attending Aristotelian essentialism. The neoclassical metaphysics of Charles Hartshorne puts at our disposal resources that provide a genuine alternative to the substance metaphysics of Aristotle and that can help untie the transworld identity knot. Specifically, neoclassical metaphysics provides three principles that together resolve the transworld identity problem: (1) the temporal interpretation of possible worlds, (2) the genetic interpretation of substantial identity, and (3) the causal interpretation of essential properties. I will comment on each of these principles to corroborate my contention that the notion of transworld identity is not unintelligible in itself, but becomes so in the context of a substance metaphysics.

The Temporalistic Interpretation of Possible Worlds.

What do we mean by "possible worlds"? Saul Kripke has pointed out that possible worlds are not places, like foreign countries, that we can visit or inspect through powerful telescopes. Rather, possible worlds are stipulated states of affairs; they refer to possible states of the world.[25] Can we stipulate just any state of affairs as a possible worlds? Clearly not; for example, we cannot speak of a possible state of affairs in which objects are, in exactly the same respects, both spherical and cubical. What, then, are the laws or conditions for stipulating possible world? What we are asking is not a logical or a semantical question; for the logical answer is "x is possible if it is not necessarily not true," and the semantical answer is "x is possible if it is accessible from the actual world." Our question, rather, is ontological: Metaphysically, what does it mean to say that a given state of affairs is possible?

Possibility and Actuality. The first thing to notice is that *possibility* is a relative term: something is possible relative to something else. While standing in Rome, it is not possible that I be in New York in the next half hour; but if I were in New Jersey or if I lived in an age of faster travel "being in New York in the next half hour" would indeed be a possible state of affairs. In other words, what is possible is relative to what is actual. (Or what is possible is relative to other possibilities that are themselves relative to actuality. Ultimately, possibility must be tethered to actual states of affairs.) What is possible is what could be actual.

What, then, does it mean to be actual? As our ordinary language shows all references to actuality involve references to time, specifically, either to the immediate past or to the remote past. It is actually the case that Napoleon lost at Waterloo, that I was born in 1946, and that I have just written these words. (Strictly speaking, the present is the realm of *becoming* actual rather than of *being actual.*) If *actuality* is a temporal term, and if possibility is related to actuality, then possibility, too, is temporal.

The modal distinction between possibility and actuality thus proves to be a temporal distinction: the actual is the past and the possible is the future. This is why we unavoidably use temporal terms when we discuss possibilities. *Is* it possible that Napoleon win at Waterloo? No. *Was* it possible that Napoleon win? Yes, at those times when "Napoleon at Waterloo" was still future.

Actuality and possibility are thus related in precisely the same way that the past and future are related: the past is externally related to the future (today has its own character regardless of what tomorrow will be); the future is internally related to the past (what may or may not happen tomorrow is at least partially in reaction to what happens today).

Logical and Real Possibility. What about the distinction between real and logical possibility? Even if we grant that the criterion for real possibility is compatibility with actuality, how shall we interpret logical possibility? Hartshorne's answer is, in precisely the same way. The criterion for logical possibility is the same as the criterion for real possibility, namely, compatibility with actuality.

To be logically possible means to be conceivable. To be conceivable, a proposition cannot be self-contradictory, the meanings involved in the proposition must not contradict one another. But meanings must have references, they must mean something. Can meaning refer only to itself? By that standard, any thought would be logically possible: the meaning of round square would refer to the meaning of round square. Can the meanings of a logical possibility refer only to other logical possibilities? Then we have an infinite regress. Rather, we should say that at some point the meanings involved in a logical possibility must refer at least to a real possibility, and that, finally, to (a real capacity of) actuality. As Hartshorne expresses the point: "If a consistent meaning means something, but something not even possible, then it means something very odd indeed. If it means only its own consistency, then it is really meaningless."[26]

On this approach, then, to say that a state of affairs is "merely logically possible" (i.e., "logically, but not really possible") means one of two things: (1) The real possibility upon which the logical possibility depends lies so far in the past or the future that it is irrelevant for present purposes. Consider, as an example, a state of affairs where a material object travels faster than 186,000 miles per second (the speed of light). According to [some] contemporary physicists, this is an impossible state of affairs. But is it *logically* impossible? The answer, on the Hartshornean analysis that I am offering, is this: *Either* "traveling faster than the speed of light" is as contradictory as "round square" and so is not logically possible (that it *seems* logically possible to us is a reminder of the fallibility of our knowledge[27]), *or* it is logically possible in the sense that the laws of physics are contingent and could really be different in different cosmic epochs. (2) There may be another sense in which something is "merely logically possible": namely, in the case of a self-contained mathematical or logical system whose axioms are not really possible. To say that concepts within the system are logically, but not really, possible is thus to say the concepts do not refer beyond the closed system.

Granting these two exceptions, the point is that compatibility with actuality is the criterion for both real and logical possibilities. Thus, even logical possibilities are temporally indexed. For example, I would contend that, strictly speaking, the concept of my twin brother is not *now* a logical possibility, because I was not born a twin. To be sure that concept was once possible (and I may now, so to speak, "borrow" it from the past and entertain the thought), namely at the time that my being born a twin was a real possibility, and that is why now any concept of my twin brother carries an implicit "if" which, given the present state of the world, could never be actualized. This interpretation of logical possibility will doubtless seem too restrictive to many. My suggestion, however, is that if we allow as logically possible now a concept (my twin brother) that refers to a state of affairs that could never, under any now really possible conditions, be the case, then we must also allow round square as a logical possibility. I will grant, however, that there is this difference between "round square" and "my twin brother": the former was always logically impossible whereas the latter has become logically impossible. This may be given a temporal interpretation: "round square" is incompatible with all futures, "my twin brother" is incompatible with some futures. The basic thesis, that even logical possibility is best interpreted in terms of temporality, remains.

Necessity. What does necessity mean on this temporal interpretation? On the neoclassical approach, necessity is defined in terms of possibility: the necessary is what is common to a set of possibilities, that whose nonactualization is not a possibility within the given set. A *conditional* necessity is what is common to a set of some possibilities; an *unconditional* necessity is what is common to the set of all possibilities. We may understand the difference between *de re* and *de dicto* necessity as follows: *de re* necessity refers to necessary or essential properties, properties that an individual would possess in any possible world in which it existed (it is just these properties which Quine has challenged). *De dicto* necessity refers to propositions; it means falsity in no possible world.[28] Combing the conditional-unconditional distinction with the *de re-de dicto* distinction, then, we have the following types of necessity:

1. Conditional *de re* necessity: essential properties of individuals denoted by rigid designators.
2. Unconditional *de re* necessity: essential properties of individuals denoted by strongly rigid designators.
3. Conditional *de dicto* necessity: falsity in no possible world; truth in some, but not all, possible worlds. For example, propositions affirming essential properties of rigid designators are conditionally necessary. (Also, certain mathematical systems may be conditionally *de dicto* necessary.)
4. Unconditional *de dicto* necessity: falsity in no possible world; truth in every possible world. Propositions affirming essential properties of strongly rigid designators are unconditionally nec-

> essary. Metaphysical truths are unconditionally necessary, for example, "something exists."

Some examples will illustrate this temporal interpretation of necessity. What does it mean to say that mortality is an essential property of human beings? On the neoclassical interpretation, this means that in every alternative future in which human beings could exist, humans would be mortal. However, because there are alternative futures that exclude human beings altogether, "human beings" is—to use Kripke's language—a rigid designator, not a strongly rigid designator. Thus, mortality is a conditional *de re* necessity and "all humans are mortal" is a conditional *de dicto* necessity (Kripke's bare necessity).

The existence of God, according to the ontological argument, is an unconditional *de re* necessity. This means that the existence of deity is a feature of all possible worlds, or—to put it in temporal terms—that there is no future or once-future state of affairs which excludes (or could exclude) the divine existence. Deity has the essential property of universal existential tolerance; it exists on any conditions whatsoever. An unconditional *de dicto* necessity is one which affirms an essential feature of temporality itself. "Necessarily, something exists" and "Necessarily, God exists" are candidates for this status.

To summarize the neoclassical approach: modal distinctions are temporal distinctions.[29] The actual is the past; the possible (logical and real) is the future; the necessary is the eternal. Expressed otherwise: The necessary is defined in terms of the possible and the possible is defined in terms of the future.

It is, I realize, particularly bold and ironic to answer Quine's challenge to the meaningfulness of *de re* necessity by sketching a metaphysical position wherein *de dicto* modality is itself defined in terms of *de re* modality: propositional necessity mirrors objective necessity. This represents a radical departure from the practice of defining necessity in terms of analyticity and then explaining "possible worlds" as worlds that do not conflict with necessary truths. Nicholas Rescher, for example, writes that: "Necessary truths are not necessary because they are true in all possible worlds; rather, possible worlds are so because they do not conflict with truths judged to be necessary on independent grounds."[30] But this is surely to guarantee by fiat that *de dicto* necessity will make sense and *de re* necessity will not. As Quine has put it so bluntly, given only a *de dicto* interpretation of necessity, one does not know what *de re* necessity even means.

It is helpful to distinguish, among *de dicto* necessities, what I will call trivial and nontrivial necessities. (Quine calls these, respectively, logical and analytic truths.) By a trivial *de dicto* necessity, I mean one wherein the descriptors are inessential to the truth of the statements. For example, in the statement, "All people are people," the reference to people is inessential. The statement is just as true if I substitute "ducks" or "zaregs" for "people." The truth of the statement has nothing to do with ontological reality. By a nontrivial *de dicto* necessity, on the other hand, I mean one in which the descriptors do play a role in determining the truth of the statement, for example, "All people are mortal." We must know the meanings or references of "people" and "mortal" in order to determine the truth of the statement.

To argue that *de dicto* necessity makes sense while *de re* necessity does not is to assimilate linguistic necessity to the trivial model, and this is just the practice that I am challenging as arbitrary and dogmatic. To say that deity necessarily exists is not just to say that "a necessary existent would necessarily exist"; it is to say that there *must be* a being that has the essential property of necessary existence, and *because* the divine necessary existence is a feature of all possible states of affairs, because it is an unconditional *de re* necessity, the proposition affirming the divine existence is itself unconditionally *de dicto* necessary.

What gains has the temporal interpretation of possible worlds purchased for solving the so-called problem of transworld identity? Several authors have pointed out that there is an analogy—although not an identity—between identifying an individual across possible worlds and identifying an individual throughout time. Alvin Plantinga, for example, briefly develops this analogy in his book, *The Nature of Necessity*, and he concludes that there is only an analogy because, although "times are linearly ordered . . . nothing like this is available in the transworld case."[31] And Quine, in addressing the comparison between the transworld and the transtemporal, concludes that "the devastating difference is that the series of momentary cross-sections of our real world is uniquely imposed on us, for better or for worse, whereas all manner of paths of continuous gradation from one possible world to another are free for the thinking up."[32]

However, if the line of reasoning which I have been developing is correct, then there is more than an analogy between the transtemporal and the transworld cases; there is an identity, because possibility *is* futurity. This means that, Quine notwithstanding, paths from world to world are not "free for the thinking up." Nicholas Rescher is closer to the truth when he writes: "Insofar as relational properties [i.e., temporal relations] are seen as built into the very essence of certain individuals we face insuperable constraints in the sorts of worlds in which they can be accommodated. They are then *not* independent of their environment, but can demand the presence of some individuals and the absence of others."[33]

The identity between transworld and transtemporal provides a crucial insight for solving the transworld identity problem, because it shows that the problem is not one of actually making identifications, for we do this regularly. I can identify a person I have not seen for a long time as the same person I knew twenty years ago. Rather, *the problem is one of specifying a criterion* according to which we regularly do make such identifications.

Individual Identity

Specifying a criterion for *identification* depends, in turn, on what we mean by individual *identity*. And on this point, Aristotelian essentialism, and indeed every substance metaphysics, is problematic.

By a "substance metaphysics" I mean any philosophy in which substance is taken to be the ultimate concrete fact, "concrete" in the sense that it is not derived from anything more fundamental, "ultimate" in the sense that everything else is explained in terms of it. Substance is that which "underlies" or "endures through" change; it is that "in" which accidents inhere. Essential properties are aspects of substantial identity; they are features of an individual that are the same in all possible worlds in which the individual exists. The important point is that, on the interpretation given by substance metaphysics, these essential features are both changeless *and concrete*: accidental change is to be explained in terms of them, rather than the other way.

One alternative to a substance metaphysics is what I will call the "event metaphysics" of Whitehead and Hartshorne.[34] According to this view, substances are not the final metaphysical facts; rather, they are abstractions from the final facts, which are occasions or events.

Ordinary language employs this distinction. Compare "I am Larry Goodwin" and "I am hungry." The first "I" refers to my *substantial self*, that which endures throughout a period of years; the second "I" refers to the *momentary self* in which my substantial self is realized and from which it has been abstracted. I (substantial) remain who I (substantial) am whether I (momentary) sleep or eat or play. The momentary selves are the final realities, and the substantial self is abstracted from them. Essential features are the recurring themes (thoughtful, industrious, optimistic) in the momentary states: these features are changeless, but—and here is the difference from the interpretation of substance metaphysics—they are not concrete. Rather, essential features are abstractions from different concrete states or momentary selves. On this view, then, substances are "in" accidents, rather than vice versa. For example, from the statement "Mary is happy today" I can infer "Mary exists" (and thus the momentary state contains the substantial identity); but from "Mary exists" I can draw no conclusion about Mary's momentary state.

Hartshorne distinguishes *strict identity*, wherein what is identical is both changeless and concrete, from *genetic identity*, wherein what is identical is changeless and abstract.[35] In a substance metaphysics, substantial identity is interpreted as strict identity; in an event metaphysics, the identity of momentary events is strict, whereas the identity of substances is genetic. Our question, then, is this: Is individual identity across possible worlds better understood on the strict or the genetic interpretation?

Let us examine a prosaic case, "Mary was sick yesterday, but she is well today." How shall we understand the claim that the same person was ill and now is well, since illness and wellness are different?

According to "Aristotelian essentialism," the solution is that illness and wellness are accidental modifications of the same person, where "same" means "the same concrete substance." So the strictly identical person was qualified accidentally in one way yesterday and is qualified in another way today. This is the way that Arthur Prior, for example, explains the point: "It is one and the same thing (the whole thing, so far as talk of parts and wholes is appropriate here) which at one time does or undergoes this and at another does or undergoes that, and at one time stands here and at another time—by which it (the same thing) *has stood* here—stands there. It is within this framework that we must try to give the language of 'chronology' its meaning; not vice versa."[36]

But this seems paradoxical: how can *the same (concrete) subject* undergo this and then undergo that, and yet be strictly identical? How can *the same (changeless) person* be sick-then and well-now, since Mary-as-sick is precisely *not* identical with Mary-as-well? The only way that a strictly identical concrete subject can entertain different characteristics is simultaneously and in different respects: "John is green in his eyes and red in his hair." To say, then, that sick-then and well-now are modifications of the *same* concrete subject is to "spatialize" temporal reality; it is to treat "then" and "now" as simultaneously existing actualities.

Another way to state this problem is to say that a strict theory of substantial identity involves a symmetrical view of substantial identity. Take S1 to be Mary-sick-yesterday and S2 to be Mary-well-today. If S1 and S2 are strictly identical with one another, then if S2 can remember S1, why cannot S1 foresee S2? This is the paradox which results when time is spatialized.

Consider now the Whiteheadean-Hartshornean interpretation of the statement "Mary was sick yesterday, but she is well today." Each *momentary* subject (concrete state, event) is strictly identical with itself; but the identity which binds them together as instances of the same *substantial* subject is genetic, rather than strict. From the different momentary subjects, Mary-sick-at-time-x and Mary-well-at-time-y, we abstract the common features that constitute Mary-as-identical. The identity of the concrete events is strict, and the identity of abstract substances is genetic. And the events contain the substance.

We have, then, two proposals for explaining individual identity: "Either there is *one* subject sick-now and well-later—that is, with sickness and health coexistent in diverse temporal parts of itself (which spatializes time and contradicts the very meaning of temporal)—or there is a sick subject actual now, and later another nonsick subject may be actualized belonging to the same genetic series."[37] My argument has been that the former option, "Aristotelian essentialism," interprets substantial identity in a way that *should* present problems to Quine and to the rest of us as well; but that the neoclassical interpretation of substantial identity provides a coherent alternative that avoids these problems.

Essential Properties

How, then, are we to understand essential properties on the neoclassical view? If possible worlds are future states of this world, and if substantial identity across worlds is genetic identity throughout time, then essential properties are those abstract features that an individual will illustrate in any of its future states.

According to what criterion may we identify an individual's essential features? According to precisely the same criterion that we use to establish possible worlds and individual identity: causality. *Essential properties are causally efficacious boundaries for individual development.* What, then, are George W. Bush's essential properties? Some obvious candidates include being human and being born at such and such a time. Thus, Bush could not have been a twelfth century theologian, because his birth in this century means that all subsequent experiences which constitute instances of "George W. Bush" must conform to his being born at such and such a time. Not that Bush's birth was unconditionally necessary, but it has become conditionally necessary in the sense that to speak of *his* birth supposes a chain of experiences sufficiently developed to abstract an individual identity—Bush—from them. It is nonsense to ask if this entire sequence could have taken place at another time, for it would no longer be *this* temporal sequence. Identity is chiefly a retrospective abstraction from a route of temporal occasions. To relocate the temporality is to change the identity.[38]

Can we successfully identify all of a person's essential properties? Perhaps not, but if we do in fact regularly identify things throughout time and if we can clearly specify the criterion for such identifications (temporal inheritance or causality), just how serious is the problem of transworld identity? What we really face is a factual problem of interpreting a criterion in a particular case, not a metaphysical problem of nonsensical properties. Essential properties, *de re* necessities, are no more mysterious than time or causality.

Conclusion

A modal ontological argument is committed to the proposition that God has the essential property of necessary existence, (Ex) N (Px). The argument is thus committed also to quantified modal logic and to the essentialism (*de re* modality) that it entails. Quine has argued that quantified modal logic is problematic, and that the possible world semantics required to interpret quantified modal logic commits us to an unintelligible metaphysics, "Aristotelian essentialism." The problem of transworld identity is used to illustrate the point. Our inability to solve this problem is taken as evidence that all talk of necessary or essential properties (including, therefore, the essential property of necessary existence) is meaningless.

I have argued that the supposed problem of transworld identity is solvable. Contrary to Quine's implicit assumption, Aristotelian essentialism is not the only metaphysical option available. Hartshorne's event ontology presents an alternative—and superior—metaphysical analysis of possible worlds, individual identity and essential properties. Temporality is shown to be the interpretive key to *de re* modality. What is unintelligible is not *de re* necessity, but a substance interpretation of *de re* modality.

What is at issue in Quine's attack on quantified modal logic and *de re* modality, and in the Hartshornean response that I have developed, is the very possibility of metaphysics. My conclusion is that the modal ontological argument presupposes metaphysics by its distinction between *de dicto* and *de re*, and that neoclassical metaphysics answers the crucial questions that this legitimate distinction raises.

Notes

1. In this essay, I will be using the terms "God," "Perfection," and "Perfect Being," interchangeably. In so doing, I am honoring Anselm's formal definition of deity as "that than which none greater can be conceived," although I would reject Anselm's material interpretation of how deity is in fact best conceived. Instead I would argue in favor of Charles Hartshorne's neoclassical interpretation of a perfect being as "the self-surpassing surpasser of all." For a careful discussion of the logic of "perfection," see Hartshorne, MVG 1–56.
2. A contingently existing being is, by definition, a dependent being. To exist independently is superior to existing dependently. Therefore, a perfect being would exist independently, that is to say, necessarily.
3. Thus the ontological argument "borrows" the conceivability of deity from other theistic arguments, such as the cosmological and teleological. These other arguments, however, should not be interpreted as *a pos-*

teriori in the sense that they rely on empirical data; like the ontological argument, all valid theistic arguments will be a priori, arguments about meaning. Thus, what supports the modal ontological argument in its assumption about the conceivability of deity are other non-ontological arguments with a modal structure.

4. "It was indeed an ill day for Anselm when he hit upon his famous proof. For on that day he not only laid bare something that is of the essence of an adequate religious object, but also something that entails its necessary non-existence." J. N. Findlay, "Can God's Existence Be Disproved?," in *New Essays in Philosophical Theology*, ed. Antony Flew and Alasdair MacIntyre (New York: Macmillan, 1955), p. 55.
5. Immanuel Kant, *Critique of Pure Reason*, trans. Norman Kemp Smith (New York: Macmillan, 1970), p. 503.
6. David L. Paulsen, "The Logically Possible, Ontologically Possible, and Ontological Proofs for God's Existence," *International Journal for Philosophy of Religion* 16 (1984): 47–48.
7. John Hick, A Critique of the Second Argument, in *The Many-Faced Argument*, ed. John Hick and A. C. McGill (New York: Macmillan, 1967), p. 348.
8. For Hartshorne's discussion of the ontological argument see especially *Anselm's Discovery: A Re-Examination of the Ontological Argument for the Existence of God* (LaSalle, Ill.: Open Court, 1965); "Ten Ontological or Modal Proofs for God's Existence," in LP 28–117; and "The Formal Validity and Real Significance of the Ontological Argument," *Philosophical Review* 3 (May 1944): 225–245. For a discussion of Hartshorne's ontological argument see my doctoral dissertation, *The Ontological Argument of Charles Hartshorne* (Missoula, Montana: Scholars Press, 1978).
9. W. V. O. Quine, "Reference and Modality," in *From a Logical Point of View*, 2nd ed. (New York: Harper & Row, 1963), pp. 139–159.
10. Quine, "Reference and Modality," p. 148.
11. Quine, "Reference and Modality," p. 148.
12. Arthur F. Smullyan, "Modality and Description," in *Reference and Modality*, ed. Leonard Linsky (London: Oxford University Press, 1971), pp. 35–43.
13. Smullyan, "Modality and Description," p. 39.
14. Quine, "Reference and Modality," p. 155.
15. Quine, "Reference and Modality," p. 155.
16. Quine, "Reference and Modality," p. 155.
17. Quine, "Reference and Modality," p. 143.
18. Alvin Plantinga raises an interesting point: An analytic proposition is a proposition that has the property of being-true necessarily or essentially.

Thus, "necessary truth is best seen as a special case of *x's having P essentially*: the case where x is a proposition and P is truth." Why, then, should it be any harder to understand the *de re* necessity that, for example, nine has the essential property of greaterness-than-seven than it is to understand the *de dicto* necessity that the proposition, "nine is three squared," has the property of truth essentially? See *Alvin Plantinga*, ed. by James E. Tomberlin and Peter van Inwangen (Boston: D. Reidl, 1985), p. 76.

19. Kripke, "Semantical Considerations on Modal Logic," in *Reference and Modality*, pp. 63–72.
20. P. van Inwagen, "Plantinga on Trans-World Identity," in *Alvin Plantinga*, p. 116.
21. D. W. Hamlyn, "Contingent and Necessary Statements," in *The Encyclopedia of Philosophy*, vol. 2, ed. Paul Edwards (New York: Macmillan, 1967), p. 199.
22. *Words and Objections: Essays on the Work of W. V. Quine*, ed. D. Davidson and J. Hintikka (Dordrecht: D. Reidl, 1969), p. 338.
23. Quine, "Reference and Modality," p. 156.
24. Tushar K. Sarkar, "Cures for the Maladies of QML," in *Mind, Language and Necessity*, ed. K. K. Bantertee; Jadavpur Studies in Philosophy, vol. 3 (Atlantic Highlands, N.J.: Humanities Press, 1982), p. 259.
25. Saul Kripke, "Naming and Necessity," in *Semantics of Natural Language*, ed. D. Davidson and G. Harman (Dordrecht: D. Reidl, 1972), p. 345, n. 15.
26. Hartshorne, MVG 304.
27. "If we had command of our ideas, we should see logical absurdity in any description that is really impossible." C. Hartshorne, "Real Possibility," *The Journal of Philosophy* 60 (1963): 594.
28. Falsity in no possible world is not the same as truth in every possible world, because, for example, a mathematical truth may be false in no possible world, but may be true only in those worlds where the assumptions of the mathematical system obtain. The point is that a contingent truth will be false in some possible world(s), whereas necessary truths will be universally immune to falsification.
29. The converse thesis is also true: Time is modal in structure. The being of the past is modally different from the being of the future. In this retrospective aspect, reality is definite preservative, cumulative, the realm of what has been; in its prospective aspect, reality is indefinite, creative, novel, the realm of what may or may not be.
30. N. Rescher, *A Theory of Possibility* (Pittsburgh: University of Pittsburg Press, 1975), p. 5.
31. A. Plantinga, *The Nature of Necessity* (Oxford: The Clarendon Press, 1974), p. 95.

32. W. V. O. Quine, "Worlds Away," *The Journal of Philosophy* 73 (Dec. 1976): 861.
33. Rescher, *A Theory of Possibility*, p. 94.
34. For the most complete discussions of event metaphysics, see A. N. Whitehead, PR, and Hartshorne's CSPM and WP.
35. C. Hartshorne, "Strict and Genetic Identity: An Illustration of the Relations of Logic to Metaphysics," in *Structure, Method and Meaning: Essays in Honor of Henry M. Sheffer*, ed. P. Henle, H. M. Kallen, and Suzanne K. Langer (New York: Liberal Arts Press, 1951), pp. 242–252.
36. A. N. Prior, *Papers on Time and Tense* (Oxford: The Clarendon Press, 1968), p. 86.
37. Hartshorne, "Strict and Genetic Identity," p. 253.
38. We may need to distinguish different types of essential properties. Some, such as enduring character traits, are best understood as *abstractions* from a series of momentary selves; others, such as birth date and lineage, are *conditions* of there being a particular series. I owe this suggestion to Professor Philip Devenish of the University of Chicago.

Chapter 10

The Second Epistemic Way

BILLY JOE LUCAS

Editor's Comment: As Lucas indicates in his concluding endnote, Hartshorne served both as a dissertation committee member and as a frequent philosophical interlocutor while Lucas was a doctoral student at the University of Texas at Austin. Apropos of the previous discussions of Quine, Lucas has mentioned to the editor that the point of origin for his own passionate interest in modal logic and its philosophical problems, issuing in his dissertation on "The Logic of Omniscience," was the famous 1979 rencontre *between Hartshorne and Quine at Boston University, which Lucas was able to attend. Hartshorne has explicitly mentioned Lucas's dissertation as the best formulation of the modal semantics underlying his (Hartshorne's) own uses of modal logic, especially regarding the appropriate contexts for S4 and S5 (see PCH 657–658). Moreover, Hartshorne cites the particular essay below as a model for formalization of ontological type arguments of which the epistemic is a variant (see WM 146). Thus, given Hartshorne's own recommendation, it seems most fitting to include such an essay in an anthology that (in part) addresses Hartshorne's relation to the analytic tradition. Nota Bene: A glossary of symbols used in this essay is provided by the editor at endnote 4.*

In order to illustrate some of the constructive uses of logic for work in the philosophy of religion as inspired by Charles Hartshorne, I make use, in this essay, of three systems of first-order modal logic to articulate, and answer, some questions concerning the nature and existence of an omniscient being. In Section I, I present, from three premises, a valid derivation of the proposition that an omniscient being exists, In Section II, I offer contextual analyses of two concepts of omniscience and show how two of the three premises of the epistemic existence argument in Section I become demonstrable truths when interpreted in the light of the definitions given in Section II. In Section III, I formulate a variation on the epistemic existence argument in Section I, and construct a proof to show that the revised argument is valid on Hintikka's semantics for a modal logic free of existence assumptions. I conclude, In Section IV, by indicating some of the general kinds of questions that can be profitably investigated when formal systems of sufficient power are applied to problems in the philosophy of religion.

An Epistemic Existence Argument

A valid formal derivation, which yields as conclusion the existence of an omniscient being, by way of deduction from the premises which concern epistemic concepts, I shall call an epistemic existence argument,[1] or an epistemic way.[2] The epistemic existence argument to be presented here has three premises.

1. $\Box(x)[Ex \supset \Box(p)(p \supset Kxp)]$
2. $(x)[(p)(p \supset Kxp) \supset Ox]$
3. $\Diamond(\exists x)Ex$

(Read 'Ex': x is an epistemically unsurpassable being. Read 'Ox': x is omniscient. 'Kxp' abbreviates: x knows that p.) An approximation of premise (1) in English: it is a necessary truth that, for any x, if x is epistemically unsurpassable then it is not even possible for there to be a true proposition that x does not know.[3] Premise (2) can be translated: anyone who knows all true propositions is omniscient. Premise (3) affirms the logical possibility of the existence of an epistemically unsurpassable being. Just what premises (1)–(3) mean will be considered in Section II, where interpretations of 'Ex' and 'Ox' will be codified that render both (1) and (2) demonstrable truths. But as interest in the concepts of epistemic unsurpassability and omniscience is in part to be motivated by their role in facilitating a demonstration of the existence of an omniscient being, we begin by justifying the claim that (1), (2), and (3) together validly yield the existence of an omniscient being. And now for the proof.[4]

(1)	$\Box(x)[Ex \supset \Box(p)(p \supset Kxp)]$	Premise
(2)	$(x)[(p)(p \supset Kxp) \supset Ox]$	Premise
(3)	$\Diamond(\exists x)\ Ex$	Premise
4.	$\Box\mid\ (\exists x)$	H $\Diamond$ E on (3)
5.	$\mid\ (x)[Ex \supset \Box(p)(p \supset Kxp)]$	SR (1)
6.	$\mid\ \mid\ Ea$	HEI on 4 a/x
7.	$\mid\ \mid\ Ea \supset \Box(p)(p \supset Kap)$	UI 5 a/x
8.	$\mid\ \mid\ \Box(p)(p \supset Kap)$	MP 7, 6
9.	$\mid\ \mid\ \Box_a\mid\ (p)(p \supset Kap)$	SR 8
10.	$\mid\ \mid\ \quad\mid\ (\exists x)(p)(p \supset Kxp)$	EG 9 x/a
11.	$\mid\ \mid\ \Box(\exists x)(p)(p \supset Kxp)$	$\Box$I 9–10
12.	$\mid\ \Box(\exists x)(p)(p \supset Kxp)$	EI 4, 6–11
13.	$\Diamond\Box(\exists x)(p)(p \supset Kxp)$	$\Diamond$E (3), 4–12
14.	$(\exists x)(p)(p \supset Kxp)$	$\Diamond\Box$E 13
15.	$\mid\ (p)(p \supset Kbp)$	HEI on 14 b/x
16.	$\mid\ (p)(p \supset Kbp) \supset Ob$	UI (2) b/x
17.	$\mid\ Ob$	MP 16, 15
18.	$\mid\ (\exists x)Ox$	EG 17 x/b
19.	$(\exists x)Ox$	EI 14, 15–18

Thus, if (1), (2), and (3) are all true, then there exists an omniscient being. Further, if (1), (2), and (3) are all *known* (or become known), then the derivation just constructed yields knowledge of the existence of an omniscient being. We record this result as Theorem 1.

T1. $[(1) \,\&\, (2) \,\&\, (3)] \supset (\exists x)Ox$

And now for an examination of the meaning of (1)–(3).

Analysis of Meanings of Premises (1)–(3)

It is not difficult to provide an analysis of 'Ex,' or of being an epistemically unsurpassable being, which suffices to make premise (1) both true and demonstrable. Consider Definition 1.

D1. E^1x for $\Box(p)(p \supset Kxp)$

According to D1, to be epistemically unsurpassable is to necessarily know all true propositions.[5] D1 offers an interpretation of 'Ex,'[6] an interpretation that renders 'E^1x' everywhere uniquely eliminable for '$\Box(p)(p \supset Kxp)$'. D1 eliminates talk of epistemic unsurpassability in favor of talk (in a language of first-order modal logic)[7] about the dyadic relation, x knows that p. Given D1, Theorem 2 follows immediately.[8]

T2. $\Box(x)[E^1x \supset \Box(p)(p \supset Kxp)]$
Proof.

1.	$\Box$ | | E^1x	HCP
2.	| | $\Box(p)(p \supset Kxp)$	D1, 1
3.	| $E^1x \supset \Box(p)(p \supset Kxp)$	CP 1–2
4.	| $(x)[E^1x \supset \Box(p)(p \supset Kxp)]$	UG 3 x/x
5.	$\Box(x)[E^1x \supset \Box(p)(p \supset Kxp)]$	$\Box$I 1–4

What T2 shows is that there is an interpretation (via D1) of premise (1) which is a demonstrable truth. We next provide a similar result with respect to premise (2).

Omniscience is a concept with a long history, and usage varies from philosopher to philosopher. But a fair literal reading would be: knowing all truths. This concept is codified in Definition 2.

D2. O^2x for $(p)(p \supset Kxp)$

Thus, on D2, to be omniscient is to know all true propositions. When premise (2) of the epistemic existence argument captured in T1 is interpreted via D2, the result is a provable truth, as Theorem 3 records.

T3. $(x)[(p)(p \supset Kxp) \supset O^2x]$
Proof: similar to the proof of T2.

From T1, T2, and T3 we get Theorem 4.

T4. $\Diamond(\Box\exists x)E^1x \supset (\exists x)O^2x$

Proof. T1 holds for all interpretations of 'Ex' and 'Ox,' and so holds in the special case when 'Ex' is interpreted via D1 and 'Ox' is interpreted via D2. This special case of T1 is strictly equivalent to T2 $\supset$ (T3 $\supset$ T4), from which T4 follows immediately (given T2 and T3).

T4 affirms that there exists a being that is omniscient in the sense of knowing all truths if it is logically *possible* that there is a being exhibiting epistemic unsurpassability in the sense specified in D1. In other words, from the possibility of the existence of a certain kind of perfect being, the actual existence of an omniscient being follows.

A Valid Variant in Free Modal Logic

In examining modal arguments for the existence of some specified kind of entity, a natural question is: will this argument hold up in a *free* modal logic, that is, in a modal logic free of existence assumptions? Hintikka's formal semantics for M + B serves as a free modal analogue of QB−.[9] Clearly the use of Existential Generalization at line ten of the derivation in Section I, while perfectly legitimate in classical modal logics, is *invalid* in a free modal logic.[10] Thus, T1 should not hold in Hintikka's M + B. And, sure enough, it does not. What is, perhaps, somewhat surprising is that there is an analogue of T1 that does hold in Hintikka's M + B. Consider the following variant of (3).

(3') $\Diamond$ Ea.

(3) affirms the possibility of the existence of a being that is epistemically unsurpassable. (3') makes the somewhat stronger claim: for some (it does not matter which) *specific* individual *a*, it is possible that *a* is epistemically unsurpassable.[11] If we keep (1) and (2) as premises and replace premise (3) by (3'), then we get Theorem 5 as an analogue of T1.

T5. $[(1) \& (2) \& (3')] \supset (\exists x)Ox$

The proof of T5 is a *reductio* and proceeds by assuming there is *some* model set m that contains (1), (2), (3'), and (x)~Ox (the denial of '(∃x)Ox'), and then shows that m is *not* an M + B model set.[12]

Proof.

(1)	$\Box(x)[Ex \supset \Box(p)(p \supset Kxp)] \in m$	Hypothesis
(2)	$(x)[(p)(p \supset Kxp) \supset Ox] \in m$	Hypothesis
(3')	$\Diamond Ea \in m$	Hypothesis
4.	$(x){\sim}Ox \in m$	Hypothesis

5.	Ea ∈ n, mRn	C.M.* (3')
6.	(x)[Ex ⊃ □(p)(p ⊃ Kxp)] ∈ n	C.N.* (1), 5
7.	Ea ⊃ □(p)(p ⊃ Kap) ∈ n	C.11. 6, 5
8.	□(p)(p ⊃ Kap) ∈ n	Lemma 1, 7, 5
9.	(p)(p ⊃ Kap) ∈ m	C.N.* 8, (3'), 5, R symmetric
10.	(p)(p ⊃ Kap) ⊃ Oa ∈ m	C.11. (2), 9
11.	Oa ∈ m	Lemma 1, 10, 9
12.	~Oa ∈ m	C.11. 4, 11

Lines 11 and 12 violate C.1. Thus, m is not an M + B model set. Hence, the epistemic existence argument of Section I easily converts to a similar argument that is valid in a modal logic free of existence assumptions. T5 records this result.

Additional Lines of Investigation

If one assumes that questions about which propositions are sufficient to prove the existence of this or that kind of entity are best discussed relative to some specified logic(s),[13] then it is obvious that results of the kind presented in Section I are to be had only when one makes use of some reasonably powerful system of formal logic. The derivation in Section I serves to show the utility of QB– for constructive work in philosophy of religion.[14] But more than this is accomplished by that derivation. The epistemic existence argument which led to T1 is formally valid in QB–, and so holds for any interpretation of 'x is omniscient' and 'x is epistemically unsurpassable.' T1 thus expresses a very general result. There are four somewhat different lines of investigation opened up by T1. The *first* is to consider a wide range of interpretations of 'Ex' and 'Ox,' and to assess the impact of each on the premises of the epistemic existence argument of Section I. Section II provides an example of this sort of investigation, and T4 an example of the sort of result to which it can lead. A *second* line of investigation opened up by T1 is to consider some variations on premises (1)–(3), looking for variations relative to which the proof that led to T1 remains valid. Just as a quick example of what I mean, consider (1'), (2') and Theorem 6.

(1') □(x)[Ex ⊃ □(p)(Kxp ≡ p)]
(2') (x)[(p)(Kxp ≡ p) ⊃ Ox]
T6. [(1') & (2') & (3)] ⊃ (∃x)Ox

When premise (1) is replaced by (1'), premise (2) is replaced by (2'), and premise (3) remains as before, '(∃x)Ox' follows by exactly the same derivation that led to T1.[15] Thus, T6 is a minor variation of T1, albeit a significant one, since D1 and D2 are not, alone, sufficient to yield theorems corresponding to T2 and T3. And this fact leads us to a third area of inquiry opened up by the proof of T1. To answer the question, What additional premise will yield, under D1 and D2, a theorem that is to T6 what T4 is to T1? is to engage in this *third* line of investigation opened up by T1. (Additional information on this issue may be found in LO, 1981.) The *fourth* line of investigation opened up by the valid epistemic existence argument of Section I is the following. Having proven, in QB−, some results of philosophical interest, results that turn essentially on the specific concepts of possibility and necessity used in the proofs, one naturally asks to what extent, if any, are the same, or similar, results obtainable in alternative systems of modal logic? Section III exhibits one result of this kind concerning the epistemic existence argument constructed herein.

In conclusion, we see then, that premises (l)–(3) are sufficient to justify the claim that an omniscient being exists—sufficient in the strong sense that there actually exists a valid formal derivation of that claim from those premises. (*Vide* T1). It is also clear that the same derivation justifies the claim that an omniscient being exists when premises (1) and (2) are replaced by analogous premises (implicitly) concerning alternative concepts of epistemic perfection and omniscience (*vide* T6). It has also been shown that, relative to suitable analyses of epistemic perfection (D1) and omniscience (D2), premises (1) and (2) are themselves provable (*vide* T2 and T3). We have also seen that there is a variant of the second epistemic way [using (3') instead of (3)] for which there is an effective proof using Hintikka model sets. (*Vide* T5). Finally, I have tried to indicate some of the issues in the philosophy of religion that can best be investigated when one works with systems of formal logic that extend classical first-order logic.[16]

Notes

1. Thus, while validity is a necessary condition for having an epistemic existence argument, it is hardly sufficient. I use the word *derivation* in the usual way, so that an argument (or derivation) can only be individuated relative to some effectively described formal system.
2. The arguments constructed in Sections I and III show the validity of the *second* epistemic way. For a discussion of the *first* epistemic way, see Lucas, “The Logic of Omniscience,” Ph.D. Dissertation, the University of Texas at Austin, 1981, pp. 117–129 (hereafter LO). The first published attempt to construct a formal derivation of the conclusion that an omniscience being exists is, I believe, by A. G. Nasser and Patterson Brown, Discussion Note, *Australian Journal of Philosophy* 47 (1969): 61–64, who attempt to formalize the epistemic argument in Hartshorne, LP, chapter 2.

For a discussion of Nasser and Brown and its relation to the argument of Hartshorne, see LO, chapter 3. Also see Hartshorne, CSPM, chapter 14.

3. This English translation of (1) makes use of the fact that (1) is strictly equivalent to the following: $\Box(x)[Ex \supset \sim\Diamond(\exists p)(p \,\&\, \sim Kxp)]$.
4. The proof which follows is constructed in QB− (Quantified B Minus), a system of natural deduction for a Brouwerian modal logic first described in Lucas, LO, chapter 2. The notation used here is adapted from I. Copi's *Symbolic Logic*, 5th ed. (New York: MacMillan, 1979); F. Fitch, *Symbolic Logic* (New York: Ronald Press, 1952); and from G. E. Hughes and M. J. Cresswell, *An Introduction to Modal Logic* (London: Metheun, 1972). [*Editor's Basic Glossary of Notation for Readers Unfamiliar with Modal Logic:* Symbols: $\Box$ = "necessarily," $\Diamond$ = "possibly," (x) = "for all x," $(\exists x)$ = "there exists an x," $\supset$ = "implies," $\equiv$ = "if and only if" or "is logically equivalent to," $\sim$ = "it is not the case that," $\in$ = "is included in the set." Derivation Rules: EG = existential generalization, EI = existential instantiation, HEI = hypothesized existential instantiation, MP = modus ponens, $\Box$I = instantiation from necessity, UI = universal instantiation.]
5. The meaning of 'E^1x' is wholly a function of the meaning of 'x knows that p', the $\supset$, the universal quantifier, and the modal operator $\Box$. Nonetheless, the reader might find the following imaginative exercise helpful. Consider two beings, b_1 and b_2, who each know all truths and differ, with respect to their epistemic traits, only in that b_2 is such that it is possible for there to be a truth unknown to b_2 whereas it is not even a possible truth about b_1 that there exists a truth unknown to b_1. Thus, while b_2 is not surpassed "in actual fact" by b_1, b_2 *is* surpassable in principle by b_1. b_1, unlike b_2, would satisfy D1.
6. 'Ex' is, of course, open to other interpretations. 'Ex' without superscript abbreviates 'x is epistemically unsurpassable'; 'E^1x' with superscript 1 is an expression replaceable in all contexts by '$\Box(p)(p \supset Kxp)$.' Similar remarks apply to 'Ox' and 'O^2x.'
7. Should one desire to make use of the propositional quantifier, (p), the logic requires admission of restricted quantification or else a full second-order logic. In this essay I make no use of quantification over propositions, and the logic remains first-order.
8. TI was proven using QB−. T2 (and T3 below), while provable in QB−, requires nothing stronger than first-order SO.5, and the proof given here is an SO.5 correct proof. T2 and T3 are, in this sense, more general than is T1. (For a discussion of SO. 5, see Hughes and Cresswell, *An Introduction to Modal Logic*.)
9. For a concise presentation of Hintikka's semantics, see J. Hintikka, "Modality and Quantification," *Theoria* 27 (1961): 119–128, which is

reprinted and expanded in Hintikka's *Models for Modalities* (Dordrecht: D. Reidl, 1969).

10. A similar comment holds for the use of Universal Instantiation at line 16. An interesting essay that touches on this very point in a related (albeit different) context is Hintikka's "On the Logic of the Ontological Argument," first published in K. Lambert, ed. *The Logical Way* (New Haven: Yale University Press, 1969) and subsequently reprinted in Hintikka, *Models for Modalities*. [Editor's Comment: Please note that Lucas's (3') ◊Ea is *not* incompatible with any theses of process *ontology*, since (3') cannot be interpreted as making any existence claims, properly speaking. Lucas's point in exploring a free modal variation is simply to make the, I think interesting, logical claim that even with *free modal* assumptions there is a valid scheme of epistemic argumentation. I issue these statements in reply to an anonymous reader.]
11. Since M + B does not require that every name denotes an existing object, (3) does not, in and of itself, require that *a* actually exist.
12. The *reduction* that follows makes some use of minor changes in Hintikka's presentation of the system: for example, the $\supset$ is eliminated in favor of [~,v, &] in Hintikka's version. *Lemma I*: for any model set m, if $p \supset q \in m$ and $p \in m$, then $q \in m$, *provided that* all individuals that occur free in p also occur free in q.
13. For a discussion that is not carried on relative to some specified set of valid rules for constructing derivations see George Mavrodes, *Belief in God* (New York: Random House, 1970).
14. Additional examples may be found in Lucas, LO.
15. Thus, T1, T4, and T6 depend on QB−. T2 and T3 depend on SO.5, and T5 on M + B. An interesting question, not to be pursued here, is: to what extent can the results recorded in T1–T6 be presented relative to weaker, or more general, systems of logic?
16. Much recent work that makes use of modal logic in the philosophy of religion has been inspired by Hartshorne (cf. LP, chapter 2). I am indebted to Professor Hartshorne, not only for generously serving on my dissertation committee while emeritus at the University of Texas, but also for unstintingly giving of his time in discussions with me during the period from 1976 to 1981. Another standard work that makes use of substantial ideas from logic, although not formal, is Plantinga (cf. his *The Nature of Necessity* [Oxford: Oxford University Press, 1974]). An interesting and elegant use of an extremely powerful extension of classical first-order logic in the philosophy of religion is to be found in C. A. Anderson, "Divine Omnipotence and Impossible Tasks: An Intentional Analysis," *International Journal for Philosophy of Religion* 15 (1984):109–124. (I am also indebted to Professor Anderson, not only for

generously serving on my dissertation committee while teaching at the University of Minnesota, but also for having read and provided valuable commentary on more versions of the present essay than either of us cares to remember.) A recent use of elementary modal logic in the field is by Robert Kane, "The Modal Ontological Argument," *Mind* 93 (1984): 336–350, to the author of which I am also indebted.

Chapter 11

The Logic of Future Contingents

GEORGE W. SHIELDS AND DONALD W. VINEY

Introduction

Charles Hartshorne is a respected figure in American philosophy, who is perhaps best known for three major achievements: with Paul Weiss, he took on the arduous project of carefully editing the papers of C. S. Peirce for Harvard University; he has resurrected serious discussion of the logic of the ontological argument; and he has presented a clear exposition and defense of much of A. N. Whitehead's philosophy, in course integrating this defense with a highly sophisticated and original systematic philosophical theology. What is perhaps less known is that Hartshorne has contributed uniquely to some issues in philosophical logic and associated issues in the metaphysics of time, particularly to a whole cluster of time-honored problems associated with the so-called logic of future contingents. In fact, we submit that one of Hartshorne's most important contributions to philosophy in general is his treatment of the future. As Eugene Peters once put it, Hartshorne's solution to the problems of future contingents is one of his genuine "philosophic insights."[1]

In this essay, we shall support Peter's claim by arguing for the following: (1) Hartshorne's position on future contingents has remarkable economy and is perfectly compatible with a libertarian doctrine of freedom (and thus with standard notions of moral accountability); (2) the major criticisms of Hartshorne's position within the critical literature—including implicit ones residing in analytic discussions of middle knowledge—are unwarranted; and (3) Hartshorne's doctrine has strong affinities with the work of a number of significant analytic philosophers who have recently treated issues concerning future contingents, in particular R. M. Adams, William Hasker, J. R. Lucas, Storrs McCall, A. N. Prior, and Linda Zagzebski. (With perhaps the exception of A. N. Prior, these affinities appear to have emerged quite independently, although Hasker has explicitly recognized the affinities, see GTK 188–189.) So far as we are aware, such connections have nowhere been previously commented upon in any sustained way.

We will proceed by first presenting the problems of future contingents in their broad historical context while introducing Hartshorne's solution and his metaphysics of time. We will then examine three major challenges to Hartshorne's view as delivered by S. M. Cahn, Michael Clark, and by a number of analytic philosophers who could be grouped under the banner of "neo-Molinism." In a third and final section, we give pointed attention to J. R. Lucas's work, which is replete with as yet explicitly unnoticed connections to Hartshorne's views.

The Problems of Future Contingents

The usually named "problem" of the logic of future contingents is really a cluster of problem*s* concerning the nature of time, knowledge—especially divine knowledge—of events in time, and the relation of truth to time. The problems arise most forcefully for those who wish to preserve the reality of contingency. For anyone happy to accept what William James famously called the monist's "block-universe," where change, motion, and time are mere appearances of undifferentiated *being*, contingency does not exist.[2] At best, for the monist, there can only be a problem of the logic of things that *appear to be* contingent. No process metaphysics, such as the one developed by Hartshorne, is monistic in this sense. Hartshorne conceives nature as a theater of interactions among ephemeral centers of creative activity, each of which comes to be objectively immortal in the memory of God. For Hartshorne, contingency is real, and thus, the problems of the logic of future contingents demand solutions.

The most elementary meaning of the adjective "contingent" is "could be otherwise," in contrast to "necessary" meaning "could not be otherwise." Philosophers have used these adjectives in both a *de re* and a *de dicto* sense. Understood *de re*, contingency applies to things, objects, processes, attributes, or states of affairs. Understood *de dicto*, contingency applies to declarative sentences. Suppose, for instance, that Charles is going bald but takes steps to retard or reverse the process. Being bald is a contingent attribute of Charles. If he allows the process of balding to continue he may lose all of his hair; but if he intervenes—say, with medication or hair implants—then he will not become bald. The state of affairs of Charles being completely bald is contingent. Likewise, the sentence expressing this state of affairs is contingent. "Charles is completely bald" is true if Charles has no hair on his head but false otherwise.

The problem of the logic of future contingents occurs on at least three levels, two corresponding roughly to the *de re* and *de dicto* meanings of "contingent," and a third involving an interplay between the two meanings. At the first level, the problem is primarily one of *de re* contingency, whether temporal events are contingent and how these might be represented in a metaphysical system. At the second level, *de re* and *de dicto* contingency combine in the problem of whether and how God knows truths about contingent events. At the third level, the problem is primarily a question of *de dicto* contingency; are there eternal truths about contingent events or how are truths about contingent events to be represented? Let us call these three levels respectively the ontological, the cognitive, and the semantic.

Ontology and the logic of future contingents. The ontological dimension of the logic of future contingents concerns the nature and reality of temporal becoming. Hartshorne notes that we often believe, or act as if we believe, that the future could turn out one way rather than another.[3] This is the sense of the contingency of the future. We experience the past differently. It is settled. As Aristotle noted in the *Nichomachean Ethics* (VI, 2), the past is not an object of choice, not even for God. No one can choose to have *sacked* Troy. The medieval thinkers agreed (*pace* Peter Damien). As Thomas Aquinas said in *Summa Theologica* (I, Q 25, a. 4), not even God can restore virginity to a woman once she has lost it. The medievals referred to the past as accidentally necessary to indicate its unchangeability. It should be noted that, although the past is not an object of choice, it often presents itself as having once been a matter of choice. James noted in his essay "The Dilemma of Determinism" that feelings of regret are an indication that the past could have been different from what it is.

The contingency of some aspects of the future and the accidental necessity of the past reflect our invariant experience of the asymmetry of temporal becoming—time proceeds from past to future. We are born before we die; we never die before being born. We grow older, but we never grow younger. We remember the past and we anticipate the future, never the reverse.[4] The past, especially the remote past, is a field where one can discover an inexhaustible detail of facts, but the future, especially the distant future, is only an object of speculation. It is true that our sense of duration varies with our moods and that experiences exist where time seems to stand still. Only in the realm of fantasy, however, are there Merlins whose lives go from future to past.[5] Hartshorne follows Whitehead in thinking that philosophy's "ultimate appeal is to the general consciousness of what in practice we experience" (PR 17). Thus, any philosophical account of time that entails the falsity of temporal asymmetry is, insofar, inadequate.

For Hartshorne, as for Whitehead, time is creation, the coming to be of actuality in the form of individual drops of processive activity. Each "actual occasion" (Whitehead's expression) is causally influenced by its immediate predecessors and causally influences its immediate successors. Hartshorne avoids determinism by construing causal influence as providing necessary conditions for the occurrence of an effect, but never sufficient conditions. The final explanation for why a concrete effect—the becoming of an actual occasion—is the way it is necessarily includes the reaction of the entity on the influences from its past. The actual occasion's own reaction upon its past is the measure of novelty in the universe. The extent of novelty is a matter of degree, from the nearly exact repetition of pattern at the inorganic level to the serendipity of artistic creation at the human level.

The asymmetry of time arises, in Hartshorne's philosophy, from the fact that an actual occasion is internally related to past actual occasions but externally related to future ones. Indeed, the expression "future actuality" is a contradiction in terms. For Hartshorne, to be fully actual is to be fully determinate, and this prerogative belongs only to the past.[6] The future is the realm of more or less unsettled possibilities. Hartshorne, following C. S. Peirce, refers to time as a species of objective modality (CAP 79). The past is actual, the present is the becoming of actuality, and the future is what may become actual.

It is instructive to compare Hartshorne's idea of temporal becoming with what McTaggart called an A-series. An A-series is an array of events running from past to present to future (by contrast, a B-series runs from earlier to later). McTaggart said that when one subtracts the determinations of the A-series, what is left is an ordered array of events without any temporal determinations—he called this a C-series.[7] The C-series is analogous to the alphabet. For example, the letter R has a definite place between Q and S; but it would be incorrect to say that R is temporally after Q or temporally before S. According to Hartshorne's theory, the past is the realm of completed acts of becoming, the future is the realm of what has yet to become, and the present is the becoming of actuality. If one subtracts the determinations of past, present, and future, in Hartshorne's metaphysics, there is no ordered array of events, no C-series; there is simply nothing.

Cognition and the logic of future contingents. It should be evident that, with Hartshorne's metaphysics of time, the future exists only as a more or less well-defined continuum of possibilities. Thus, if God knows the future perfectly, then it is these possibilities that are the objects of God's knowledge. However, the dominant tradition in Jewish and Christian thought has been that God's knowledge of the future is more like our knowledge of events fully determinate in themselves. For Augustine, time itself is a creation of God and does not affect the divine being. Augustine proclaims in the *Confessions* (XI, 13), "Your [God's] today is eternity . . ." In *The Consolation of Philosophy*, (book 5, prose 6), Boethius gave philosophy its most famous definition of eternity, "The complete possession all at once of illimitable life." According to Boethius, God is eternal, surveying events, which to us occur successively, in one unchanging and simultaneous instant. Boethius (*Consolation*, book 4, prose 6), and following him Thomas (*Summa Contra Gentiles*, book I, 66.7), used the analogy that time is to eternity as the points on a circle are to its center. Just as the center is equidistant from all of the points on the circumference, so God is equally present, equally creative, equally knowing at each moment of time.

The Augustinian-Boethian-Thomistic synthesis has a certain elegance but did not go unchallenged. John Duns Scotus, who retained the doctrine of God's timelessness, questioned the circle analogy on the grounds that things not yet in existence could not be present to God.[8] Luis de Molina made essentially the same point.[9] These views prefigure Hartshorne's objection:[10]

> [Classical theism] assumes that events future are yet in themselves real and determinate, or that time is analogous to a circle and not to an endless line whose points are added to it from moment to moment and form no complete sum.

A different, but related, concern was how an eternal, and therefore unchanging, God could know a temporal world. Maimonides, Peter Aureoli, and William of Ockham despaired, albeit for different reasons, of knowing *how* God could know future contingents.[11] The view of Thomas that "the knowledge of God is the cause of all things" (*Summa Theologica* I, Q 14, a.8) seemed only to aggravate the problem by jeopardizing the freedom of the creatures.[12] A desire to preserve a robust sense of human freedom was behind the denial of some philosophers that God knows future contingents. This denial was voiced by Levi ben Gerson and Faustus Socinus, but was most imaginatively expressed in a dialogue of Jules Lequyer.[13] Hartshorne follows the lead of Gerson, Socinus, and Lequyer. Like his forerunners, Hartshorne makes clear that, because future contingents are not actual, it is no limitation on God not to know them as actual.

The Hartshornean position on God's knowledge of the future entails that there is no account of the mechanics of omniscience that can reconcile God's eternal knowledge of the future and human freedom, construed along libertarian lines.[14] Molina demurred. He argued that between God's "natural knowledge" of what *could be* and God's "free knowledge" of what *is* or what God decides to create, God has "middle knowledge" of what *would be*. Molina construes middle knowledge as being similar to natural knowledge in being prevolitional (i.e., independent of anyone's will, including God's) but similar to free knowledge in being contingent. According to this view, God knows, prior to the decision of what world to create, what every possible creature would do under any possible set of circumstances. By creating the creatures, and knowing the circumstances in which they are created, God has perfect knowledge of what they *will do*.

Molinism has generated much excitement among contemporary analytic philosophers of religion.[15] It represents not only the most promising way in which traditional theism can salvage human freedom and divine foreknowledge of future contingents, but it also allows for a strong concept of divine providence. Indeed, as William Hasker says, for anyone committed to libertarian freedom and to a doctrine according to which no detail of the world is outside of God's providential control, "Molinism is the only game in town" (GTK 118). Molinism, however, comes with considerable metaphysical baggage. First, middle knowledge entails the existence of *possible individuals*. Second, Molinism requires that there be enough "counterfactuals of freedom"—truths about what individuals would do under different circumstances—to serve as the basis for God's decision of which world to create. Finally, middle knowledge conditionals are a strange hybrid: they are contingent truths about finite wills, but they are not grounded in the will of any individual, including God. We shall see that Hartshorne, anticipating the objections of some analytic philosophers to middle knowledge, questions each of these assumptions.

Semantics and the logic of future contingents. The idea of an eternal God cognizant of the entire course of history neatly dovetails with the intuition of some logicians that truth is unchanging, or more precisely, that the truth values of propositions do not change. The tenses used in ordinary language *seem* to contradict this intuition. For instance, the sentence, "Neil Armstrong set foot on the moon" is now true but was not true prior to July 20, 1969. To preserve the intuition of the eternity of truth it is necessary to introduce a tenseless copula and to rewrite the sentence in a way that explicitly marks the temporal location of the event: "Neil Armstrong *sets foot* on the moon *on July 20, 1969*." This is an example of what W. V. O. Quine calls an eternal sentence.[16] With the device of eternal sentences, truth can be treated as unchanging. The rewritten sentence can be understood as true whether uttered before the event (as by someone wagering), during the event (as by an eyewitness), or after the event (as by an historian). The tenseless copula serves as the semantic equivalent to the eternity of the medieval God.

The idea of timeless truth troubled some of the ancients for what they saw as its fatalistic implications. Both Diodorus Cronus and Aristotle suspected that eternal truth posed problems for free will (see FLT, chapters 2–3). As we have seen, Aristotle argues that it is impossible to change the past. On the other hand, the future, in so far as it contains real potency for alternate possibilities, has yet to be decided. The truth about it should reflect this openness. Aristotle says in *De Interpretatione* (IX, 19a 33–34):

> Since propositions correspond with facts, it is evident that when in future events there is a real alternative, and a potentiality in contrary

> directions, the corresponding affirmation and denial have the same character.

The problem is that what is eternally true does not admit of an alternative. Consider the sentence, "The sea-battle will occur tomorrow or the sea-battle will not occur tomorrow." The doctrine of eternal truth says that one of the disjuncts, suitably rewritten as an eternal sentence, is true. Thus, the disjunct is true. The most common interpretation of Aristotle is that he believed that the disjunct is true but that neither of the disjuncts can be true, for the sea-battle is a contingent occurrence and tomorrow has not yet arrived (FLT 24–25).

An unhappy consequence of Aristotle's solution is that it seems to suspend the law of excluded middle where propositions about the future are concerned. Certainly this is the case if "The sea-battle will occur tomorrow or the sea-battle will not occur tomorrow" is symbolized "*p* or *not-p*." If Aristotle means to say that *p* and *not-p* are both false, then by the rules of the propositional calculus, "*p* or *not-p*" should be false, which is absurd. If, as seems more likely, he means to introduce a third truth value then he must explain why "*p* or *not-p*" should not be interpreted as neither true nor false. Excluded middle is, after all, simply a restatement of bivalence. Thus, none of the multivalent systems—for instance, those of Łukasiewicz, Bochvar, or Keene—accept excluded middle as a tautology.[17]

Hartshorne is sympathetic to Aristotle's solution. Indeed, in an early article, and for a brief time, he defended it.[18] Within two years, however, he hit on the idea of representing the indeterminacy of the future not in truth values but in predicates pertaining to the future (MVG 100f; IO 45).[19] As Hartshorne puts it (CSPM 145):

> We need no third truth value, but we do need a third type of predicate for future moments of process besides 'definitely P' and 'definitely not P', namely, 'indefinite with respect to P.'

Hartshorne's triad of predicates, "definitely-definitely not-indefinite," is meant to refer to the extent to which the future is causally open or closed with respect to a given event P. If all causal possibilities include P then P will definitely occur. If no causal possibilities include P then P will definitely not occur. If P is included by some and excluded by other causal possibilities then the future is indefinite with respect to P. Hartshorne's solution retains the advantage of Aristotle's insight that the future is, in some respects, open while it avoids the complications that Aristotle's view imposes on logic. We shall expand on and sharpen Hartshorne's triadic scheme immediately in the next section as we place it in the context of an important critique of his view issued by S. M. Cahn.

Major Challenges to Hartshorne's View

Cahn's Challenge

In a reissued contemporary classic entitled *Fate, Logic, and Time* (FLT), Steven M. Cahn presents a provocative defense of Aristotle's solution to the problems of future contingents. In course he gives an interesting commentary on Hartshorne's views. Basically Cahn rejects Hartshorne's position on the grounds that his (Hartshorne's) effort to save the Law of Excluded Middle does so only at the cost of giving up the most hallowed of all logical principles, namely, the Law of Non-Contradiction. Given the stature of FLT in the field of logicofatalism studies and the fact that it serves, in our view, as an excellent critical foil for bringing out the *significance* of Hartshorne's contributions, Cahn's discussion merits close consideration.

Cahn is concerned to respond to a variety of logical arguments that favor the metaphysics of fatalism, including the celebrated Master Argument of the Stoic logician Diodorus Cronus. It is in this context that his critical discussion of Hartshorne occurs. Very roughly stated, the Master Argument asserts that the Law of Excluded Middle (hereafter LEM) compels us to say that either it is true or it is false that an event X will occur, in which case the future is "fated" either to include or exclude X. In his paper entitled "The Meaning of 'Is Going to Be,'" published in *Mind* 74 (1965), Hartshorne sums up his (implicit) case against this argument as follows (cited by Cahn at the beginning of his evaluation of Hartshorne, FLT 60f):

> Any will, will-not, or may-or-may-not statement, if not true, is definitely false; it can only be right or wrong to say that all, or that only some, or that no possibilities at a specified present or past time for a later time include A [a future event]. But whichever of the three statements is true, the others both are false . . . The third "value" is thus in the statement forms, not in their truth status.

Now, according to Cahn, Hartshorne (like A. N. Prior) is here arguing that the LEM, that is, "the law" that any unitary statement is either true or false, need not be compromised "in order to avoid reaching fatalistic conclusions" (FLT 61). Surely Cahn is correct in attributing this view to Hartshorne. This is quite clear from a more rigorous presentation of what has been asserted in the above passage. If we "flesh out" the mentioned future tense statement forms, abbreviated as "any will, will-not or may-or-may-not statement," and represent these by sentential variables, we produce the following statement schemas:

Let X stand for "x will occur."
Let $\overline{X}$ stand for "x will not occur."[20]
Let M stand for "x may-or-may-not occur."

Following Hartshorne's assertion that "whichever of the three statements is true, the others are both false," we produce the following veridical conditionals:

(a) If "X is true," then ("$\overline{X}$ is false" and "M is false").
(b) If "$\overline{X}$ is true," then ("X is false" and "M is false").
(c) If "M is true," then ("X is false" and "$\overline{X}$ is false").

This analysis of future tense statements does not vitiate the LEM, as defined above, since Hartshorne has used *only* the notions of truth and falsehood in his account of the purportedly exhaustive statement forms X, $\overline{X}$, and M. We should add that Hartshorne has also explicitly asserted his desire to avoid violation of the *Law* of Excluded Middle when treating future tense statements on occasions other than the above. For example, he asserts that, since there are other options available for avoiding fatalism, one need not go the way of Łukasiewicz's three-valued logic, whose sacrifice of the law "seems to involve serious inconvenience, at the least."[21] And, although Hartshorne agrees with Cahn's main contention in FLT that "some form of excluded middle must be given up" (CSPM 16, n. 1), he again qualifies this as applying *not* to truth values of statements (hence not applying to the *law* of excluded middle as expressed, say, in the tautologous sentential schema p v~p), but "to predicates and their negatives" (CSPM 17).

Now, Cahn asserts that such an analysis, although it preserves the LEM, does so on the intolerable pain of giving up the Law of Non-Contradiction (Cahn uses the traditional terminology "law of contradiction" that we take to be a misnomer, FLT 63, our italics):

> Hartshorne asserts that it is false that a sea-fight will take place tomorrow and it is false that a sea-fight will not take place tomorrow [note the alternative (c) in the schemata above]. *If* we represent the proposition 'a sea-fight will take place tomorrow' by *p, then* Hartshorne seems to be affirming that *p* is false and *~p* is false. But this is surely to deny the law of contradiction, for *p* and *~p* are certainly contradictories, and as such, one must be true and the other false.

Cahn is well aware that Hartshorne's response to this is that, in the peculiar case of future tense statements, statements of the form "x will occur" and "x will not occur" are contraries *not* contradictories (FLT 63). Yet, he responds to this immediately by asserting that, "at this point it is no longer clear what Hartshorne means by a contradictory or what he means by affirming that one proposition is the contradictory of some other proposition" (FLT 63). For consider: since "there was a sea-fight" and "there was not a sea-fight" are contradictories (and no one challenges *this*), why should a mere change in tense from "there was a sea-fight" to "there will be a sea-fight" remove the status of contradiction (FLT 63)? On this basis, Cahn concludes that Hartshorne avoids fatalism and preserves the LEM only by rejecting the Law of Non-Contradiction. Thus, Hartshorne cannot be correct, according to Cahn, in his claim to have avoided fatalism without giving up *any* fundamental principle of formal logic.

We want to argue that this assessment will not at all do since it can be pointed out *exactly* why Hartshorne wishes to contend that "x will occur" and "x will not occur" statement forms are not strict contradictories. Moreover, he can contend this while assuming the standard truth-functional notion of contradiction as negation of truth value. In fact, Hartshorne's reasoning follows quite orthodox logical considerations, as time-honored as the medieval logician's "square of alterns." We will proceed to show this, and to show in course that the root difficulty with Cahn's criticism resides in his incorrectly representing or mirroring the object-language expressions "x will occur" and "x will not occur" as p and $\sim p$ (respectively) in the metalanguage of unanalyzed sentential schemas. In fact, his so "mapping on" to sentential schemas in this way betrays a begging of the question.

First of all, let us get clear as to what Hartshorne means by "x will occur" and "x will not occur" statement forms. This will involve simply a more rigorous restatement of his assertion that, "it can only be right or wrong to say that *all*, or that only *some*, or that *no* possibilities at a specified present or past time for a later time include A." What Hartshorne seems to have in mind is that: "x will occur" means "all causal conditions for actualization of x (a projected event under some more or less general description) from the utterance about x (to the occurrence of x) are such that x is going to occur." These renditions employ the universal quantifiers "all" and "no," and as such they suggest alternatives on the traditional square of alterns. Note that when an A-type statement and E-type statement having the same terms (say S and P) are both false, this entails that "some S and P" and "some S are not P" are *each* true, and hence are conjunctively true. Employing this analogy with the square to translate into future tense schemata, we could say that, "some causal conditions are and some causal conditions are not, from the utterance about event x, such that x is going to occur, and which *one* set of conditions (as *opposed* to the other) obtains is not decided at the time of the utterance about event x, since *both* sets obtain at the time of the utterance (i.e., if it is *false* that all causal conditions . . . and no causal conditions . . .)."[22]

Hartshorne is here exploiting the fact that our ordinary, common sense notions about the future include a *trichotomy* of expression forms; what might be called "necessitating," "excluding," and "merely permitting" expressions. Such expressions have analogies in present or past tense as well as future tense ordinary scenarios: "She commands (commanded) it," "she forbids (forbade) it," and "she gives (gave) no commands regarding it" (see CSPM 135). Or note the following legal analogy: the law *requires* that you do x, the law *forbids* that you do x, or there is no legal precedent with respect to x.

It seems to us that Cahn has decided without careful consideration that "x will occur" and "x will not occur" *must* map on to sentential metalanguage expressions as *p* and *~p*. For, taking Hartshorne's lead that we employ the "square of alterns" in thinking about this issue, observe the following distinct mapping:

Let (∀p) stand for "all causal conditions at (an arbitrarily selected present time) t"; let (Ep) stand for "there is at least one causal condition at t"; and let "øp" stand for a dispositional predicate expression, "e is going to occur," which predicates of or says something informative about p, that is, the causal conditions relative to t. Given such notation, we produce the following square of alternatives:[23]

> (∀p)øp: All causal conditions at t are such that e is going to occur.
> (∀p)~øp: All causal conditions at t are such that it is not the case that e is going to occur.
> (Ep) øp: There is at least one causal condition at t such that e is going to occur.
> (Ep)~øp: There is at least one causal condition at t such that it is not the case that e is going to occur.

It is important to note that ~[[∀p) øp] ↔ [(Ep) øp]], that is, the A-type and I-type, and respectively, E-type and O-type forms are not semantically equivalent, as we have defined them, since the causal condition in the particularly quantified statements *might not* be included in the scope of conditions covered by (∀p). Whether the condition ranged over by (Ep) is or is not included in the conditions ranged over by (∀p) *depends on the conditions existing at t* such that they either require, exclude, or neither require nor exclude the occurrence of e. Put another way, (∀p)øp if true is a sufficient condition for (Ep)øp, but (Ep)øp if true is *not* a sufficient condition for the truth of (∀p)øp, since, if (Ep)øp happens to be true, this is logically *compatible* with there being at least one possible state relative to t in which it is *not* the case that e is going to occur. In other words, it is at least logically possible that the future relative to t might develop in such a way that conditions come into being that will *then* require the occurrence of e, but it might also develop in such a way that conditions come into being that will *then* exclude the occurrence of e, and this indefiniteness as to which possibility obtains at t is extramentally real.[24] This reasoning is perfectly compatible with the square of alterns model in which particularly quantified statements can *both* be true, in which case the universally quantified statements are *both* false.

On the basis of all this, we should say that "there will be a sea-fight" [symbolically (∀p)∅p], and "there will not be a sea-fight" [symbolically (∀p) ~∅p] map onto sentential meta-language expressions simply as p and q, where p → ~ q and q → ~ p. It is to be noted that [(p → ~ q) • (q → ~ p)] mirrors the truth value semantics of contrariety, not contradiction (which is mirrored by [p ∧ q] where ∧ is *strong* disjunction).[25]

This analysis reveals that Cahn's argument against Hartshorne is in fact question begging. While surely Cahn is correct in holding that "*p* is false" and "*~p* is false" represents a breach of the Law of Non-Contradiction, *the question at issue* is whether or not the future tense "x will occur" and "x will not occur" can be correctly formalized as *p* and *~p, a fortiori* given common sense or ordinary language assumptions about future tense statements. Indeed, we should not assume hastily or naively that syntactical affinity (was/was not—will/will not) translates into semantical affinity (see paragraph below). Put another way, in order to adopt Cahn's assessment of Hartshorne one must *assume* a metaphysics of fatalism, that is, one must assume the position that every event which in fact occurs is fixed *for all time* to occur in order to collapse the alternatives into an exhaustive dichotomy such that at some time t the possibilities are limited to "x will definitely occur" or "x will definitely not occur." If one argues that *on the basis of this exhaustive dichotomy* fatalism follows, this is just to beg the metaphysical question of fatalism, since that very dichotomy already contains fatalism. However, such a begging of the question occurs unwittingly when Cahn asserts that tense *should* make no difference to the contradictory status of the statement forms in question, and that consequently *p* and *~p* correctly represent Hartshorne's interpretation of "a sea-fight will occur" and "a sea-fight will not occur."

Indeed, it seems quite odd that, in the light of other things he says in FLT, Cahn would suggest as the main point in his rejoinder to Hartshorne that a shift in tense will have no effect on the logical status of the statements in question. For example, Cahn presents (in our estimation at least) a powerful argument against any "atemporalistic metaphysical" interpretation of Quine's proposal that all logical constructions be made tenseless by employing a tenseless copula and then by moving any required chronological descriptions into predicate expressions (see FLT 34–35). In effect, he argues that, while one can certainly do what Quine suggests without incurring any formal logical infractions, one cannot interpret such a procedure as disconnecting the *meaning* of statements from temporal references—temporal references are at least sometimes semantically uneliminable. As he sums this up at FLT 127:

> A proposition's tense may be shifted from the verb to the adverbial phrase, but the tense cannot be altogether eliminated without altering the meaning of the proposition. A proposition's tense is thus an integral and uneliminable part of the proposition.

This passage makes it quite clear that Cahn is committed to a temporalistic theory of truth, and so his critique of Hartshorne cannot take the form of argumentation based on any timeless theory in which things can be viewed only from the standpoint of *how matters turn out* (as Rescher and Urquhart phrase it[26]).

But if the semantical uneliminability of temporal references is true as a general principle, then why treat without significant qualification or comment "there *was* a sea-battle" and "there *was* not a sea-battle" as having the *same* logical status as the future tense counterparts of such statements? Indeed, we have some reason to think that tense makes a difference *precisely* in this case. Common sense assumes that the past *is* definite and does not admit "may-be-or-may-be-not" expressions with respect to past *states* themselves as distinct from our *knowledge* of those states. Common sense assumes that it *is* the case that definitely George Washington was elected first U.S. president or he was not so elected. However, we do not often regard the future in the same way, at least from the point of view of commonsense assumption encoded in ordinary language expression. The future states themselves are often conceptualized in terms of "may-be-or-may-be-not" expressions as in, say, the case of discourse about the future result of a game that the players of the game will decide. It is at least logically possible that this applies not just to our knowledge of the future, but to the future itself or *in re*; to assume otherwise would surely beg the metaphysical question of fatalism.

We conclude that what Hartshorne means by a contradiction conforms to its meaning in standard logical theory. There is no reason to think otherwise given our alternative sentential mapping. In fact, Hartshorne's whole manner of handling this issue comports with ordinary language usage and common sense assumption. Now, of course, "common sense" might well be productive of notions which are in fact metaphysically incorrect. But the issue *contra* Hartshorne, as stated by Cahn, is not metaphysical but formal logical, and there is simply no reason why formal logic must exclude the expressions of common sense intuition from the scope of formalization. Hence, for all Cahn has shown in FLT, Hartshorne apparently can avoid fatalism without giving up either the LEM or the Law of Non-Contradiction. Hartshorne's views about future contingents cannot be faulty for any reasons brought against him by Cahn and predicated on the assumptions made by Cahn.

Clark's Challenge

Another analytic philosopher who has published a critique of Hartshorne's 1965 *Mind* essay is Michael Clark.[27] Clark is sympathetic to Hartshorne's ultimate objective of affirming an open future, but he thinks that Hartshorne's analysis of logicofatalism is both flawed and unnecessary. For reasons of economy, we will here briefly examine what we regard as two of the most interesting of Clark's reasons for thinking that Hartshorne's position is flawed. (A full treatment of his detailed objections would require at least an article length discussion, but we hold that each of these can be effectively addressed from a Hartshornean perspective.)

Succinctly stated, Clark issues at least two main objections to Hartshorne's view as follows:

(1) Hartshorne's analysis confines our talk about the future to a strict construction of the "simple future tense" such that a projected future event either definitely will occur, definitely will not occur, or may-or-may-not occur. But, according to Clark, this construal leaves out of account other modes of discourse about the future such as conditional facts that are currently settled. Consider it causally settled at t (8 A.M., August 1) that, "if I get in my car at 8 A.M., August 2, I shall be blown up" (label this conditional proposition A). How should this assertion be handled on Hartshorne's analysis? Because Hartshorne's notion of "definitely will occur" imputes necessity of a future event, Clark suggests that Hartshorne is committed to an odd modal construal that loses the sense of contingency we intend in asserting A (notice that getting in my car at a specified time is, in and by itself, a contingent matter as Hartshorne would certainly agree). That construal runs as follows: "If I *must* be in my car at 8 A.M., August 2, than I *must* be blown up." Hartshorne's triadic scheme for the future thus cannot capture the full intended meaning (senses of contingency included) of a large class of locutions about the future and is consequently inadequate.

But is this really so? While Hartshorne does not treat such conditionals in the *Mind* essay, we hold that it is clear that his triadic scheme allows us to say that, if at t causal conditions are such that this conditional state of affairs *is* necessitated, then such a conditional is true of the future relative to t: All causal conditions at t are such that "if c, then b" and this is precisely contradicted by the statement that some causal conditions at t are not such that "if c, then b" (where c = "I get in my car at 8 A.M., August 2" and b = "I shall be blown up"). What is at stake here is whether this *conditional* state *will be, will not be, or may-or-may-not be*. This seems to preserve the contingency enclosed in the conditional while at the same time preserves Hartshorne's essential metaphysical idea that the creative advance has *narrowed* the alternative futures by virtue of the causal conditions settled at t. Why then are we compelled to interpret

Hartshorne's view here as "If I *must* be in my car at 8 A.M., August 2, then I *must* be blown up"? Such an interpretation hardly seems required.

Perhaps Clark is directed to it because of the modal theorem he appeals to at n. 1, p. 176:

$$[\Box (c \supset b)] \supset (\Box c \supset \Box b)$$

(Here the consequent represents his rendition of Hartshorne's modal construal of A.) But surely this will not do. For consider: If the causal conditions which necessitate $c \supset b$ obtain *only* at some time t, this means that there are at least some possible worlds (say, some prior to t) in which $c \supset b$ is *not* necessitated and thus $\Diamond \sim (c \supset b)$. (Obviously, the context-appropriate modal semantics here cannot allow the "nontemporal" construction of necessity in S5 where any possible world W is accessible from any other W^1 and conversely. Only modal semantics restricting access to possible worlds from the actual world will thus serve, for example, as in Kripke's intuitionist construal of S4.) However, if that is the case, then $\Box (c \supset b)$ cannot characterize Clark's initial assumption that "at t it is causally settled that $c \supset b$." However, Clark would need $\Box (c \supset b)$ in order to get to the entailed $(\Box c \supset \Box b)$, which he thinks represents Hartshorne's "odd" construal of the conditional proposition A. Thus, it remains quite puzzling as to why Hartshorne's concept of the conditional future as implied in his triadic scheme must be interpreted in Clark's fashion.

(2) Clark also objects that, if Hartshorne's analysis is correct, no logical asymmetry between past and future is established, contrary to Hartshorne's underlying intentions. This is because, if we accept Hartshorne's analysis of the future, it can be applied to the past such that the past, like the future, is "open." Clark states (p. 178):

> Given present states of affairs and laws of nature, there are many different detailed courses which the future might take. But equally, given the laws of nature, if we consider present conditions as effects, there are many detailed pasts from which they might have arisen. There are past events which are contingent with respect to the present, which are not retrodictable even in principle from present conditions using laws of nature.

But this is quite mistaken from the standpoint of Hartshorne semantics and process metaphysics. At a present time t, there are in fact no "detailed different *pasts*," and, on Hartshorne's view, there are certainly no *past* events that are contingent in their relation to the present. As Hartshorne makes clear in an important paper,[28] both prediction and deductive inference run retrodictively. A present "effect" such as "I am writing on Clark's analysis" implies propositions true of the past such as "I learned of the existence of Clark's analysis," but there is no converse implication (if with Clark and Hartshorne relative indeterminism is assumed), and this relation of retrodictive implication is not itself contingent. We *could not now* be writing about Clark's analysis if it were not first true that we had encountered such an analysis. To say this expresses the very meaning of the doctrine of *cumulative becoming*. Moreover, properly speaking, there is only one past relative to t. On Hartshorne's metaphysics, the very meaning of "the past" is that it is that modal condition of actuality such that *once future* alternative possibilities have been eliminated so as to achieve actual choice among those alternatives. At best, then, we could say that there are many detailed different *past futures* (a subset of "the past" given the ontological principle's assertion that possibilities are always possibilities of actuality). In fact, Clark can suggest to us an "openness" of the past only by referring to *the future* in a retrodictive way. But no *ontological* openness of the past relative to some present time t is established by any of Clark's considerations, since the past relative to t is in fact *immutable* at t and any time subsequent to t, that is, the past at t just *is both* the set of actualities at t *and* the set of past futures at t. In effect, any assertion about states of affairs at t, made at any time in the future of t is ontologically closed (given Hartshorne's metaphysics of time). Whatever has been achieved at t and whatever possibilities attended that achievement are forevermore. This is something that *cannot* be said of the set of possibilia in the future of t. In fact, since (on the Hartshorne-Peirce theory of future possibilia as dense continua[29]) possibilia are protean, novel possibilia for future actualization—new determin*ables*—have emerged at t. Herein lies an irreducible asymmetry.

Futhermore, Clark's explanation of his statement about retrodiction is put in epistemic terms, in terms of evidence (p. 178):

> Consider all the cases of suicide in Britain this year. After the suicides have occurred there remains evidence of them; the year after, the evidence is enough to determine precisely who killed himself, but hundreds of years later, perhaps, the remaining evidence is enough to establish roughly how many suicides there were but not precisely who they were. The openness of the future is matched by a corresponding openness in the past.

But this is again confusion. Statements about the condition of our evidence for making retrodictions are not at all statements about the past. Rather, they are about the present or (in the case of Clark's scenario) the future! No *ontological* openness of the past is established by any present or future human *epistemic* limitations.

In so far as we have reviewed Clark's critique here, we conclude that Hartshorne is both modest and correct in his only published comment on Clark's essay: Clark's objections are indeed "inconclusive."[30]

Hartshorne and the Challenge of Molinism

A number of contemporary analytic philosophers are convinced by Molina's construal of future contingents (or some variation of it). But, as pointed out earlier, Molina's view denies that the future is "open" for God. So, any defense of Molinism carries an implicit rejection of Hartshorne's position on future contingents in relation to God's knowledge. Thus, recent efforts to resurrect Molina ought to be carefully examined. Moreover, since (outside of some brief work by the authors and two other articles[31]) process philosophers have been slow to address the now long-standing "Neo-Molinist" developments in recent analytic philosophy, the following represents a much needed execution of, as it were, "unfinished business."

According to Luis de Molina, God knows, antecedent to the decision to create the universe, what any creature *would do* in any situation that the creature might face. This is called middle knowledge. If the actual world is the created world, then it is not *actual* creatures about which God has middle knowledge but *possible* ones, for God's knowledge is antecedent to, or logically prior to, the decision to create. Thus, once the universe is created, God knows what the actual creatures in it *will do* because God knew what their possible counterparts *would do*. To clarify, let S be a possible creature and let C be a situation in which S could be placed. Let A and not-A be the decisions (for A, or for not-A) that S might exercise. We can imagine two possible worlds, P1 and P2, such that:

P1: S is in C and decides A.
P2: S is in C and decides not-A.

Molina maintains that God knows which of these possible worlds would occur if S were created to be in C. For the sake of argument, let us suppose that S in C would decide A. This yields a middle knowledge conditional—MK-conditional for short—with the following form, MK/P1:

MK/P1: If S were in C then S would decide A.

This is the sort of proposition that God is said to know according to Molina's theory.

Philosophers generally follow David Vriend in referring to MK-conditionals as "counterfactuals of freedom" (VF 91). We prefer the more neutral and descriptive expression "MK-conditional." First, we wish to be explicit in leaving open the question whether MK-conditionals are counterfactuals of *freedom*. Above all, however, we want to emphasize that the logical subjects of MK-conditionals, unlike counterfactuals of freedom, are *possible* individuals.[32] To ignore the distinction between the actual and the possible is to invite modal confusion. Examples of what actual individuals would do under varying circumstances have an air of plausibility that is lacking when one speaks of what merely possible individuals would do. This is because possible individuals, unlike actual ones, are themselves counterfactual and thus have no actual characteristics, properties, or life histories in terms of which to anchor judgments about what they would do, or even what they might do.

Molina's theory is specifically designed to safeguard a strong sense of the libertarian free will of the creatures and God's infallible knowledge of their decisions. That is to say, Molina means to preserve a doctrine of freedom according to which one's decision is free only if one could have decided otherwise in the same circumstances. In our example, S decides A in C; but if S is free in this libertarian sense, S *could have* decided not-A in C. Put differently, P2 is not an impossible world. Molina therefore construes MK-conditionals as contingently true. If God creates S in C then S *will* decide A and God knows this because God knows a MK-conditional that says S *would* decide A in C. God also knows, however, that S could have decided not-A in C. Thus, the MK-conditional, "If S were in C then S would decide not-A" could have been true.

Not least among the attractions of Molinism is that it promises, in Thomas Flint's colorful language, a theoretical basis for preserving a "real, red-blooded providence and genuine, true-blue freedom" (DP 99). Flint goes so far as to claim that, from the standpoint of those who take traditional Christianity as normative, anti-Molinism carries a heavy burden of proof (DP 107–108).[33] W. L. Craig, an enthusiastic proponent of middle knowledge, explains the attraction of Molinism (OWG 134):

> Think then of God's planning the entire course of world history so as to achieve his purposes! Given middle knowledge, the apparent contradiction between God's sovereignty, which seems to crush human freedom, and human freedom, which seems to break God's sovereignty, is resolved. In his infinite intelligence, God is able to plan a world in which his designs are achieved by creatures acting freely. Praise be to God!

This is not to say that Molinism permits God the ability to create any possible world. In our example, P2 is a possible world. If we make an additional assumption that S is free in C, then we must say that God cannot create P2, for the MK-conditional—stipulated for the sake of argument—is that S *would decide* A in C.[34]

A question that figures prominently in discussions of Molinism is, What or who brings it about that a MK-conditional is true? Molinists agree that God is not responsible for their truth, for that would compromise the very freedom that the theory was designed to preserve (cf. DP 123).[35] This leaves only two alternatives:

1. MK-conditionals are made true (or false) by *possible* persons or by the properties that possible persons possess.
2. MK-conditionals are not made true by anyone; they simply are true (or false).

Fransisco Suarez, Molina's younger contemporary, defended the first alternative. Suarez postulated in possible creatures a property (a *habitudo*) of freely acting in specific ways in specific situations (VF 81). David Basinger argues that Molinists should adopt the second alternative.[36] Craig apparently agrees, for he refers to God's middle knowledge as a form of innate knowledge (OWG 133). Fredosso also seems to recommend that MK-conditionals are not made true by anyone (LMDF 74–75).

It is important to understand why Molinists cannot say that MK-conditionals are made true by *actual* persons. Flint outlines four reasons for this, but two stand out as most significant (cf. DP 124). First, if God is to be able to use MK-conditionals in deciding which universe to create, then the conditionals must be true independent of the existence of the persons God chooses to create. Second, and more fundamentally, MK-conditionals are true (or false) whether or not the possible individual who is their logical subject ever exists. If a statement is true (or false) whether or not S exists, then it is difficult to understand how S could in any way be responsible for its truth value. Flint remarks that some MK-conditionals refer to people who never get created, "*uninstantiated creaturely essences*" (DP 124). More precisely, on Molinist principles, *no* MK-conditional refers to an instantiated creaturely essence *apart from God's decision to create particular persons*.[37]

Hartshorne never explicitly addresses Molinism in his writings—he noted in personal correspondence, "I have not gone into Molina" (letter to Viney, 27 August 1988). There can be no doubt, however, that his understanding of the logic of future contingents leaves no room for MK-conditionals. This is not at all to say that Hartshorne rejects all *would-be* conditionals as false (see discussion of Clark above) or that he denies God's knowledge of them. He writes (PCH 662):

> God, I suppose, knows what "would be true" if this or that happened tomorrow, but this would be is no very definite history. Tomorrow will define itself, it cannot be defined in advance plus some universal trait of "actuality." It will have new predicates, not merely new applications of old predicates.

When Hartshorne speaks of "tomorrow" adding "new predicates" to what already exists, he is reaffirming his conviction of the reality of creative becoming. He says, "'Reality' means 'as of now,' and the 'now' acquires new reference each moment" (CSPM 118; ZF 124). The would-be conditionals that Hartshorne acknowledges lack the specificity to count as genuine MK-conditionals.

At the heart of Hartshorne's denial of MK-conditionals is his denial of the existence of merely possible individuals. He says, "There is an unutilized possibility of individuals, but not an individuality of unutilized possibility" (MVG 308). It is the nature of possibility, according to Hartshorne, to leave some details unspecified. For example, fictional characters, unlike actual people, have *no fully detailed biography* (MVG 308):

> Mr. Micawber is a quasi-individual, with some of the aesthetic properties of an individual, but not an individual in the strict sense. He is a class, specific enough to simulate an individual for the purposes of the aesthetic illusion or "make-believe."

A similar observation can be made about future persons. Fictional characters, however, are unlike our descendants in that they form *a class of variables* tied to our creative imagination. Our descendants, on the other hand, form *a class of variables* tied to our reproductive potentialities. One's first child—to consider one variable of reproductive potential—could be male or female, and this *variable* becomes a *constant* only at conception. Another variable is quantity. One's "first" child may be twins!

The idea of future generations is most usefully contrasted with the idea of generations past. Our ancestors are fixed points of reference in an array of past events. There are facts about them that can be discovered, but none that can be created (setting aside ersatz properties like "born 300 years before the invention of the airplane"). One's paternal grandmother, for example, refers to a fully definite individual about whom one may have accurate or inaccurate memories and whose life one could research. One's descendants, however, leave no traces in the future to be discovered. At best, one can speak of a range of characteristics that may be true of them depending on the actual causal conditions of the past and present (e.g., one may refuse to have children for fear they would inherit a severe genetic defect). The asymmetry between ancestors and descendants can be expressed this way: to speak of one's ancestors is to speak of the ancestors one had; but to speak of one's descendants is not perforce to speak of the descendants one will have. Thus, Hartshorne says, apart from the special case of God, "individuals have to be identified partly by some empirical reference or other" (LP 62).[38]

Hartshorne takes the actual world as a primitive notion and defines possible worlds, or more precisely, possible world-states, as ways that the actual world could be or might have been. As noted in our introduction, the actual world presents itself as an integrated but multifarious process of becoming, and this is the sense of actuality operative in Hartshorne's philosophy. Thus, Hartshorne's understanding of "actual world" differs from those who think of the actual world in abstraction from its temporal flux, imagining the future to be on the same ontological footing as the past. Hartshorne asks, "If all the definiteness there could ever be were laid up in eternal arrays of definite qualities, why would there be any point in actual instances?" (PCH 609). Hartshorne maintains that the concept of merely possible individuals destroys the distinction between the possible and the actual, and with it, the notion of becoming (LP 165):

> Before events happen, they lack nothing except a totally transparent, featureless something called "actual occurrence." To some of us this is truly an absurdity. If becoming does not create new quality and quantity, new determinateness, then, we argue, it creates nothing, and nothing ever really becomes.

Doubtless, convinced Molinists do not share Hartshorne's sense of the absurdity of the idea of merely possible individuals. However, it is worth noting that, as a matter of intelligibility, possible worlds—which possible individuals are imagined to inhabit—are defined or identified as variations of the actual world. For example, Alvin Plantinga, for whom the actual world is one of the possible worlds, must construct *all* of his examples of possible worlds—"maximally complete states of affairs"—from descriptions of the actual world (NN 45). In practice, Molinists must be Hartshorneans, *always* grounding talk of possible worlds in the actual world. If one is to gain an inkling of what God's prevolitional knowledge is like, on Molina's view, it is necessary to omit *all* mention of what is actual—save the existence of God—and think only of galaxies of fully definite possible worlds inhabited by fully definite individuals.[39]

If possible individuals do not exist in the sense required by Molinism then there can be no agents to serve as the explanations for why MK-conditionals are true (or false). Suarez's theory of *habitudos* also falters if possible individuals do not exist. This is not to say that counterfactuals pertaining to possible decisions of actual creatures can have no truth values. We often know how people will react under given conditions and this serves to guide our own decisions in ways that bear a distant analogy with the way Molina conceives God to employ MK-conditionals in the creation of the cosmos. For example, one purchases a rare recording of Caruso for a friend known to have a fondness for great tenors. One's knowledge of the friend's tastes in music, of his character as so far formed, allows one to *predict*, with reasonable certainty, how he will respond (cf. MVG 103). Of course, here we are speaking of counterfactual conditionals for actual persons. Moreover, *no* MK-conditional presupposes a probability about what a person would do whereas *many* of our ordinary projections about how someone would respond to a situation are shot through with fallibility and judgments of probability. The friend who loves tenors, for instance, may also be so fastidious about sound quality that he cannot appreciate the gift. Adams presses the objection to Molinism that counterfactuals of freedom are all false, or more precisely, that he does not understand what it would be for them to be true (VF 79, 91, note 4). Hasker also defends the view that there are no true counterfactuals of freedom (GTK, chapter 2). Both Adams and Hasker opt for the view that counterfactuals about free decisions should be couched in terms of what the agent *would probably do*. This is close to Hartshorne's view, although he introduces an important qualification (LP 171):

> When we feel morally responsible for an act, this need not mean that we think that, as we were the instant before, we had the psychological capacity to refrain from it. It may only imply that at some time previously we could have entered upon a different course from the one which led to the act.

It is in the spirit of Hartshorne's qualification on libertarian freedom to adopt a position like that of Robert Kane. According to Kane, "*Not all* of our morally responsible choices or actions (those for which we are truly praiseworthy or blameworthy) have to be such that we could have done otherwise with respect to them directly" (SFW 40). Free will, for Kane, involves being the ultimate creator and sustainer of one's own ends and purposes, and this requires only that *some* of our decisions could have been otherwise (SFW 4, 43).

It should come as no consolation to Molinists if Adams and Hasker are wrong in claiming that no counterfactuals of freedom hold true. Both defenders and detractors of Molinism give plausible counterexamples to the Adams-Hasker view. Plantinga, a defender of middle knowledge, gives this example: "If Adams were to ask me to go climbing at Tahquiz Rock the next time I come to California, I would gladly (and freely) accept."[40] Zagzebski, a critic of middle knowledge, gives this example: "If I had taught a course on Aristotle last semester, I would not have primarily assigned readings from Hegel" (DFF 136). Each of these examples is easily accommodated by Hartshorne's (or Kane's) modified libertarian model of free choice. The examples only defeat the claim that counterfactuals of freedom are not possible; they do not support the more extravagant position that *all* counterfactuals of freedom can be expressed as *would-be* conditionals. Zagzebski rightly concludes, "The defense of the truth of certain carefully selected examples of counterfactuals of freedom is nowhere near sufficient to show the truth of the theory of middle knowledge, or even its plausibility" (DFF 141).

Thus far we have considered Hartshorne's rejection of MK-conditionals. Yet, even granting the generous assumption that possible individuals exist to serve as subjects of MK-conditionals, Hartshorne's metaphysics provides reasons for thinking that Molinism cannot do what it promises, to wit, preserve both libertarian freedom for the creatures and divine foreknowledge of their decisions. A consequence of Hartshorne's view of actuality and possibility, where the decisions of the creatures are concerned, is that what was or is possible is coterminous with what *could have been actual* or what *could yet be actual*. In a word, to be actually possible is to be (or to have been) possibly actual. In contemplating the past we consider what might have been had our choices been different. The feelings of relief (at disasters avoided) or regret (at opportunities missed) reflect our sense that the past was once a realm of alternatives awaiting our decisions. Our anxiety (over important decisions) reflects our sense that the shape of tomorrow depends on what we do today. Our feelings betray our beliefs that the past might have taken a different course and that the future might take one course rather than another, all depending on our decisions.

The Hartshornean equation of *the actually possible* and *the possibly actual* is inconsistent with the doctrine of middle knowledge. Recall the possible worlds labeled P1 and P2:

P1: S is in C and decides A.
P2: S is in C and decides not-A.

We stipulated that God knows the following MK-conditional:

MK/P1: If S were in C, S would decide A.

On Hartshorne's view, if P2 is indeed a possible world, or a possible world-state then, at some time prior to the actualization of S being in C, the state of affairs described by "S decides not-A" could have become actual. On Molinist principles, however, the only possible worlds that can become the actual world are worlds that God can create. Because MK/P1 is true, any world that God creates in which S is in C will also be one in which S decides A. Therefore, P2 is not a world that could become actual. If P2 is not a world that could have been actual then the requirement of libertarian freedom that S in C could decide A or not-A cannot be met.[41] We do not deny that, on the Molinist account, P2 is a possible world. However, because it is a possibility that could never become actual, it is not enough to guarantee S's libertarian freedom. As far as S's freedom is concerned, P2 is, to borrow a phrase from James Felt, an "impossible world" (IW). Thus, the MK-conditional MK/P1 is not a counterfactual of *freedom*. If we ask, "Could S have decided not-A in C?" the Molinist answer must be, "Not in any world God could have created."

Within analytic circles, the closest parallels to the Hartshornean argument we have proposed are in Adams's and Zagzebski's discussions of middle knowledge.[42] According to Zagzebski (DFF 140):

> [The] relation between the antecedent and the consequent of a counterfactual conditional is like the relation between the present and the future. Given that the present is what it is, there are many ways the future might be. [. . .] There are also some ways the future *would* be, given that the past is what it is, so every branching path may include the same event.

Zagzebski singles out the principle of conditional excluded middle (CEM) for criticism. CEM states that the contradictory of "If X then Y would occur" is "If X then Y would not occur." Adams notes that the negation of a conditional is not obtained by denying its consequent, but by denying the entire conditional (VF 79). Zagzebski agrees. Her analysis treats these statements as contraries, analogous to universal categorical propositions on the square of opposition. If the statement "If X then Y might or might not occur" is true then the *would* and *would not* statements are both false. This is very similar to, and is in fact a variation on, Hartshorne's claim, discussed in our Introduction and earlier (under "Cahn's Challenge"), that "P will occur" and "P will not occur" are contraries, with "P may or may not occur" as the proposition that completes the triad.

By tying the truth values of counterfactual statements to the asymmetry between past and future, Hartshorne and Zagzebski can explain why counterfactuals about actual persons are true or false. Hartshorne maintains that causal conditions of the universe at any given moment delimit the range of possible effects that can issue from those conditions. Zagzebski agrees, although she believes that the counterfactual relation involves more than causal and logical necessity (DFF, chapter 4). Both philosophers agree that the truth or falsity of counterfactuals are not mere brute facts about existence but are, in part, explained by a network of causal relations in the creative advance from past to future. In our previous example, the friend's decision to make a gift of the Caruso recording was grounded in the knowledge that the recipient loved tenors.

The familiar complaint against Molinism that MK-conditionals are "groundless" surely has its source in the common practices that Hartshorne and Zagzebski can cite in support of their accounts. Counterfactuals about actual states of affairs and actual individuals are clearly not groundless. Our assessments of *what could be* and *what would be* are grounded in our knowledge, or at least our claims to knowledge, of *what is actual.* This serves to highlight a striking difference between ordinary counterfactuals and MK-conditionals. A very plausible theory, like that of Hartshorne or Zagzebski, explains, in principle, the truth conditions for ordinary counterfactuals. The MK-conditionals posited by Molinism, on the other hand, are contingently true, but there is no explanation of their truth. Thus, the (stipulated) truth of "If S were in C then S would (freely) decide A" is a metaphysical surd—not a necessary truth, not a truth derivable by axioms of a metaphysical system,[43] not a consequence of God's will, and not even a consequence of S's decision.[44] The lack of an explanation for these odd truths must surely count as a mark against Molinism. As Hartshorne says, "Contingent possibilities not in time, conceivable accidents in eternity, make no more sense to me than they evidently did to Aristotle" (IO 47).

We thus conclude that the examined contemporary efforts at resurrecting Molina's position fail. Consequently, Hartshorne's position on future contingents stands unscathed for any reasons presented on behalf of middle knowledge.

Hartshorne and J. R. Lucas's *The Future*

As we have just seen, a number of important analytic philosophers have arrived independently at positions quite close and sometimes identical in important respects to Charles Hartshorne's (R. M. Adams, W. Hasker, R. Kane, and L. Zagzebski). We add that one of the most rigorous treatments of the logic of future contingents in the entire analytic literature—J. R. Lucas's formidable *The Future: An Essay on God, Temporality, and Truth* (F)—also exhibits a remarkable alignment with Hartshorne's position, so much so that we devote a separate and final section to discussion of it. To our knowledge, no such comparative commentary exists in the critical literature.

Lucas's *The Future* develops a modal tree semantics approach to the logic of future contingents. The tree with its branches is an apt image for expressing the processual nature of reality: the trunk represents the actual past with branches representing the possible paths that the future might take. Using the diagrammatic device of trees, Lucas's general program is to express quite precisely a metaphysics of time that is very much akin to Hartshorne's with its stress on the irreducible asymmetry of the temporal modes.[45] More specifically, there are at least three junctures in Lucas's treatise where he constructs Hartshornean positions on future contingents: (1) setting out an implicit Hartshornean modal square, he develops an accessibility model of tree semantics that resists "pressure from the Principle of Bivalence" while preserving Excluded Middle and that resists "necessitarian" overtones (F 153–154); (2) in his discussion of "Defeasible Truth" (F 177–180), he provides a model for discussing Aristotle's sea battle based on two accessibility relations (a "weaker" relation labeled Q_1 and a "stronger" relation Q_2), which closely approximates Hartshorne's discussion of future contingents in *Creative Synthesis*; and (3) in a chapter on "The Vulnerability of God," Lucas argues for an implicitly dipolar conception of deity, a deity that logically cannot know all the details of the future given a universe containing free creatures and governed by the laws of quantum mechanics. We will explicate each of these items in turn:

(1) Lucas develops a dynamic view of time and temporal becoming, which, like Hartshorne's, resists necessitarian or strict deterministic conceptions of the future. At F 153, he explicitly rejects "pressure from the Principle of Bivalence" in so far as it leads us to hold that, necessarily, if it isn't true that there is going to be a sea battle tomorrow, then it can only be false that there is going to be a sea battle tomorrow. (This, of course, is Hartshorne's view as well.) In light of this rejection, Lucas constructs the modal logic of his so-labeled "future operator" in a way that resists "necessitarian overtones." This logic lines up neatly with the Hartshornean square explicated in the section on "Major Challenges to Hartshorne's View" as it produces a fourfold scheme of veridically cast future-tense propositions. Stated in abbreviated form, and assuming Lucas's tree semantical qualifications cited below, we have:

1. It is true that L_t PR. 3. It is true that M_t PR.

2. It is false that L_t PR. 4. It is false that M_t PR.

(where L_t = "temporal necessity," M_t = "temporal possibility," and PR is an arbitrary proposition about the future). These can be arranged into the following square of alternatives having analogies with the nonmodal Aristotelian categoricals A, E, I, and O:

It is true that L_t PR. ↔ It is false that M_t PR.

It is true that M_t PR. ↔ It is false that L_t PR.

It is true that L_t PR.	It is false that L_t PR.
It is true that M_t PR.	It is false that M_t PR.

We cite the appropriate passage from Lucas's text in full (F 153–154). Note that the A and E analogues in Lucas's tree semantical construction carry, so to speak, universal quantification over all Q-accessible and Q^{-1}-accessible worlds of date R in the tree T (t) with node at t (i.e., truth can be assigned to L_t PR *iff* L_t PR holds in *every* Q-accessible and Q^{-1}-accessible world, etc.), while the I and O analogues carry, so to speak, particular quantification (i.e., truth can be assigned to M_t PR *iff* M_t PR holds in *some* Q-accessible or Q^{-1}-accessible world):

> We assign TRUE to L_t PR, iff *every* Q-accessible and Q^{-1}-accessible world W_{iR} of date R in the Tree T (t)with node at t is one in which PR be True, and otherwise we assign FALSE to L_t PR.

Similarly we assign TRUE to M_t PR, iff *some* Q-accessible or Q^{-1}-accessible world of date R in the Tree T (t) with node at t is one in which PR *be* true, and otherwise we assign FALSE to M_t PR.

(2) In a chapter on "The Actual Future," Lucas develops a tree semantical approach to two ways in which we can regard the future. These two ways are characterized by Lucas in terms of two kinds of accessibility relations to possible worlds which he labels Q_1 and Q_2. He develops these ideas in something like the following way in a section on "Defeasible Truth" (F 177–180):

Suppose an admiral at a time t gives an order to attack the enemy at 5 P.M. the following day (label this subsequent time t^1). The subordinate captains may predict with reason that "there will be a sea battle tomorrow." For practical purposes, we might say that the prediction is "properly grounded." This involves us in the assumption of a narrow range of possibilities prior to t^1 such that the possible worlds (represented by tree branches) at t^1 contain the predicted event. That is to say, the subordinate captains at t consider the future sea battle at t^1 to be contained in the present moment t by virtue of the admiral's order. Because of the admiral's order, for all practical purposes, the sea battle has "got to" occur. This kind of accessibility relation to possible worlds can be regarded as a weaker Q_1 relation. On the other hand, a full or metaphysically comprehensive perspective takes into account a much wider range of possibilities prior to t^1: at 4:59 p.m. on the day of t^1 the admiral might change his mind and order the subordinates to stand down; at 4:50 P.M. on the day of t^1 (because of disturbances in the weather noticeable only at 3 P.M. on the day of t^1), a severe storm blows the naval vessels out of firing range; the admiral's order might be countermanded prior to t^1 by the Secretary of the Navy; and so on and on. In other words, given a complex indeterministic universe that includes the existence of deliberating agents who might change their intentions at any time prior to a predicted event at t^1, there are very many possible worlds at t^1 that do not include, say, a sea battle. Here there is no "got to" at time t as allowed in the Q_1 relations model. The kind of accessibility relation which takes into account these wider possibilities can be regarded as a stronger Q_2 relation. Thus, we employ in our discourse about the future two distinct modalities, Q_1 and Q_2.

However, the actual future should be represented by a tree semantical diagram which corresponds to the wider Q_2 modality with the narrower Q_1 mapped on to it. Assume that u is the time of the event and t a "posterior present" time of utterance about u. The line ending at the box represents the past, while the various branches with nodes (the nodes are represented by the small circles and are intended to indicate possible events) represent possible worlds or pathways. Some of these branches at their nodes contain a sea battle and others do not. The set of possible worlds which includes a sea battle is circled. The narrow Q_1 view of the future is a subset of the larger Q_2 view; Q_1 is thus represented by the bold lines inside the whole Q_2 tree. Thus, we have the following diagram (F 179):

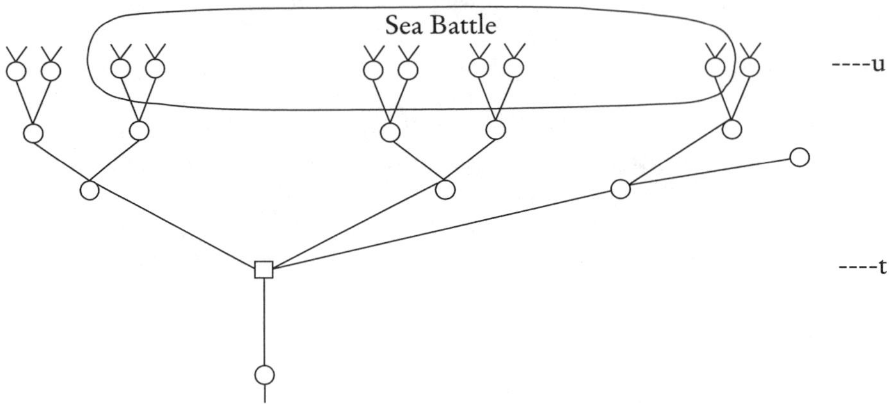

The point of this is to show that truth-claims about the future can "be defeated only by the passage of time" (F 180). Thus, only at u or "only *ex post facto*" can we determine that any Q_1 predictions would not be defeated by the course of events (F 180). As such only valedictory truth can be ascribed to Q_1 predictions.

This significantly matches Hartshorne's discussion at CSPM 135–136 where he treats the complications for logic introduced by his rejection of the notion that "truth is timeless." Here he considers Frederick Waismann's contention that the notion of "temporal truth" implies the purportedly "absurd" question, "*when* did it become true that a certain date and place definitely includes, say, rain?" Hartshorne retorts that in principle this question is not at all absurd. It becomes true at just that time when causal conditions definitively require rain and exclude nonrain at the mentioned date and place (CSPM 136). In terms of Lucas's vocabulary, it becomes true at just that node in the semantical tree of the actual future in which all branches or possible worlds traceable to that node contain rain. Moreover, Hartshorne clearly implies just such a wider Q_2 tree semantics of the actual future when he makes the following three points: (a) the passage of time is an *essential* factor in determining the probability or propensity for the occurrence of an event, (b) as in Lucas's Q_2 tree semantics, the dates t and u are *both* essentially required, and (c) the truth concerning a projected event can only be determined in a definitive way ("indefectibly" in Lucas's terminology) by the occurrence of the event (or events near the occurrence of the projected event). Consider the following passage from CSPM 136 (which we have correlated with points a–c).

> Years before a suicide happened there was only a probability or mild probability that the suicide would take place [thus, as in Q_2, allowing many possible worlds containing no suicide]. But a few seconds before, it may have been impossible, considering the laws of nature, including human nature, that the man should not take his life [a]. And at any rate we know that *the truth of an occurrence comes into being with*, or at some finite time before, *the occurrence* [c, our italics] . . . To say, 'it happens at time t' is only a proposition schema, not a definite proposition. To become a proposition it must read, 'As of, and after, time t, a certain feature definitely belongs to time t^1.' Two dates, date of affirmation and date of the event, are in principle required [b].

(3) After completing his discussion of the modal logic of time, and in words that appear almost as if they had been written by Hartshorne himself (minus the use of "Him" for the deity), Lucas offers this summation of the implications of his view for metaphysics and theology (F 209, our italics):

> If time is a perpetual becoming, a weaving rather than an unrolling, we cannot take a static view of the universe, but must see it as dynamic, in which something is always happening, *vague possibilities crystallizing out into sharp actuality*. Reality is through and through temporal. Equally, God is temporal, though not merely that. Although we can properly say that God is more than merely temporal, that He transcends time, and to that extent is beyond and outside time, we cannot say that He is timeless, or that for Him there is no difference between future and past.

While Lucas speaks of divine action in clearly unilateral, interventionist ways that are alien to Hartshorne's model of divine action (e.g., raising Jesus from the dead, F 210)—and he clearly accepts the notion of omnipotence that holds that God *chose* to create a world with entities possessing libertarian freedom and with quantum mechanical "dice playing," rather than the process notion that a world of entities possessing zero freedom is logically and metaphysically impossible (F 227–231)—the above and other passages commit Lucas to familiar themes of the Hartshornean doctrine of God, namely, an affirmation of divine temporality and the "dipolar" temporal/timeless distinction, and a concomitant rejection of the traditional doctrines of timeless immutability and impassibility on both philosophical and religious grounds.

In consonance with Hartshorne, Plato's celebrated argument for timeless immutability from the idea of divine perfection is clearly rejected by Lucas (F 216) as is the effort of Stump and Kretzmann to secure timelessness through the device of "ET-simultaneity" (ET-simultaneity is not transitive and so is not a "genuine species of simultaneity" at all, F 218). Like Hartshorne, Lucas sees divine temporality as part and parcel of a properly biblical, Judeo-Christian understanding of God, as contrasted with Greek philosophical notions of divinity, which are in fact the ultimate cultural sources of the idea of timeless immutability and impassibility in traditional Christian theology (see especially F 214–216). Like Hartshorne, he regards divine love as the core value to be found in the idea of deity, a love which is specifically characterized in tacitly process theological terms as both "creative" and "vulnerable" (F 232). Thus, for Lucas, like Hartshorne, a religiously viable concept of God entails emotional passibilism. Moreover, Lucas regards God to be best characterized metaphorically as "parent" and explicitly rejects in this context the metaphor of "absolute monarch" (of course, one of Hartshorne's favorite targets of derision in classical Christian thought). In light of these various connections, it is no wonder that Lucas explicitly mentions in his Preface a potential relationship between his own ideas and "those of the Process Theologians," although he defers the discussion to a later occasion.

Conclusions

If we have argued the above matters correctly, we submit that two basic conclusions ought to be drawn: (1) Eugene Peters was indeed correct in suggesting that Hartshorne's solution to the problems of future contingents counts as one of his truly great "philosophic insights." The whole Hartshornean package here delivers an extraordinary "unified" achievement: it preserves contingency and becoming, preserves libertarian freedom of the will and with it moral responsibility in the standard sense, preserves the most fundamental principles of logic without resorting to the complications of multivalence, and at the same time preserves the idea of omniscience defined as "perfect adequacy of knowledge" without resorting to metaphysically extravagant and logically difficult notions of merely possible individuals. (2) In light of the uncovered connections between Hartshorne and work on the problems of future contingents presented by a variety of analytic philosophers, we submit that two important observations apropos of the aims of this book are in order: First, such connections strongly support an important thesis of Chapter 1, namely, that analytic philosophy simply cannot be identified with anti-process logical theory and metaphysics. The Ramsey-Russell-Quine "eternal sentences" view represents only one tradition within the rich field of analytic philosophy of logic and time. Second, the notion that the authors have encountered repeatedly in conversations with some other professional philosophers—to quote one such interlocuter at a conference, "what on earth do analytic and process philosophers have to say to one another?"—must be viewed as glib, superficial, and simply uninformed.

References

Works frequently cited have been identified by the following abbreviation:

DDF Zagzebski, Linda Trinkaus. *The Dilemma of Freedom and Foreknowledge*. New York: Oxford University Press, 1991.

DP Flint, Thomas. *Divine Providence: The Molinist Account.* Ithaca and London: Cornell University Press, 1998.

F Lucas, John R. *The Future: An Essay on God, Temporality, and Truth*. Oxford: Oxford University Press, 1989.

FLT Cahn, Steven M. *Fate, Logic, and Time*. New Haven: Yale University Press, 1967.

GOK Viney, Donald Wayne. "God Only Knows? Hartshorne and the Mechanics of Omniscience," in *Hartshorne, Process Philosophy and Theology*, edited by Robert Kane and Stephen Phillips. Albany: State University of New York Press, 1989, pp. 71–90.

GTK Hasker, William. *God, Time, and Knowledge.* Ithaca and London: Cornell University Press, 1989.

IW Felt, James W. "Impossible Worlds," *International Philosophical Quarterly* 23, no. 3 (September 1983): 251–265

LMDF Molina, Luis de. *Luis de Molina on Divine Foreknowledge* (Part IV of the *Concordia*). Translated Alfred J. Freddoso. Ithaca, New York: Cornell University Press, 1988.

OWG Craig, William Lane. *The Only Wise God: The Compatibility of Divine Foreknowledge and Human Freedom.* Grand Rapids, Michigan: Baker Book House, 1987.

RPFC Shields, George W. "Some Recent Philosophers and the Problem of Future Contingents," *The Midwest Quarterly* 34, no. 3 (Spring 1993): 294–309.

SFW Kane, Robert. *The Significance of Free Will.* New York: Oxford University Press, 1996.

VF Adams, Robert Merrihew. "Middle Knowledge and the Problem of Evil," in *The Virtue of Faith and Other Essays in Philosophical Theology*. New York: Oxford University Press, 1987, pp. 77–93. Originally published in *American Philosophical Quarterly* 14 (1977).

1. E. Peters, "Philosophic Insights of Charles Hartshorne," *The Southwestern Journal of Philosophy* 8 (Feb. 1977): 169.

2. The Eleatics, Parmenides, and Zeno gave the first philosophically sophisticated defense of extreme monism. This monistic strain reappears in the works of the Stoics, Spinoza, and more recently, in the works of F. H. Bradley and J. M. E. McTaggart.
3. C. Hartshorne, "A Metaphysics of Universal Freedom," in *Faith and Creativity: Essays in Honor of Eugene H. Peters*, ed. George Nordgulen and George W. Shields (St. Louis: CBP Press, 1987), pp. 28–29.
4. Some philosophers have suggested that no asymmetry of *time* is shown by this apparent empirical truth about the actual world. This truth is only a consequence of the second law of thermodynamics, which just *happens* to hold in the actual world. In a possible world with different physical laws, the order of events could be reversed and thus time could be reversed. We reject this line of reasoning as a morass of confusion. Karl Popper has pointed out that any proof of the complete reversibility of physical process would not undermine the "arrow of time." Let S be a system with a reversible process P occurring at time t_1. Let P be reversed at t_2. This means that S returns at t_2 to its *state* at t_1, not that *time* returned from t_2 to t_1. An underlying asymmetry of time is presupposed even in the very act of conceptualizing the reversibility of a physical system. See K. Popper, "Replies to My Critics: Gruenbaum on Time and Entropy," in *The Philosophy of Karl Popper*, book II, ed. P. Schilpp (La Salle, Ill.: Open Court, 1974), pp. 1140–1142.
5. Time dilation in Einstein's special theory of relativity does not violate temporal asymmetry as we have characterized it. In the so-called twin paradox, one twin travels at speeds approaching the speed of light. Relative to his earthbound brother, his aging process is much slower. Special relativity dictates that there is no single inertial frame of reference according to which the twins must age at the same rate. However, nothing in the theory allows a person to grow younger. Also, see the footnote discussion (n. 45) of Storrs McCall's recent work on special relativity and the objectivity of the tensed modalitites.
6. Hartshorne and Whitehead part company on the nature of possibility. Whitehead's eternal objects are "forms of definiteness." For Hartshorne, possibility is always more or less indefinite. Put differently, Hartshorne, unlike Whitehead, makes no distinction between definiteness and determinateness (see D. R. Griffin, "Hartshorne's Differences from Whitehead," in *Two Process Philosophers: Hartshorne's Encounter with Whitehead*, ed. Lewis S. Ford (Tallahassee: American Academy of Religion, 1973).
7. J. M. E. Mc Taggart, *Philosophical Studies* (New York: Longmans, Green & Co., 1934), p. 116.
8. Cf. Douglas Langston, *God's Willing Knowledge: The Influence of Scotus' Analysis of Omniscience* (University Park: Pennsylvania State University Press, 1986), p. 18.

9. LMDF 124. Molina sees with clarity that what Thomas called God's "visionary" knowledge of the actual as illustrated in the circle analogy, when coupled with the divine will (which cannot be separated from divine knowledge by virtue of God's simplicity), strictly implies determinism.
10. C. Hartshorne, "Foreknowledge, Divine," in *An Encyclopedia of Religion*, ed. Vergilius Ferm (Secaucus, N.J.: Popular Books, 1945), p. 284.
11. Shields, RPFC 297–298.
12. Cf. William Occam, *Predestination, God's Foreknowledge, and Future Contingents*, trans. Adams and Kretzmann (New York: Appleton-Century-Crofts, 1969), pp. 49–50.
13. Jules Lequyer, *Translation of Works of Jules Lequyer*, trans. D. W. Viney (Lewiston, N.Y.: Edwin Mellen Press, 1998), pp. 51–152.
14. The qualification is barely necessary since, by definition, there is no difficulty in reconciling a *compatibilist* account of freedom and causal determinism. At a minimum, the libertarian maintains that the principle of alternate possibilities must hold for *some* free decisions (on this see Robert Kane, SFW 4, 43).
15. Recent exchanges between William Hasker and Thomas Flint and those among Robert Adams, Hasker, and William Lane Craig are of particular interest. Flint and Hasker crossed swords in a discussion of Hasker's *God, Time and Knowledge* (GTK), in *Philosophical Studies* 60 (1990): 103–126. Flint then devoted a chapter to Hasker in *Divine Providence* (DF 138–158). Adams gave an anti-Molinist argument that is related to but different from Hasker's in "An Anti-Molinist Argument," *Philosophical Perspectives 5: Philosophy of Religion*, ed. J. Tomberlin (Atascadero, Calif.: Ridgeview Publishing Co., 1991), pp. 343–353. Flint attempted to defuse Adams's criticism (DP 159–176). Craig responded to Hasker and to Adams in (respectively) "Hasker on Divine Knowledge," *Philosophical Studies* 67 (1992): 89–110, and "Adams's New Anti-Molinist Argument," *Philosophy and Phenomenological Research* 54, no. 4 (Dec. 1994): 857–861. Hasker responded to Craig and defended Adams's argument against Craig's criticisms in "Middle Knowledge: A Refutation Revisited," *Faith and Philosophy* 12, no. 2 (April 1995): 223–226, and "Explanatory Priority: Transitive and Unequivocal, A Reply to William Craig," *Philosophy and Phenomenological Research* 57, no. 2 (June 1997): 389–393. Craig again replied in "On Hasker's Defense of Anti-Molinism," *Faith and Philosophy* 15, no. 2 (April 1998): 236–239, but Hasker has rejoined in "Anti-Molinism is Undefeated!," *Faith and Philosophy* 17, no. 1 (January 2000): 126–131.
16. W. V. O. Quine, *The Pursuit of Truth*, rev. ed. (Cambridge, Mass.: Harvard University Press, 1992), p. 78.
17. Susan Haack, *The Philosophy of Logics* (Cambridge: Cambridge University Press, 1978), chapter 11.

18. C. Hartshorne, "Are Propositions About the Future True or False?," *Proceedings of the American Philosophical Association-Western Division* (April 20–22, 1936): 26–32.
19. Craig's criticisms of Hartshorne depend on interpreting him as denying or suspending the Law of Excluded Middle (see Craig's "Divine Foreknowledge and Future Contingency," in *Process Theology*, ed. R. Nash [Grand Rapids, MI: Baker Book House, 1987], pp. 93–115, and his "Process Theology's Denial of Divine Foreknowledge," *Process Studies* 16, no. 3 [Fall 1987]: 198–202). For a critique of Craig's reading of Hartshorne and a rebuttal of some of his arguments see D. W. Viney, "Does Omniscience Imply Foreknowledge?: Craig on Hartshorne," *Process Studies* 18, no. 1 (Spring 1989): 30–37, as well as GOK 71–90; also, see G. W. Shields, "Fate and Logic," *Southern Journal of Philosophy* 26, no. 3 (Fall 1988): 376–377, notes 4 and 10. It is also worth noting at this juncture that Hartshorne understands omniscience, in its primary signification, as a knowledge of events not a knowledge of truths about events. In the language of Bertrand Russell, it is a *knowledge by acquaintance* (Hartshorne, "Foreknowledge, Divine," p. 547). In this respect, Hartshorne's view diverges significantly from most analytic discussions for which "talk about the future [is] . . . talk about propositions and their truth values" (Johnathan Kvanvig, *The Possibility of an All-Knowing God* [New York: St. Martins Press, 1986], p. 3).
20. We deliberately use the class-complement bar over the variable X rather than the truth-functional tilde in order to make it clear that "X will occur" and "X will not occur" are *not* to be taken as contradictories.
21. MVG 140, n. 3. Hartshorne admits that some form of excluded middle must be conceded, but not the *analytic law* of excluded middle, since this would conflict with accepting noncontradiction: [(A v ~ A) ≡ ~ (A • ~ A] is tautologous. In his concluding chapter in FLT, Cahn concurs that the analytic LEM cannot be rejected.
22. Granted, this involves quantifying over causal possibilities, and that violates Quinean restrictions. However, Hartshorne and Cahn are committed to the extramental *reality* of possibilities; so, on such metaphysical assumptions, there *is* something over which we are quantifying. We submit that this is no more logically extravagant than quantifications involved in probability calculus (p = 1, p = 0, p = <1, >0). Moreover, *contra* Quine, we simply contend that *de re* modality *is* intelligible (see chapter 9 in this volume) and, consequently, that quantified modal and deontic logics are perfectly permissible.
23. This "temporalized" square of opposition has a precise analogue in A. N. Prior's "square of equipollence and opposition" constructed for

deontic logic as an extension of the logic of modality. "A is obligatory" is not contradicted by "Not-A is obligatory," but by "A is not-obligatory." To see the analogy to the present context simply add "to occur" after the obligation predicate. See A. N. Prior, "The Logic of Modality," in his *Formal Logic* (Oxford: Oxford University Press, 1973), section 6 on "Deontic Logic," pp. 220–229.

24. This way of putting the matter brings out a basic feature of Hartshorne's ontology of the future. For Hartshorne, futurity contains three generic ontological strata or types: immediate future events that are determined (in the "soft" sense explained below), immediate future possibilities for events that are determined not to become actual, and future probabilities or propensities that then can *become* relatively determinate. *Process is essentially a matter of selecting and narrowing scopes of vague possibility.* For Hartshorne, then, a future event can be determined in the sense that antecedent conditions for the event can be such that the event under some more or less general description cannot be *prevented* from occurring, although for any such "determined" event there will be at least *some* aspect of it that is not determined by the antecedent conditions (cf. LP, chapter 6). No future possibility is therefore absolutely definite.
25. Note that $(p \wedge q)$ has a truth table in which the schema is true only when exactly one statement variable is true, otherwise it is false. This, of course, is a veridical analogue for contradiction. $[(p \rightarrow \sim q) \bullet (q \rightarrow \sim p)]$ has a distinct truth table. $[(p \rightarrow \sim q) \bullet (q \rightarrow \sim p)]$ is false only on one set of truth assignments, namely, when p and q are both true. The conjunction is true when p and q are both assumed to be false. This, of course, is a veridical analogue for contrariety.
26. N. Rescher and A. Urquhart, *Temporal Logic*, Library of Exact Philosophy 3 (Berlin: Springer- Verlag, 1971), p. 211.
27. M. Clark, "Discourse About the Future," in *Knowledge and Necessity*, ed. G. N. A. Vesey (London: MacMillan and St. Martin's Press, 1970). All page references in the discussion under "Clark's Challenge" are to this text.
28. C. Hartshorne, "Creativity and the Deductive Logic of Causality," *The Review of Metaphysics* 27, no. 1 (Sept. 1973): 62–74
29. For a detailed presentation of this theory, see G. W. Shields, "Hartshorne and Creel on Impassibility," *Process Studies* 21, no. 1 (Spring 1992): 44–59. Also see Richard Creel, *Divine Impassibility: An Essay in Philosophical Theology* (Cambridge: Cambridge University Press, 1986), esp. chapter 3: "Continuity, Possibility, and Omniscience," and James A. Keller, "Continuity, Possibility, and Omniscience: A Contrasting View," *Process Studies* 15, no. 1 (Spring 1986): 1–18.

30. C. Hartshorne, "Von Wright and 'Hume's Axiom,'" in *The Philosophy of G. H. von Wright*, Library of Living Philosophers, vol. 19, ed. Lewis Hahn (La Salle, Ill.: Open Court, 1989), p. 75.
31. See Viney's GOK and Shields, RPFC; also see, Eugene Peters, "Divine Foreknowledge," *Encounter* 40 (Winter 1979): 31–34, and Felt's IW.
32. Flint would seem to agree with our main reasons for preferring the expression "MK-conditional" even though he retains the misleading expression "counterfactuals of freedom." According to Flint, "the antecedent of such a conditional needs to be stated in such a way that no assumption is made that the agent being described is a genuinely free, action-performing creature" (DP 46). He also notes that, "middle knowledge needs to include not only counterfactuals about actual free creatures, but also conditionals about merely possible but nonfactual creatures" (DP 46). He argues that MK-conditionals are best thought of as conditionals that refer to *individual essences*, which is to say, the set of properties essential to a creature (DP 47).
33. Hartshorne endeavored to make *Deus est caritas* the center of his philosophical system, but he had no interest in privileging orthodox Christian beliefs (see R. Auxier and M. Davies, eds., *Hartshorne and Brightman on God, Process, and Persons: The Correspondence*, 1922–1945 [Nashville: Vanderbilt University Press, 2001], p. 14). From an early age he ceased to believe explicitly in the Christian doctrine of the incarnation (DL 147). Thus, the burden of proof of which Flint speaks can have no purchase on Hartshorne and it is not assumed in this essay.
34. Alvin Plantinga introduces the concept of *transworld depravity*, a property of possible individuals such that they would produce moral evil in any world in which they might exist (NN 184–189). Although Plantinga does not refer to Molina in this context, his view is clearly a version of the doctrine of middle knowledge. Moreover, transworld depravity highlights the fact that middle knowledge puts restrictions on the worlds that God can create.
35. Alfred Freddoso notes that the doctrine of middle knowledge is *not* what distinguished the Jesuit Molina from his Dominican rivals, the followers of Domingo Bañez. The Bañezians accepted the existence of MK-conditionals, but they maintained that God is responsible for their truth values. God's knowledge of them, therefore, is postvolitional rather than prevolitional (LMDF 23–24).
36. David Basinger, "Divine Omniscience and Human Freedom: A Middle Knowledge Perspective," *Faith and Philosophy* 1 (1984): pp. 291–302.
37. Zagzebski argues that, for the purposes of attempting to solve the dilemma of human freedom and divine foreknowledge, God only needs to know MK-conditionals about *actual* free creatures. She says, "the

well-known difficulties with individuating possible but nonactual beings, while a problem for the full theory, are not a problem for that part of it relevant to foreknowledge" (DFF 126). We disagree. Even if God's knowledge were restricted to actual creatures, it is an actual creatures' counterpart as a possible individual that figures into a MK-conditional. God's free knowledge, the knowledge of what God actually creates, is what determines whether the *possible individuals* in MK-conditionals are also actual ones. A MK-conditional is "middle" precisely because it is not a consequence of God's creative acts. Thus, only a possible individual can serve as its subject. In any event, as already noted, middle knowledge customized to fit only actual individuals deprives the theory of its usefulness as an explanation of divine providence. It is the divine knowledge of all possible outcomes, on Molina's theory, that allows God to select the best.

38. Hartshorne maintains that God is the one individual identifiable *a priori* or by concepts alone (see D. W. Viney, *Charles Hartshorne and the Existence of God* [Albany: State University of New York Press, 1985], pp. 131–132). Nevertheless, Hartshorne denies that God is pure actuality. Thus, God's "biography," like those of the creatures, is also not written in advance.
39. The concept of a galaxy of possible worlds is Flint's (DP 51f). The metaphor itself illustrates our point. Galaxies are clusters of *actual* stars, so that talk of possible worlds as forming galaxies is itself possible only by an oblique reference to the actual world.
40. A. Plantinga in *Alvin Plantinga, Profiles*, vol. 5, eds. J. Tomberlin and P. van Inwagen (Dordrecht: D. Reidl, 1985), p. 373.
41. Hartshorne's conclusion can also be derived using what Hasker calls the power entailment principle (PEP):

> PEP: If it is in one's power to bring it about that *P*, and "*P*" entails "*Q*" and "*Q*" is false, then it is in one's power to bring it about that *Q* (GTK 49).

The Molinist wants to say that, the truth of MK/P1 notwithstanding, it is in S's power to decide not-A in C. However, S's power to decide not-A in C entails the falsity of MK/P1. Thus, by PEP, if it is in S's power to decide not-A in C then it is in S's power to render MK/P1 false. We have seen that contemporary Molinists deny that MK-conditionals are made true by anyone, including God. Hence, the truth of MK/P1 and "S has the power to decide not-A in C" are strictly inconsistent.

42. Zagzebski, unlike Hartshorne, is a theological compatibilist. We intend here only to draw a comparison between the positions of Zagzebski and Hartshorne on middle knowledge.

43. In essence, we are arguing that the falsity of MK-conditionals follows from the axioms of a metaphysical system like Hartshorne's. We are also arguing that Hartshorne's metaphysics has clear advantages over Molinism. A similar argument has already been outlined by Felt (IW 260–261).
44. The followers of Molina came to speak of God's *supercomprehension*, God's ability to be certain about the truth of MK-conditionals when they are not metaphysically, logically, or causally necessary. Craig's suggestion that God's "infinite understanding" of what every possible free creature would do in every possible circumstance seems to be a variation on *supercomprehension* (OWG 133–134). Freddoso concedes that the doctrine of *supercomprehension* is the weakest link in Molina's theory. He suggests that the doctrine is superfluous if MK-conditionals can be shown to obtain and if God is essentially omniscient (LMDF 53). Flint calls the doctrine "a rather murky and unhelpful concept" (DP 56). We agree. It is, at best, a property applied to God that begs the question of middle knowledge.
45. It should be observed that a strikingly analogous use of tree semantics can be found in Storrs McCall's important paper, "Time flow, nonlocality, and measurement in quantum mechanics," in *Time's Arrow Today*, ed. S. F. Savitt (Cambridge: Cambridge University Press, 1995). McCall presents a (non–Many Worlds Interpretation) "branching" quantum relativistic model of space-time. This model is extremely congenial to a process perspective: his notion of "branch attrition"—where possible world states "fall off the tree," as it were, according to the actualization of events as time unfolds—accommodates Special Relativity, while providing "a precise and objective meaning" to temporal asymmetry, temporal becoming, and the A-series modes of "past," "present," and "future." Anyone who suggests that a process theory of "cosmic time" is somehow undermined by relativity theory should certainly read this essay. Also consult the Special Focus on Process Thought and Natural Science, edited by Tim Eastman, *Process Studies* 26, nos. 3–4 (Fall–Winter 1997): esp. C. Papatheodorou and B. J. Hiley, "Process, Temporality, and Space-Time," 245–277.

Notes on Contributors

James Bradley is associate professor of philosophy at the Memorial University of Newfoundland, St. John's, Newfoundland, Canada. He is the author of numerous articles in professional journals, including *Process Studies* and the *Journal of Speculative Philosophy*, among many others.

Richard M. Gale is professor of philosophy at the University of Pittsburgh. Among his many publications are the much-discussed classic, *The Language of Time, Negation and Non-Being, The Existence and Nature of God*, and (as editor) *The Philosophy of Time.*

George L. Goodwin is president of the College of Saint Scholastica in Duluth, Minnesota. He is the author of *The Ontological Argument of Charles Hartshorne* and is coeditor of *Witness and Existence: Essays in Honor of Schubert Ogden.*

John W. Lango is professor of philosophy at Hunter College in New York City. He is the author of numerous articles appearing in such professional journals as the *Australian Journal of Philosophy* and *Transactions of the C. S. Peirce Society*, among many others. He is the author of *Whitehead's Ontology.*

Billy Joe Lucas is professor of philosophy and chair of the Philosophy Department at Manhattanville College in Purchase, New York. He is the author of numerous papers published in the *Journal of Symbolic Logic* and the *International Journal for Philosophy of Religion*, among others. He is a past president of the Society for Philosophy of Religion.

George R. Lucas Jr. is professor of philosophy in the Department of Leadership, Ethics, and Law at the United States Naval Academy in Annapolis, Maryland. President of the American Association for Liberal Education, he is editor of the SUNY Press Series in Philosophy and author of *Two Views of Freedom: Hegel and Whitehead, The Genesis of Modern Process Thought*, and *The Rehabilitation of Whitehead: An Analytic and Historical Assessment of Process Philosophy.* He has contributed to the Open Court Library of Living Philosophers volumes on Hans-Georg Gadamer, Charles Hartshorne, and Paul Weiss.

Leemon McHenry teaches in tthe Department of Philosophy at Loyola Marymount University in Los Angeles, California. He is the philosophy review editor for *Process Studies*, and is the author of *Whitehead and Bradley: A Comparative Analysis*, along with numerous publications in scholarly journals.

Willard Van Orman Quine is the late Edgar Pierce professor of philosophy emeritus at Harvard University. Among his prolific and much discussed publications are *Methods of Logic, From a Logical Point of View, Ontological Relativity and Other Essays, Word and Object, The Pursuit of Truth*, and *Quiddities: A Philosophical Dictionary*. He is the subject of the Open Court Library of Living Philosophers Series, volume 18, *The Philosophy of W. V. O. Quine.*

Nicholas Rescher is university professor of philosophy at the University of Pittsburgh. Perhaps America's most prolific living philosopher, he is editor of the *American Philosophical Quarterly* and the *History of Philosophy Quarterly* and has been appointed to the Board of Advisors of *Process Studies.* Among his scores of books are *The Philosophy of Leibniz*, *Essays in Philosophical Analysis*, *Topics in Philosophical Logic*, *Satisfying Reason*, *A Theory of Possibility*, and *Process Metaphysics: An Introduction to Process Philosophy.*

George W. Shields is 2000–2001 university distinguished professor, professor of philosophy, and chair of the Division of Literature, Languages, and Philosophy at Kentucky State University in Frankfort, Kentucky. In addition to numerous publications in a wide variety of professional journals, he is coauthor/coeditor with the late George Nordgulen of *Faith and Creativity: Essays in Honor of Eugene H. Peters* and with Mark Shale of *Science, Technology, and Religious Ideas.* He is a past president of the Kentucky Philosophical Association.

Donald W. Viney is professor of philosophy at Pittsburg State University in Pittsburg, Kansas. He is author of *Charles Hartshorne and the Existence of God*, and has published a translation of the work of nineteenth-century French philosopher Jules Lequyer. He serves on the editorial board of the *Midwest Quarterly* and has published widely in anthologies and journals ranging from *Faith and Philosophy*, the *Journal of Mind and Behavior*, and *History of Philosophy Quarterly* to *Process Studies* and *Teaching Philosophy*, among others.

Index of Names